Der Rosenkavalier

The Metropolitan Opera Classics Library

THE METROPOLITAN OPERA CLASSICS LIBRARY

RICHARD STRAUSS

Der Rosenkavalier

COMEDY FOR MUSIC IN THREE ACTS

LIBRETTO BY

HUGO VON HOFMANNSTHAL

STORY ADAPTATION BY

ANTHONY BURGESS

INTRODUCTION BY

GEORGE R. MAREK

GENERAL EDITOR

ROBERT SUSSMAN STEWART

MICHAEL JOSEPH LONDON

FIRST PUBLISHED IN GREAT BRITAIN BY MICHAEL JOSEPH LTD
44 BEDFORD SQUARE, LONDON WC1
1983

ISBN 0 7181 2210 0

PRINTED IN THE UNITED STATES OF AMERICA

Foreword

The Metropolitan Opera Classics Library, which honors the Metropolitan's centennial, was born out of the often expressed idea that opera is, at one and the same time, music *and* drama. Those familiar with the managing of opera houses know from hard-won experience that few, if any, operas ever earn a permanent place in the repertory if they do not bring "good stories" to their music. Indeed, the majority of our most beloved operas have been inspired by the narratives of either ancient myth or legend, or of novels, or of classical comedies and great tragedies.

Yet the historical fact that opera is, essentially, European in its tradition has meant that, for much of the English-speaking world, the use in opera of these literary treasures in languages other than our own narrows rather than expands their immediacy and their hold over us. We are all aware of having to "read up" on the story of an opera before attending a performance — or, drearier still, of having to sit through three or four acts without ever really knowing who is saying what to whom. Far too often the drama is lost completely, and the whole opera itself becomes clouded over, dusty like a museum piece, truly "foreign."

It is with this in mind that The Metropolitan Opera Classics Library has asked some of the most renowned writers of our time to retell the stories of operas in their own way, to bring the characters and the action to life. This is, of course, in no way to take away from, or diminish, the central role of music in opera; but rather to enrich or enhance it, so that, ultimately, the marriage of music and drama will be fulfilled, and opera will become more clear and more available — to more people.

Anthony A. Bliss
GENERAL MANAGER
METROPOLITAN OPERA

Acknowledgments

Many members of the staff of the Metropolitan Opera must be thanked for their contribution to this first volume in *The Metropolitan Opera Classics Library.* The largest indebtedness is to Michael Bronson, Director of the Media Department, who, from the outset, has been tireless in the encouragement he has given and in the enormous amount of work he has done.

I must also thank Clemente D'Alessio in the Media Department for his unflagging support, and I am grateful to Sue Breger and Vivienne Contrera for their help.

Robert Tuggle, Director of the Metropolitan Opera Archives, has provided invaluable assistance with research materials and illustrations. Others who have been helpful in the selection of photographs and technical illustrations are Nina Keller in the Press and Public Relations Department; Catherine Mallary in the Production Department; James Heffernan, the Metropolitan's Official Photographer; Winnie Klotz, Assistant to the Official Photographer; and Clarie Freimann, Presentations Coordinator at the Metropolitan Opera Guild. I would also like to express thanks to Michael Rubinovitz of the Metropolitan Opera Guild for preparing the *Rosenkavalier* discography.

Special thanks must go to Franco Zeffirelli, whose vast knowledge of opera and opera production has been a continued source of inspiration. Mrs. Dorle Soria has been gracious enough to lend material from her private collection of opera memorabilia. For supplying material from other opera houses, I would like to thank Helen O'Neill of the Glyndebourne Festival Opera, and Francesca Franchi of the Archives of the Royal Opera House, Covent Garden.

I am also especially indebted to Gerald Fitzgerald, Associate Editor of *Opera News,* for his editorial acumen, to Marcia Lazer, Marketing Director of the Metropolitan Opera, for her perceptive ideas, and to David M. Reuben, Director of the Met's Press and Public Relations Department, for his considerable efforts on behalf of this project and, in addition, for his reading of the entire manuscript. In preparing the libretto, David Hamilton's expertise is greatly appreciated. Jack Beeson, composer and MacDowell Professor of Music at Columbia University, has also read the entire manuscript and has made many useful suggestions.

My sincere thanks to Barry Lippman of Little, Brown and Company — a patient and insightful editor.

— Robert Sussman Stewart

All things must pass, like mist, like dreams.

(THE MARSCHALLIN, ACT I)

Introduction

The Music of Poetry or the Poetry of Music?

Two months after the premiere of *Der Rosenkavalier* in Dresden on January 26, 1911, Hugo von Hofmannsthal, writing to Richard Strauss, drew a retrospective estimate of the work on which both of them had spent the intensive labor of the past two years. Hofmannsthal wrote that now that he understood more intimately the nature of Strauss's music, he hoped to accomplish a new large work in which the text and music would be better mated. *Der Rosenkavalier* did not entirely satisfy him, though taken as a whole he rather liked the opera; and, he dared to hope that it would retain its place on the stage for several, perhaps for many, decades. At least, that is, on the German stage — the reception of *Der Rosenkavalier* that March at La Scala had been anything but encouraging. "It is true," wrote Hofmannsthal, "that my libretto contains the *heavy* defect that much which goes to make up its individuality and its charm disappears in translation." It was, then, as a German opera on German stages that Hofmannsthal envisioned the future of the work.

To be sure, of the two collaborators Hofmannsthal was the more modest. Yet even the confident Strauss could, in 1911, hardly have foreseen the extent of the *international* success of their comedy, the one opera of his not only most often performed within but also outside Germany and Austria, an opera which is part and parcel of the standard repertoire in London and New York, Buenos Aires and San Francisco.

Indeed, the rules of common logic — however nearsighted a guide on the road of art — offered more than enough reasons why *Der Rosenkavalier* could not be, and would never be, popular on foreign shores. The first and strongest of these reasons lies in language. Much of the opera's fun, its wit, its irony, is verbal. The language used, or rather the several languages used, by Hofmannsthal are gradations of German, ranging from the precious "candy-box" language of the aristocrats, liberally interspersed with French, to the Viennese street dialect of the suburban tradesman. Unlike *The Marriage of Figaro,* to which *Rosenkavalier* has often been compared — a comparison which is unfair to Strauss's work — the jokes are frequently found in the turn of a phrase rather than in the turn of a melody. What is Ochs's lecture on his amatory prowess in Act I — only sparsely underscored by music — if it is not a verbal piece of humor? The same can be said for the scene between Ochs and the Notary (descendant of a long line of stuttering legal pedants). Faninal's rage after the Baron is pinked is the comic rage of a talkative *nouveau riche.*

Hofmannsthal's language is so finely wrought that one can read the libretto with the fullest of pleasure — if one knows German. Observe how the Marschallin, for example, expresses herself. In eighteenth-century German three forms of address were used: the formal *Sie,* the familiar *Du,* and a third form, *Er,* often employed in speaking to a person of lower rank. In the very first scene the Marschallin uses "Du" to Octavian when she professes her love for him ("Du bist mein Bub") and "Er" when she teases him ("Beklagt Er sich über das, Quinquin?"). When others are present she calls him "Rofrano" or "Der Herr Graf." In the third act, when she dismisses Ochs, she tells him, in French, to make "bonne mine à mauvais jeu," which the Police Commissar probably does not understand. When she soliloquizes she speaks Hochdeutsch — with a Viennese accent. These shadings of speech help to give her scenes humor and pungency; it is a choreography in words. Ochs mixes up sundry expressions: Italian (he calls a sword a "spadi"), French, and words taken from the gutters of slang, such as "Palawatsch" or "Glumpert."

Not only the verbal wit, but also the thought content which lies behind it and which gives this remarkable text its body and fullness, make it necessary that we understand. Octavian's self-centered, self-assured reflections on youth need language as much as music for their expression. The philosophy of the Marschallin, her probing of the passage of life and the inconstancy of feeling, lose the subtler part of their savor if the words remain incomprehensible, eloquent though her music undoubtedly is. At its best, the music of *Der Rosenkavalier* is poetic and the poetry is musical.

How very much to the past does this poetry belong! It was written by a man whose skill lay in the exquisite tooling of a phrase, in the romantic sheen of expression, in the lambent coloring of verse. He belonged to a group of artists who delicately analyzed their own souls, souls which, if I may so express it, swayed in the wind when the wind blew mildly on an autumn evening. All was transient. Grace was the one essential.

In present-day theater gentle self-examination has given way to the harsh cut into the ego and psychic dredging. The silver mirror has been replaced by a surgical lance. Hofmannsthal's plays, such as *The Fool and Death* (*Der Tor und der Tod*) or *The Theater of the Little World* (*Das kleine Welttheater*) or *Christine,* or his famous comedy *The Difficult Man* (*Der Schwierige*), are now out of fashion, even in Austria. The Austrian dramatists of the turn of the century, the Hofmannsthals and Bahrs and

Schnitzlers, have now passed into a limbo which seems laid in faraway, almost fabled history, as the Austro-Hungarian Empire in which they lived seems far away and fabled. But does the *vieux jeu* quality in *Der Rosenkavalier* bother us? Not at all.

Finally, we are up against the social structure of *Der Rosenkavalier,* which, one would think, is strange to modern audiences. The action of the opera takes place earlier than the action in *The Marriage of Figaro,* that is, before the French Revolution. But *Figaro* seems timeless and indefinite in locale, while *Der Rosenkavalier* is closely linked to Vienna's court politics, to the degree and rank of Hapsburg hierarchy. It is specific in locale and so archetypically Viennese as to appear parochial. When anybody speaks of "His Imperial Royal Majesty" he does so with a low bow, while mocking the court and its corruption. Faninal has become wealthy through being a war profiteer. Ochs is quite willing to trade off a bit of his nobility for the possession of twelve houses, not to mention the palace in the inner city. That Hofmannsthal was able to create so vivid a panorama of eighteenth-century Vienna is a pleasure for spectators who know their history and know the glamorous city on the Danube. But what about those who have never been to Vienna?

All these reasons for *Der Rosenkavalier* to have forfeited international appeal count for nothing. The objections are invalid, the logic does not hold. The opera continues to be one of the half-dozen most beloved comedies in the repertoire. Part of the explanation for such world-wide acceptance lies in the simplicity of the plot. It *is* simple, for all its sophistication and complication. After Hofmannsthal broached the subject to Strauss, who feared that it would be "a little too fine for the mob," the former replied: "The action is simple and understandable even to the most naive public: a fat old arrogant suitor favored by the father of the bride is bested by a young and handsome one — isn't that the *non plus ultra* of simplicity?" (Not so different from Donizetti's popular comic opera *Don Pasquale,* is it?)

A more important reason comes to us in the essential word used by Hofmannsthal in another passage of the letter quoted above: "charm." The play has charm. It can be said of a comedy what Barrie said of a woman's charm: "If you have it, you don't need to have anything else; if you don't have it — it doesn't matter what else you have."

What are the ingredients of this charm? Of the several that may be enumerated, the readiest is the liveliness of the characters of the comedy; not one of them, not even a minor character, is pallid. Most of them thoroughly enjoy themselves, transmitting that enjoyment to us. The best time is had by that tourist from the hinterland, Baron Ochs. When Hofmannsthal and Strauss began the work, they conceived of the big bad bouncing Baron as the central character; for a long time the title of the opera remained *Ochs*. In the beginning, the other protagonists were subordinated to the fat provincial whose visit to Vienna and *mariage de convenance* were to be the main action. Hofmannsthal and Strauss wanted to create another Falstaff: at least, Falstaff's name crops up in their correspondence. Hofmannsthal worried about the casting of the part, protesting that if the role were to be played by a thin, "specter-like" actor instead of an expansive, "comfortable" interpreter, it would mean the death of the opera. He wanted it done in *buffo* style and, if need be, a foreigner, an Italian, was to sing it. (Hofmannsthal mentioned Antonio Pini-Corsi, a surprising choice, for how could an Italian have handled the Austrian dialect? Carl Perron, a German, played the role at the Dresden premiere in 1911. But Strauss's and Hofmannsthal's favorite Ochs was Richard Mayr. They told him he *was* Ochs, although Mayr replied that he wasn't sure if he should take that as a compliment.)

Ochs is, of course, no Falstaff. He is not only not that witty in himself but does not produce that much wit in other men. Still, he is a funny creation, being a double spoof on the chaser who thinks himself irresistible and the boor who thinks himself a diplomat. He turns out to be one of those "villains" of the theater whom, though he combines in himself a lot of traits we dislike, we end up liking. He is, as Octavian describes him (though in a moment of fury), "a *Filou,* a dowry hunter, an out-and-out liar, a dirty peasant, a fellow without decency or honor." Octavian might have added that he is a coward, stingy, a snob, and, like most snobs, subservient to those who outrank him. He comes from "up north," presumably near Bohemia. That is a local Austrian joke: the ignoramuses hail from Bohemia. So Ochs is the hayseed who has shown up in the big city, with his airs, his ignorance, his bad German and his worse French. Yet he is so expansively and rotundly drawn that we laugh at him with easy tolerance. He even shows one good trait: as he says, he is "no spoilsport never." We are not at all sorry that he loses his bride, but wouldn't have minded if he had captured her dowry.

Octavian, with his seventeen years and two months, is the dashing hero of the opera, romantic from his white wig to his satin shoes, carrying with him in well-born poise all the attractiveness that only unprincipled youth can bestow. Though more experienced in love, he is obviously modeled on Cherubino — a *travesti,* or trouser role of the first order. (From the outset, Octavian was always envisioned by Hofmannsthal as "a graceful girl dressed as a man, *à la* [Geraldine] Farrar, or Mary Garden.") Octavian is predictable. But that does not make him any less attractive. Not only to Sophie and the Marschallin but also to the audience that attraction is largely a physical one. Octavian does not say anything very witty or profound. He bears a light heart in a lithe body — that is enough. He makes love well, differently to the older than to the younger woman; Hofmannsthal writes these scenes with delicate contrast. Octavian is courageous, as he has been brought up to be. He is headstrong; that is to be expected from somebody who must have been everybody's favorite. The poet named him Rofrano and tells us that the Rofranos were a very noble family. It is not a Viennese name and, I believe, Hofmannsthal meant to suggest that in Octavian's character some volatile Italian traits can be found. At any rate, he acts impulsively — and loves playacting. He does the part of "Mariandel" to perfection, and we can guess that the elaborate scenario in the inn was his own idea.

Sophie is a product of the eighteenth-century equivalent of a finishing school for young ladies: she comes "fresh from the convent." She is young and pretty and innocent. Her innocence is relieved by a good deal of spunk. She stands up for herself, convent or no convent. The playwright Hermann Bahr criticized "the ordinariness" of Sophie's speech. Hofmannsthal replied that her way of expressing herself — a mixture of what she had learned in the convent and the jargon of her father — is consistent with her character, a girl like dozens of others. In that lies the irony of the situation. Octavian falls for the first "nice" girl of his own age who comes along. Sophie has to be as she is, says Hofmannsthal, if she is not to detract from the dominating figure of the Marschallin.

Marie Therese, Princess of Werdenberg, wife of the Field Marshal of the Imperial Austrian Army, grew to be the central character of the opera as the work progressed. I mentioned that it was not so planned in the beginning; but even fairly late in the development of the scheme we find her still merely one of the protagonists, not the unique personality which she was to become. She became central and dominant almost by accident, as if she had a life of her own which pressed and enlarged the boundary of the poet's and the composer's imagination. This is not an isolated phenomenon in art, though it is usually the work itself, not just one character, which grows beyond the plan. Thomas Mann's *Magic Mountain* was planned as a short story. *Die Meistersinger* began as a "short, light opera." *Der Rosenkavalier* itself, when Hofmannsthal first proposed it, was to be "extremely terse, playing time two and a half hours, that is, half as long as *Die Meistersinger*." Perhaps the fascination which Hofmannsthal and Strauss felt for the Marschallin contributed to the final length of the opera, which is, in fact, only an hour shorter than *Die Meistersinger*.

However it happened, the Marschallin turned out to be one of the loveliest, most individually endowed, most human of the human beings of operatic literature. She has offered a never-ending challenge to a score of well-known singing actresses — Lotte Lehmann, Florence Easton, Elisabeth Schwarzkopf, Lisa Della Casa included.

It is easy to become sentimental about the Princess, to call her, as several critics have done, the female Hans Sachs. We need no such fulsome comparison. She is an experienced, wise, and understanding woman, but she is certainly not all-wise, devoid of foible or vanity. More important, she is certainly not beyond the pale of life, beyond error and passion, looking back from a vantage point of tranquillity. Strauss himself has told us that the Marschallin should be "a pretty young woman, no older than thirty-two years. True enough, in a bad humor she calls herself an 'old woman' in comparison to the seventeen-year-old Octavian, but surely she is not David's Magdalena, who by the way is likewise portrayed too old. Octavian is neither the first nor the last lover of the beautiful Marschallin, and she must not act the closing of the first act too sentimentally, as tragic farewell to her life, but must retain some measure of Viennese grace and lightness, with one mournful and one joyous eye."

Those "thirty-two years" — we must take them in eighteenth-century terms (I am reminded of Jane Austen's novels, where a woman of thirty is considered almost beyond marriageable age), not in terms of twentieth-century life span. At thirty-two, which might be the modern equivalent of forty or forty-five, she has learned her lesson that neither time nor love can stand still. She knows that Octavian must be passed on to one who is "younger and prettier." Undiplomatically she tells him so, though he chases the thought away, only to make it come true a day later. The Princess has clear eyes and she knows "when a thing has come to an end." She isn't going to spoil those eyes by weeping, however. Even when she is sad she refuses to become lachrymose. It is her humor, her sense of life played as a game — serious now and then, but still a game — which endears her to us. If we are not quite dealing with a Viennese masquerade, as the Marschallin calls the affair in the last act, neither are we dealing with a triangle in which she becomes a point of tragedy. Some of us do not understand this and we often feel more sorry for this wonderful woman than we ought to.

What other traits can we discern which account for the Marschallin's having so strong a hold on the audience that this comedy, originally entitled *Ochs,* could in the end be entitled *Marie Therese* — and this in spite of the fact that she is absent for one whole and one half an act? She belongs to the loftiest aristocracy, the Field Marshal's office being one of the highest in the realm. She takes her social position for granted. She possesses the elegance of simplicity; she is naturally gracious in all she says and does, equally at ease with the bourgeois Faninal and the suburban policeman. We can be sure that her staff of servants are devoted to her. Her genuine kindness is part of her elegance. How we would like to be like her!

Der Rosenkavalier is a comedy, not a burlesque. The difference between burlesque and comedy was described by Joseph Addison in the *Spectator:* "'The two great branches of ridicule in writing are comedy and burlesque. The first ridicules persons by drawing them in their proper characters, the other by drawing them quite unlike themselves." Proper characters, full-dimensional characters — that is why the play continues to hold our interest. Curiously enough, Hofmannsthal considered calling the work a "Burlesque Opera." Strauss squashed the title peremptorily: " 'Burlesque Opera' is impossible. There is nothing burlesque in it." They then settled on the final "Comedy for Music."

Thus far I have spoken mostly of Hofmannsthal and his play. But now I must turn to Richard Strauss and note, obvious though it is, that the most important reason, the all-important, the decisive reason for the popularity of the work lies in its music. In this opera the magician from Munich is perhaps at his most joyful, most ebullient, most brilliant, and, so to speak, at his greatest ease. That the orchestration is fascinating — that we expect from Richard Strauss! Orchestral effects such as those in the Prelude to the first act, the philosophic scene between Octavian and the Marschallin, the close of Act I, the beginning of Act II with the background chorus, the scene of the Presentation of the Rose, the scoring of the final Trio and the final Duet, and many, many more such moments prove that all Strauss learned, assimilated, thought about, and originated in the handling of the orchestra in his symphonic tone poems has been put to service in *Der Rosenkavalier.* One constantly marvels at the sheer virtuosity with which Strauss manipulates the apparatus. It is a huge orchestra, so pliantly used that it ranges from chamber music intimacy (the first monologue of the Marschallin) to the grandest grand opera exaltation (the Trio in Act III). But what is more important, most of the musical substance of the opera is of first quality, rich in singing melodies, original and bold in harmony. The music blooms, luxuriates, flourishes. In its thrall the listener is suffused with the glow, the sense of participation, the concern for what happens next, the bond of sympathy with the characters, which mark the vitality of musical drama.

The romance is there in full; nothing in the music sounds middle-aged. If we speak of charm in the text — the music has it, and in what abundance! The waltzes, which have been so highly praised and which help to give the opera its popularity, while excellent as waltzes, do not seem to me to represent the musical pinnacle of the work. The high points, rather, are to be found where they dramatically belong, in the ecstatic moments, the scenes of tension and resolution, culminating in the Finale of the last act, from the moment on when the Baron and the mocking crowd have departed.

I think it is significant that Strauss wrote the best music for those scenes in which the Marschallin is present. No doubt Octavian and Ochs fascinated him, but he seems to have devoted his finest inspiration to Marie Therese. As the Prelude, as explicit a description of love-making as there is in music, which Strauss wanted played as if it were "a parody," nears the end, the love of the Marschallin for Octavian is expressed in a beautiful quiet, round theme, a sigh enclosed in a ring of melody. That theme sets the stage for much that follows: the colloquy of the lovers, the breakfast "minuet," the relief of Marie Therese when she realizes that the voice outside is not that of her husband and she breaks out into a triumphant waltz — "Quinquin, es ist ein Besuch" — through the fun she has fooling Baron Ochs.

Can anybody resist this inundating feast of melody? Oddly, the narrator in Iris Murdoch's novel *The Black Prince* feels this about it:

> The two women were conversing in pure sound, their voices circling, replying, blending, creating a trembling silver cage of an almost obscene sweetness . . . these were not words but the highest coinage of human speech melted down, become pure song, something vilely almost murderously gorgeous. . . . I was definitely going to be sick.

I wonder if anyone ever really got sick while listening to these passages?

After the hustle and bustle of the levée scene (inspired by Hogarth's painting in the *Marriage à la Mode* series), in which Strauss seemed to want to prove that if he set out to compose an Italian tenor aria he could compete with the likes of Bellini, follow the introspective scenes, the Marschallin's thoughts on growing old, which by the music are lifted to pure truth. Every one of her words finds the right setting. They touch feelings we all have. How is it possible that we become old, when inside ourselves we continue to feel so young? Octavian does not understand, being too young. Then the notion of lunching with her lame uncle as an act of kindness, followed by the subtle promise that perhaps she will ride in the Prater in the afternoon and he, Octavian, may ride next to her carriage, a promise which the orchestra elucidates with the theme of her love. Finally — that ineffable soft close of the first act.

Only the Presentation of the Rose and the Octavian-Sophie duet stand on a similarly high musical level in the second act. It is the third act which attains the apogee, from the entrance of the Marschallin on. Those suggestive recitatives, those whispered exchanges, those broken phrases, all of which reveal her unhappiness, though even in this scene of renunciation she remains wordly-wise, a figure of comedy not of tragedy. Octavian is now nothing but an awkward boy, stammering in embarrassment. This leads to the exalted Trio, then to the "old-fashioned" Duet of the two young people and the final frill when the Princess's little page looks for Sophie's handkerchief, a close which serves as an exclamation point at the end of a long, long love letter.

The Marschallin says that "the whole thing was a Viennese masquerade, and nothing more." Yet she knows that it was something more, much more than a kaleidoscope. Like all great comedies, *Der Rosenkavalier* touches the roots of tragedy. It is a tale that deals with the heart, and its music engages our hearts. Which is not to say that *Der Rosenkavalier* is unflawed. Isn't it curious that Strauss, highly intellectual, a profound student of Mozart and Wagner, a musician who understood the principle of form, was a poor self-critic? The good fairies standing at his cradle, who gave him much, failed to give him a blue pencil. None of his best works, except certain songs and *Till Eulenspiegel* — not *Don Juan* or *Zarathustra* or *Salomé* or *Elektra* or even *Ariadne,* three quarters of which is delightful, but which then sinks into blatant Wagnerism without Wagner's genius at the end — none of them is unblemished. *Der Rosenkavalier* is too long. Worse, at certain moments the music is too fulsome and boisterous and grandiloquent. At others — stretches of the second act and the beginning of the third — it coasts. But the defects of the opera can be counted on the fingers of one hand. Its joy remains intact after a lifetime of hearing.

Almost three-quarters of a century has elapsed since its premiere, yet *Der Rosenkavalier* has suffered less from "new" and perverted stage interpretations — now so ubiquitous — than many another opera. That is its good luck, and ours, and is due to Strauss's and Hofmannsthal's acumen in preparing the original performance. Strauss quickly realized that this comedy could not be staged by the usual operatic stage director, that a new light and winged style had to be taught to the singers, that they needed to be shown how to comport themselves in the boudoir and town house of eighteenth-century Vienna. He knew that the stage director at Dresden, Georg Toller, who had done very well with *Elektra,* was inadequate for *Der Rosenkavalier.* So Strauss took two steps. He begged Hofmannsthal to come to Dresden and supervise the acting rehearsals, giving him full authority to cancel or postpone the premiere should he be dissatisfied. The second step was to invite the great director Max Reinhardt to take over the production. This was, of course, a slap in Toller's face, and, to make the insult worse, Toller did not learn of Strauss's move until he read the news in the morning paper. To Toller's protests Strauss answered somewhat petulantly that he could not understand why anyone would not be glad to have the help of a Reinhardt. To smooth matters over, Reinhardt was called a "consultant." On the first day he did not go up on the stage, but conferred with the actors in the auditorium. He took them one by one into a remote corner of the auditorium and explained and mimed each part.

He wrought the usual miracle. He taught the Marschallin to spring to life exactly as the two partners had envisioned her. He showed the plump Octavian how to behave like a boy of seventeen. He filled the comedy with bits of amusing business. He staged the levée scene reproducing the figures from the Hogarth painting. He even overcame the lack of humor in Carl Perron, who had been used to singing the Dutchman and Wotan. From the second day on, Max Reinhardt was on the stage, no longer "consultant" but the stage director, inspired and inspiring, with his infinite capacity for taking up each detail.

Before the public dress rehearsal, Perron became ill and was able only to walk through his part. A very nervous Strauss apologized to the audience, but it was clear that even with a Baron who had a head cold the work was going to be a success. That success proved to outrank any of the previous successes Strauss had experienced. It was clamorous, warm, growing from scene to scene, act to act, reaching one climax at the end of the second act, another and stronger climax at the end of the Trio, and breaking out in shouts, bravos, and hurrays at the fall of the curtain. Strauss grinned from ear to ear. Hofmannsthal, for once smiling as well, occupied himself with repeatedly shaking Reinhardt's hand.

And since that night, again and again in opera houses throughout the world, *Der Rosenkavalier* has almost never been received without a loving smile.

George R. Marek
NEW YORK, NEW YORK

Contents

Richard Strauss and Hugo von Hofmannsthal

A REEVALUATION

by

GEORGE R. MAREK

I.

In 1864 a nineteen-year-old boy named Ludwig Wittelsbach ascended the Bavarian throne. One of his first acts as "His Royal Majesty Ludwig II" was to find and rescue Richard Wagner from penury. Very soon rehearsals for a new work, *Tristan und Isolde,* were begun, Hans von Bülow conducting the Munich Court Orchestra. The first hornplayer of that orchestra was a certain Franz Strauss, whose nerves just then were in a rather jittery state. At any moment, the birth of his first child was expected. Luckily the baby came punctually, on June 11. It was a boy. He was christened Richard, but decidedly *not* after Wagner.

As soon as young Richard showed musical aptitude, which he did early on (he wrote his first musical composition when he was five and a half), Franz determined that he was to become a musician — *provided* that he study "real" music: Bach, Mozart, Beethoven, and stay strictly away from the overblown, overripe, and overloud sounds Wagner was loading on the orchestra. Franz loathed Wagner. At fifteen, Richard hid the score of *Tristan* from his father and studied it in secret.

When he began to compose in earnest, Wagner was his most immediate inspiration. True, some of Strauss's apprentice compositions which were written in his early twenties — such as *Wanderers Sturmlied* (The Wanderer's Storm Song), the First Symphony, *Burleske* — are music for which Brahms stood godfather, and that was due to Bülow's teaching of Strauss; but when he embarked on the creation of his famous tone poems — *Macbeth,* then the more important *Don Juan,* then the still more ambitious *Death and Transfiguration* — echoes of Bayreuth floated into the scores, however original and daring they were. All three were composed before Strauss was thirty years old. In his letters to his father, he tells him that during the rehearsals for *Don Juan,* the orchestra "huffed and puffed," the brass blew "with death-defiance," and one musician, dripping with perspiration, asked in what way he had sinned that God now visited such a scourge upon him.

The first performance of *Don Juan* took place on November 11, 1889, in Weimar. It proved to be an historic occasion. We may imagine the excitement of the audience sitting up straight in their chairs as they heard the first bars, when the strings throw out that bold upward leap, as if the hero were to bound in one jump to the center of the stage. We may imagine the delight of the listeners as they heard for the first time the seductive theme of love sung by the oboe, from which they were then roused by the proud assertion of the theme of Don Juan himself. As the last sounds died away, the audience began to shout its approval. Five times Strauss, who conducted the piece himself, had to acknowledge the applause. There was an immediate clamor for a *da capo,* which the composer shrewdly did not grant.

The news spread immediately. Bülow was in Weimar and reported that *Don Juan* had a "quite extraordinary success." Frankfurt, Dresden, and, later, Berlin asked for the composition. From being something more or less of a local celebrity, Strauss now became a figure of national importance; he became one of the spokesmen of the young generation. He had touched a beating vein; he had expressed in music what the writers were expressing in words, had found a new language with which to speak openly of erotic desire, of voluptuousness, of rebellion. Both virility and femininity are to be found in the score and, at the close, weariness and satiety, death in a useless duel. How well did this accord with the spirit of the times!

As he composed each of the following tone poems he found in each a greater certainty of individual style, a greater skill in making the means serve the content. *Till Eulenspiegel* is, I believe, his one totally delightful orchestral work. *Don Quixote* is a fine musical mixture of sadness and comedy, about three to one, in the same proportion of Cervantes's novel. *Also Sprach Zarathustra* — that is a puzzle. Strauss attempted the impossible, setting a philosophic doctrine to music. Though it contains beautiful passages, the composition becomes pretentious and stuffy. It lectures at you as often as it lifts you.

Strauss turned to opera early. His first, *Guntram,* is not interesting, but his second, *Feuersnot,* which had its premiere in Dresden in 1901, already contains a love scene of remarkable erotic feeling. (Thomas Beecham was fond of the work; he called it "gay and audacious.") Passion and eroticism bloomed like a marsh flower in *Salomé.* We must imagine Strauss sitting at his desk and methodically setting to music such dithyrambic lines as "Thy mouth is like a band of scarlet on a tower of ivory." When he had an evening free from his conducting chores, he would stay with *Salomé* until one in the morning, to arise the next day and, without hesitation, continue where he had left off. No outward transport, no wringing of hands, accompanied the composition of this frenzied work. He merely reported to his parents that he was "grinding away at it."

What a phrase to use about such music. Seldom, I think, has so turbulent a creation been brought forth by so calm a creator. The manuscript is set down in a neat handwriting, suitable for a Haydn minuet.

Strauss played the nearly completed score to two men whose opinions he valued. He played it first for his father. "Oh God!" the old man said, "What nervous music! It sounds as if a swarm of ants were crawling in the seat of your trousers." But Franz Strauss did not live to witness the triumph of the opera, for he died on May 31, 1905, at the age of eighty-three, to the last both admiring his son's genius and fearing for his future.

The other man was Gustav Mahler. According to Alma Mahler, Gustav's wife, Strauss played and sang the entire opera with fine expression. (Romain Rolland, far from paying tribute to Strauss's ability as a player and demonstrator of his own operas, said that he played and sang "very badly.") When he arrived at the place where Salomé dances, Strauss said in a broad Bavarian accent, "That I haven't managed yet." Mahler wanted to know whether it was not dangerous to omit the dance in this fashion and to attempt to recapture the mood later on. Strauss answered with a smile, "Don't worry!" Mahler was overwhelmed by the work. That, at least, is how Alma Mahler told the story in her reminiscences. How trustworthy a witness she was, we cannot be sure — more than one of her stories has been known for its obvious exaggeration.

A month before Strauss completed the score, he was ready to open negotiations with his friend Schuch, Intendant of the Dresden Opera. After *Feuersnot,* it was natural that Dresden should get the first opportunity. Schuch accepted with alacrity, though Strauss pointed out that *Salomé* was about twice as difficult as *Feuersnot.* As Salomé, the two men chose a singer of prominence, and curiously enough, one of ample girth, whom they had heard in Wagnerian roles. This was Marie Wittich, a Bayreuth Isolde. Strauss recalled the first rehearsal:

> At the first piano run-through the singers assembled in order to hand back their parts to the conductor — all except the Czech singer Burian, who, when asked last of all, answered, "I already know the role by heart." Bravo! At this the others felt rather ashamed and the work of the rehearsal actually started. During the acting rehearsals the dramatic soprano Frau Wittich went on strike. She had been entrusted with the part of the sixteen-year-old princess with the voice of an Isolde on account of the strenuousness of the part and the thickness of the orchestration — "one just doesn't write like that, Herr Strauss; either one thing or the other." In righteous wrath she protested, like any Saxon Burgomaster's wife, "I won't do it, I'm a decent woman. . . ."

The decent woman soon decided that the indecent role was too tempting to pass up. But two months before the date for the premiere, further troubles arose. Strauss learned that Frau Wittich had not as yet seriously studied the role. How could she master so difficult a part by the end of November? What is more, she had become fatter than ever during the summer. This worried Strauss less: "It doesn't matter," he wrote to Schuch. "Voice, Horatio, voice, and once again voice." But when the devil was she going to learn the role? By the end of October, Strauss was still dissatisfied with her progress; he now threatened to withdraw the opera from Dresden. He told Schuch that Grete Nikisch was already hard at work on *Salomé* in Leipzig and that Mahler had finally pushed the work past the censors. (This turned out to be wishful thinking. Mahler had accomplished nothing.) Strauss gave Schuch a deadline: December 9 — if not by then, he would give the work to whichever opera house could first get it ready.

We do not know how the suffering Schuch managed it, but he came through. The premiere of *Salomé* took place precisely on the day of Strauss's deadline, December 9, 1905. Wittich, corpulence and all, sang the part of the "sixteen-year-old princess" forcefully, though she could not dance it, and as in many subsequent performances a dancer was substituted for the Dance of the Seven Veils. Karl Burian was a magnificent Herod, and Carl Perron was Jokanaan. (Later it was Perron who created the role of Baron Ochs in *Der Rosenkavalier.*)

Enormous excitement pervaded all musical Germany and indeed all of Europe. Musical pundits, colleagues, people of the theater, and the socially prominent had come from far and wide to be present, and the audience, many of whom were of course familiar with Wilde's play, was in a high state of expectancy, an expectancy in which were mingled curiosity about hearing new music by the eminent composer and the fear — or the hope — that something shocking and scandalous was to be experienced. There was no scandal. The audience was swept away by the force of the music. They listened in absolute silence, broken only by a few whispers as the ballerina shed her veils and, again, as the severed head was handed from the cistern. For the final scene Schuch and his orchestra, as well as Frau Wittich, summoned every ounce of strength they possessed. The sound inundated the house and drew even the skeptical into its vortex. At the end of the performance the house went wild and vented its excitement in an ovation during which people stood on the seats, shouted, waved their hats, threw programs — and called the artists and composer before the curtain thirty-eight times.

Elektra did not really begin the partnership with Hugo von Hofmannsthal, since Strauss took an established play, Hofmannsthal's adaptation from Sophocles, for his purpose. Though *Elektra* marks a progress from *Salomé,* it enjoyed less of a success, the reason being that the work is pitiless in its demands on the audience, immersed in pitch-darkness, shrieking with dissonance, grim and graceless in its setting. In vain do we look for the full complement of love melodies we have come to expect from Strauss. This is as atypical of Strauss as the play is atypical of Hofmannsthal. There is but one moment when bitterness melts, hate dissolves into love, and Strauss let us hear an old-fashioned cantilena: that is, in the Recognition Scene. Yet in the driving and punishing music of *Elektra,* Strauss reaches new heights. It pulsates with the blood of tragedy, setting before us with new force the old truth that hatred destroys not only the hated but those who hate. The tragedy, Greek locale or not, contains no Greek consolation. It is a thoroughly twentieth-century work. When Strauss was chided that he made the music "needlessly ugly," he replied, "When a mother is slain on the stage, do they expect me to write a violin concerto?"

Three-quarters of *Elektra* lies in the orchestra. That orchestra is huge — one hundred and eleven strong — and it was said that for his next opera Strauss planned to augment it still further, by "four locomotives, ten jaguars, and a couple of rhinoceroses." They also quipped that at the Dresden premiere half the orchestra by mistake played the score of *Salomé,* half that of *Elektra* — but that it didn't make any difference! Afterwards Strauss said to Hofmannsthal he had had enough of matricide. Could the poet give him "a Mozart opera"? Something melodious "and uncomplicated."

Der Rosenkavalier was the result, the true beginning of the remarkable relationship with Hofmannsthal. In more aspects than one, *Der Rosenkavalier* marks the apogee of Strauss's operatic creations. *Ariadne auf Naxos* may equal it in charm — it is Hofmannsthal's best libretto — but not in full musical satisfaction. Its end, from the entrance of Bacchus, is a disaster. But Act I and most of Act II are unmitigated joy. Not so *Die Frau ohne Schatten:* the libretto is sesquipedalian with various symbolisms clashing all over the place. *Die aegyptische Helena* is even less convincing, and *Arabella* is a rehash of *Der Rosenkavalier,* where one has to wait until the third act to hear truly fine music.

The post-Hofmannsthal operas — *Die schweigsame Frau,* with a libretto by Stefan Zweig; *Der Friedenstag, Daphne,* and *Die Liebe der Danae,* which he created with Joseph Gregor; and the final opera, *Capriccio,* to a libretto of Clemens Krauss — all contain moments of beauty, but none has won a permanent place in the repertoire. One little opera, *Intermezzo,* for which Strauss wrote both words and music, is in its own way a masterpiece.

To his detractors, Strauss is only a clever craftsman, a minor talent.

Yet I believe he is much more than that. He dealt youthfully with youth; these passages will remain green as the laurel tree. He gave daring expression to sexual attraction, his music being pervaded by hedonistic eroticism. He was bold. If this boldness eventually assumed respectability, as was inevitable, it still has the power to excite us. In *Elektra* he summoned a tragic power which, with all its nervousness, cleanses the bosom of perilous stuff. He could soar, as in the beginning of *Don Juan* or the Trio of *Der Rosenkavalier.* He could spin an ironic yarn or tell a joke gaily, as he did in *Till Eulenspiegel.* He created characters so explicit that they have become part of our standard literature, part of life. Life would be poorer without the Marschallin, Octavian, Zerbinetta, the Composer, or even "naughty" Salomé. This sanest of composers gave us "mad scenes" frightening and pitiful. The Klytemnestra scene is fraught with terror, and Don Quixote touches our sense of pity.

It is Strauss's exuberant romantic spirit that remains the part of him we like best. We seem to need it more than ever. Melody is an essential tool of romanticism. It must have tunes, not just ejaculations of sound. That Strauss was a melodist he proved early in *Don Juan* and proved again, after sixty years, in the *Four Last Songs.*

His songs are part of his romantic gift. The best of them continue the tradition of the Lied, the tradition of Schubert, Schumann, and Brahms. In addition to such famous songs as "Morgen" and "Traum durch die Dämmerung" and "Ständchen" — how wonderful they are! — he composed such fine though less famous songs as "Die Nacht," "Breit' über mein Haupt," "Du meines Herzens Krönelein," "Ach Lieb', nun muss ich scheiden," "Ich trage meine Minne," "Heimkehr," "Freundliche Vision"; such wistful songs as "Die Zeitlose" and "Wozu noch, Mädchen."

What will last? My guess is *Don Juan, Till Eulenspiegel, Tod und Verklärung, Don Quixote, Salomé, Elektra, Der Rosenkavalier, Ariadne auf Naxos,* many songs including the four last ones, and, for a special audience, *Capriccio.* Enough to assure Strauss an important place in music's living repertoire. For such music we are willing to accept the blots that spot even his best conceptions, a touch of vulgarity — indeed more than a touch — an occasional sugariness of melody and harmony, a tumult noisier than the thought warrants, and here and there polyphonic nodules, which his conservative father criticized in the early days. Strauss himself said that polyphony was Satan's gift to the Germans.

His gods were Wagner and Mozart — not such bad deities to worship. He understood Mozart profoundly. He said, "I wish I could compose as simply as Mozart." He knew he couldn't. His love embraced virtually all of Mozart's music, not only the operas. He particularly admired the piano concertos. Mozart brought him solace: when his wife, Pauline, was lying ill with pneumonia, Strauss went to Karl Böhm one day. Tears were streaming down Strauss's face. Böhm took him to a concert in which some Mozart Serenades were performed. He lost himself completely in the music.

But it was Wagner who was the mentor from whom he could not escape entirely. Protest as he would that he had shaken off Bayreuth's shackles, he never did, not entirely. He idolized Wagner not merely as a composer but also as a theoretician and even as a philosopher. He said, "*Opera and Drama* is perhaps the most significant scientific book in world history."

When I was young I heard Strauss conduct *Tristan.* He was an excellent conductor and when it came to *Tristan* he was a man possessed. One can understand this affinity in a sense. *Tristan* is the most "modern" of Wagner's works. Its intensely articulated eroticism would touch the composer of *Don Juan;* its preoccupation with death — which Gabriele D'Annunzio had apostrophized — would touch the composer of *Death and Transfiguration.* Georg Solti remembers that after the war, in 1949, he traveled to Garmisch to discuss *Der Rosenkavalier* with the old Strauss. Strauss was not interested, but took down the score of *Tristan* from the shelf and said, "Let's talk about this."

As for Strauss the man — he can be summarized by a well-known Toscanini anecdote. When Strauss called on Toscanini in Toscanini's dressing room in Milan, Toscanini was getting ready to return home. He said to Strauss, "For Strauss the composer, I take my hat off. For Strauss the man, I put it on again." (Zweig, who admired both Strauss and Toscanini — he wrote an appreciative essay on Toscanini — denied that Toscanini was capable of forming such a judgment. Walter Toscanini confirmed that his father did, in fact, say it.)

Yes, in judging Strauss as a man we must alternatively take our hats off and put them on again. His contradictoriness is exemplified in his self-judgments, which ranged from the ridiculously modest to the overweeningly assured. Almost at the end of his life he summarized: "I know very well that my symphonic works do not touch the giant genius of Beethoven. I know exactly the distance (in greatness of conception, elemental melodic invention, and cultural wisdom) which separates my operas from the eternal works of Wagner. . . . Yet I claim an honorable place at the end of the rainbow."

On the other hand, he wrote to Hofmannsthal: "I am really the only composer alive who has true humor, wit, and a talent for parody." Of *Ariadne* he wrote: "My score, considered as a score, is truly a masterpiece which nobody is going to surpass soon."

Strauss earned a great deal of money from concertizing as well as from his performance fees. (His earnings have been estimated at $2,500,000, though some of his fortune was lost after each of the world wars.) Rarely did he write only for money. Instances of that are the additional music he composed for a *Rosenkavalier* film, and late in life, in 1945, a suite from *Der Rosenkavalier* for orchestra, both of these being potboilers cooked up for financial gains. He made copies of his scores to sell these manuscripts at high prices. Occasionally he composed for the sake of "diplomacy": a military march during World War I, a hymn or two for the Third Reich.

He was scrupulously honest in his dealings with librettists and publishers. He did not attempt to drive a hard bargain with his collaborators, even after Hofmannsthal. His interest in being adequately compensated was partly responsible for the organizational work he did, which was to benefit all German composers. (At a lunch in Paris he tried to explain his plan to Debussy. The lunch was given at the home of the music publisher, Jacques Durand, who had promised himself that the meeting of the greatest composer of France and of Germany would prove a stimulating occasion. He was disappointed. Strauss spoke of nothing but financial matters, while Debussy, who did not understand a word of what Strauss was talking about, kept silent and pretended to be lost in his dreams.)

Personally he was not particularly generous. When he entertained people he liked (or those he thought were important to his career) at his home, he was a gracious host, champagne flowing freely. When he went to a restaurant — he liked small restaurants where he could not be recognized — he scrutinized the bill carefully and sometimes left an insufficient tip. Barbara Tuchman, in her book *The Proud Tower,* which devotes an excellent chapter to Strauss, tells the story that at the first Parisian performance of the ballet *Joseph* "the evening ended happily in a gala supper at Larue's given by the composer for his friends who had come from Germany, Austria and Italy for the premiere. After feasting on early strawberries and exquisite wines, each guest was presented by the waiter with his share of the bill." (This, however, is not quite so shocking as Miss Tuchman thinks; in Germany and Austria it was often the custom to "invite" friends for a meal and have everybody pay his share.)

On his concert tours, he was quite capable of camping in the house of friends, accepting their hospitality, knowing that their social standing could not fail to be enhanced by his presence. If he was in a good mood, he regaled everybody with stories and gossip of the opera house. If he was not, he would make a nest for himself of many pillows, stretch out on the couch, and go to sleep or pretend to. One hostess who invited him said, "Please come. It will be quite an informal evening — no fuss." To which he replied, "You may make a fuss when Richard Strauss comes."

What he really liked to do — next to composing and conducting — was to play cards: Skat, a difficult game at which he was expert. Like an expert, he played with passion and he was a poor loser.

Politically, when all is said and done, he was far from heroic, far from admirable. He secretly despised the Nazis and came to detest Hitler, but was perfectly willing to play along with the gang. He accepted the post of president of the Reichsmusikkammer, until the Gestapo intercepted an incriminating letter he had written to Zweig (who was Jewish) and forced him to resign for "reasons of health." Strauss's position was that he had been a German composer under the Kaiser, that he had been one under the Weimar Republic, that he was one now under Hitler, and if the Soviets were to take over Germany he would become a Commissar. Not for a moment did he think of emigrating.

Did the flaws of his character, as well as the disgrace of his environment, contribute to a weakness as he grew old? One cannot be certain, since it is difficult to trace the connection between talent and character. At any rate, few will doubt that he gave us much. He gave us one of the rosiest comedies in music. Octavian gives the silver rose to Sophie; the music gives a bouquet to everybody.

II.

The coffeehouses were the public libraries of Vienna. Each *Kaffeehaus* had its own clientele: the members of the opera claque gathered in one and the medical students in another, the *Fiaker* coachmen in one and the cavalry lieutenants in another, the struggling journalists in one and the arrived authors in another. But all coffeehouses had one thing in common: they had to make available a copious assortment of current newspapers, periodicals, and journals. These were mounted on wooden reading racks, and you could take possession of and hoard them for hours, just for the price of "*einen kleinen Schwarzen,*" a demitasse of coffee. That was the cheapest thing you could order. (You also got free two glasses of delicious ice-cold Vienna water.) The Austrian newspapers and periodicals, heavily censored, were short on news but long on literature; they, rather than the expensive books, furnished the prevalent intellectual reading matter.

In the late 1890s there began to appear in them a number of poems of sensitivity and beauty which were signed Loris. The name was an obvious pseudonym. Who was Loris? The poets and writers in the vanguard, such men as Richard Beer-Hofmann, Felix Salten, Peter Altenberg, and Arthur Schnitzler, were curious. They guessed from the autumnal tone of the poetry that Loris must be an older man, a man of experience who had acquired mellow wisdom. Presently they discovered that the poetry had been written by a youth in his teens, that the reason for the pseudonym was that he was still attending school — schoolboys were not permitted to publish under their own names — and that the real name of Loris was Hugo von Hofmannsthal.

At sixteen he began to write, at eighteen he was famous. Stefan Zweig described his appearance: "With his sparse and not quite developed moustache and his elastic figure he looked even younger than I had expected. His profile was sharp and his face, darkly Italian, seemed nervously tense. His deep, velvety, but very myopic eyes added to this impression. He threw himself into speech with one jump, as a swimmer does into familiar waters, and the longer he spoke, the surer he became of himself, the freer his gestures."

His ancesters were Austrians, Italians, and Swabians. One grandfather was a Jew. By the time Hugo was born, the family could be considered old and patrician; it had been ennobled and sported the "von" with pride. His father had trained for the law but had become a banker, and as such was highly successful. The elements were so mixed in Hugo that he was the very model of a pure Austrian, representative of the Austro-Hungarian Empire, which was made up of heterogeneous nationalities and many languages. He was so fully aware of his Austrianism that he acknowledged not only the virtues of the inheritance but its defects as well. He knew better than to be taken in by the vaunted Austrian "*Gemütlichkeit*"; long before Hitler walked in and was welcomed he wrote of "Austrian brutality."

He was never put to the necessity of earning a living, able always to live in reasonable luxury, at least until the German-Austrian inflation of 1920 swept away his fortune in a tornado of paper money. Then he asked his friend Carl Burckhardt to sell for him a van Gogh, a Picasso, and a sculpture by Rodin. This sale and the foreign royalties from his operas permitted him to live on halfway decently.

He lived in a little rococo castle of Austrian style in Rodaun, near Vienna. No modern touch spoiled its authenticity; he never permitted central heating to be installed in place of the white porcelain stove, and often he suffered from the cold of the Austrian winter. There was no modern bathroom in the entire castle. In his study, he sat on an uncomfortable antique chair all white and gold, dressed in a severe black suit, and thought his thoughts and wrote his words. He kept a set of colored glass balls on his desk; he liked to look at them when he was writing.

His culture was prodigious. What did he not know? He was forever

"The Presentation of the Rose."

1. Maria Jeritza as Octavian, the Metropolitan Opera, 1922. (COURTESY OF THE METROPOLITAN OPERA ARCHIVES)

2. Richard Strauss, late 1890s. (COURTESY OF THE ROBERT TUGGLE COLLECTION)
3. Hugo von Hofmannsthal. (COURTESY OF CULVER PICTURES)
4. Strauss's study at Garmisch. (PHOTO: B. HIMMLER. COURTESY OF DORLE SORIA)

5. The first performance of *Der Rosenkavalier*. Scene from Act II. Royal Opera House, Dresden, January 26, 1911. (COURTESY OF *Opera News*)
6. Margarethe Siems, soprano, the first Marschallin. (COURTESY OF THE ROBERT TUGGLE COLLECTION)
7. Bass-baritone Richard Mayr was the "ideal" of Baron Ochs for both Strauss and Hofmannsthal. The part had actually been written with him in mind. Although Mayr did not play Ochs at the premiere in Dresden, he did become identified with the role in Vienna and, later, in 1927, in New York at the Metropolitan Opera. (COURTESY OF THE ROBERT TUGGLE COLLECTION)

8. "The Presentation of the Rose." Act II, 1913 production at the Metropolitan Opera. The sets were designed by Robert Kautsky, an associate of Alfred Roller who designed the original production in Dresden. (COURTESY OF THE METROPOLITAN OPERA ARCHIVES)

9. *Left*: Program of the first performance of *Der Rosenkavalier* in London at the Royal Opera House, Covent Garden, January 29, 1913 (COURTESY OF THE ARCHIVES, ROYAL OPERA HOUSE, COVENT GARDEN) *Right*: Program of the first performance of *Der Rosenkavalier* in America at the Metropolitan Opera, December 9, 1913. (COURTESY OF *Opera News*)

Royal Opera House, Covent Garden

Lessee and Manager . Mr. FRANK RENDLE

For Autumn and Winter Season

THOMAS BEECHAM OPERA SEASON, 1913

THIS EVENING'S PERFORMANCE

OPENING NIGHT OF THE SEASON

Wednesday, January 29th, at 8

FIRST PRODUCTION IN ENGLAND

STRAUSS' OPERA

DER ROSENKAVALIER

(In German)

Princess von Werdenberg .	MARGARETE SIEMS
Baron Ochs of Lerchenau . .	. PAUL KNUPFER
Octavian	EVA VON DER OSTEN
Herr von Faninal . .	FRIEDRICH BRODERSEN
Sophie	CLAIRE DUX
Mistress Marianne Leitmetzer . .	ELSA JULICH
Valzacchi	. HANS BECHSTEIN
Annina	ANNA GURA-HUMMEL
A Commissary of Police . .	ERNST VON PICK
Major-Domo of the Princess . .	HERMAN KANT
Major-Domo of Faninal .	GEORG NIERATZKY
The Princess's Attorney . .	ARTHUR PACYNA
Landlord	DENIS BYNDON-ARYES
A Singer	. FREDERICK BLAMEY
Conductor . .	Mr. THOMAS BEECHAM

The Opera produced by HERMANN GURA

For future Announcements see inside

FIRE NOTICE: *Look around now and choose the nearest exit to your seat. In case of fire walk (do not run) to that exit. Do not try to beat your neighbor to the street.* J. JOHNSON, *Fire Com.*

TUESDAY EVENING, DECEMBER 9TH, AT 8 O'CLOCK

SPECIAL PERFORMANCE

FIRST TIME IN AMERICA

DER ROSENKAVALIER

OPERA IN THREE ACTS

(IN GERMAN)

BY HUGO VON HOFMANNSTHAL

MUSIC BY RICHARD STRAUSS

FELDMARSCHALLIN FÜRSTIN WERDENBERG . .	FRIEDA HEMPEL
BARON OCHS AUF LERCHENAU	. OTTO GORITZ
OCTAVIAN, GENANNT QUINQUIN	MARGARETE OBER
HERR VON FANINAL	. HERMANN WEIL
SOPHIE, SEINE TOCHTER	. ANNA CASE
JUNGFER MARIANNE LEITMETZERIN	. RITA FORNIA
VALZACCHI, EIN INTRIGANT	. ALBERT REISS
ANNINA, SEINE BEGLEITERIN	MARIE MATTFELD
EIN POLIZEIKOMMISSÄR	CARL SCHLEGEL
HAUSHOFMEISTER DER FELDMARSCHALLIN	. PIETRO AUDISIO
HAUSHOFMEISTER BEI FANINAL	. LAMBERT MURPHY
EIN NOTAR	. BASIL RUYSDAEL
EIN WIRT	. JULIUS BAYER
EIN SÄNGER	CARL JÖRN
DREI ADELIGE WAISEN	. LOUISE COX . ROSINA VAN DYCK . SOPHIE BRASLAU
EINE MODISTIN	. JEANNE MAUBOURG
EIN LAKAI	LUDWIG BURGSTALLER
EIN KLEINER NEGER	RUTH WEINSTEIN
CONDUCTOR	ALFRED HERTZ
STAGE MANAGER	FRANZ HÖRTH
TECHNICAL DIRECTOR	EDWARD SIEDLE
ASSISTANT STAGE MANAGER . . .	LOOMIS TAYLOR
CHORUS MASTERS .	GIULIO SETTI AND HANS STEINER

CONTINUED ON NEXT PAGE

CORRECT LIBRETTOS FOR SALE IN THE LOBBY

HARDMAN PIANOS USED EXCLUSIVELY

10. Frieda Hempel as the Marschallin and Margarete Ober as Octavian in the first performance of *Der Rosenkavalier* at the Metropolitan Opera, December 9, 1913. (COURTESY OF THE METROPOLITAN OPERA ARCHIVES)

11. Otto Goritz, the first Baron Ochs at the Metropolitan Opera. (COURTESY OF THE METROPOLITAN OPERA ARCHIVES)

12. Strauss's "favorite" Marschallin was the legendary Lotte Lehmann. Starting in 1935, she sang the role at the Metropolitan Opera in eight of the next ten seasons. (COURTESY OF THE METROPOLITAN OPERA ARCHIVES)

13. Florence Easton, who won considerable acclaim as the Marschallin in the decade which followed World War I, first appeared in this role at the Metropolitan Opera in 1922. (COURTESY OF THE METROPOLITAN OPERA ARCHIVES)

14. Lotte Lehmann, earlier in her career in Vienna, as Octavian. (COURTESY OF THE ROBERT TUGGLE COLLECTION)

15. Another of Strauss's "favorites" was Elisabeth Schumann as Sophie, a role which she first sang in Hamburg in 1911 and then, in 1914, at the Metropolitan Opera. (COURTESY OF *Opera News*)

16. Along with Otto Goritz, Richard Mayr, and Michael Bohnen, Emanuel List became memorable as Baron Ochs. He first appeared in the role at the Metropolitan Opera in 1935 and went on to repeat his performance seventy-four more times. (COURTESY OF THE METROPOLITAN OPERA ARCHIVES)

browsing among long-dead writers, particularly the dramatists, from Middleton to Molière. He loved the antique, the fables and myths of ancient civilizations. He had a perceptive eye, and though he professed himself unmusical, he responded to music and knew much music. He could recall all he knew. In moments of animation he could summon to his mind every book he had read, every picture he had seen.

He was familiar not only with the literature of his country and of Germany but also with the literature of France, England, Spain, and Italy, all of whose languages he spoke. His thesis for the Doctor of Philosophy title was an investigation into the linguistic usage of a group of sixteenth-century French poets. Above all, he was a master of his own language, one of the supple stylists of German literature.

He was married to a woman who was "beautiful, exceptionally clever in a feminine way, courageous and humorous." He had three children. Fame and fortune, respect and love, surrounded him; yet he was given to terrible self-doubts, to brooding melancholy, to picayune touchiness. He was something of a snob, inordinately proud of his aristocracy, and secretly ashamed of the Jew in his ancestry. This did not prevent him from marrying someone Jewish.

Withdrawn and aloof, he hated crowds, including those that gathered for after-theater festivities. He refused to attend an official banquet after the premiere of *Ariadne auf Naxos,* if he would be forced to rub elbows with "smeary journalists and Stuttgart nonentities." Yes, he would come, but only if he were assigned to his own table with his own friends. "I am a liberal-minded person," he wrote to Strauss, "but when it comes to social intercourse I won't play along." On the other hand, with all his contempt for the "smeary journalists," he was quite avid for publicity and quite willing to make propaganda for his work, penning many an essay and newspaper article to explain what he had in mind. And the weaker his work became, the longer became his explanations.

Vacillating between a knowledge of his worth and a sense of insecurity, he was quick to take umbrage, to imagine a slight when none was intended, to feel convinced that his work was not appreciated. Many a time Strauss had to soothe him, particularly when adverse criticism disturbed him, or worse, when Strauss himself was chary of praise. One time Hofmannsthal found out that Strauss had played some of the music of the *Joseph* ballet to a friend, but not to him, the co-author. He was hurt, sat down and wrote Strauss that during their conference in Berlin he, Hofmannsthal, had so much wanted to hear this music but could not bring himself to ask Strauss straight out to play it. Did Strauss not think it worthwhile to show his music to a man who understood little of music? Nevertheless, as the collaborator, wasn't he entitled to hear the music? Strauss answered: "You are a real Viennese. Instead of telling me simply, 'Dear Doctor, please play me something from *Joseph,*' you wait for a propitious turn in the conversation. When that didn't happen to arrive, you write me a letter later. Serves you right!"

To an abnormal degree he was dependent upon the weather. A gray day was to him a lost day. When the south wind blew and carried heat, he suffered severe headaches. The barometer had to be steady before he could write. Yet he was never idle. A dozen projects were always gestating in his head. His ideas he sketched in helter-skelter fashion, covering every inch of paper across, around, diagonally, scribbling on margins. His handwriting is difficult to decipher. (Strauss's was always neat, even in the preliminary sketches.) In addition to his own output, which was considerable, he took an active part in such large enterprises as the establishment of the Salzburg Festival, he and Max Reinhardt being the guiding spirits.

To nourish his talent, he frequently became a vine clinging to strong trees, adapting other men's work; he drew on Sophocles, on Calderón (whom he especially admired), on Otway (*Venice Preserved*), on Molière, on the old morality play *Everyman.* To that extent he was a collaborator, even before Strauss. Perhaps he was too self-critical for his own creative good. Several of his works remained half-completed, most regrettably of all his *Andreas*, which is considered his masterpiece, and which indeed is a story of the most subtle implications set in a menacing Venetian atmosphere. He worked on this novella for more than ten years, then left it unfinished. Similarly, he never managed to produce the final version of his major play, *The Tower* (*Der Turm*).

He was a mystic, though his mysticism did not exclude humor and insouciance, typically Austrian. He believed that illusion is all-pervading, that awake and asleep we dream, that we playact, that we are bound by ritual and legend and are least original when we think ourselves most independent. "Weariness of long forgotten races I cannot brush off my eyelids," he wrote. Like Schnitzler, he believed in the power of mood, and wrote of the havoc or ecstasy which an *Augenblick,* an instant, can cause in our hearts. To an edition of Schnitzler's *Anatol,* Hofmannsthal (under the name of Loris) wrote some dedicatory verses, which characterized not only Schnitzler's but his own writing:

Thus we play theater,
Playact our own feelings,
Ripe before their time,
Tender and triste,
The comedy of our soul. . . .
A few listen but not all,

A few dream, a few smile,
And a few sip a sherbet. . . .

(*Also spielen wir Theater,*
Spielen uns're eignen Stücke,
Frügereift und zart und traurig,
Die Komödie uns'rer Seele. . . .
Manche hören zu, nicht alle,
Manche träumen, manche lachen,
Manche essen Eis. . . .)

Was he a great writer? I think not. His lack of clarity, his inchoate mysticism, and a touch of theatricality in his verses prevented him from being more than a minor, though a fine-grained talent.

Allardyce Nicoll, in his book *World Drama,* judges him "a blind prophet":

> In all his work Hofmannsthal reveals himself as a poet of high distinction, although a poet whom sheer love of beauty frequently leads astray and whose writings have but little message of hope. Despite his "philosophy," he is only a blind prophet whose ears are intoxicated with music.

J. B. Priestley, in *Literature and Western Man,* disagrees:

> He is ultra-sensitive, deeply serious; the mystical strain in him may not be strong, but it is not false, not a literary device like Maeterlinck's, and his feeling that catastrophe is on its way, that the world is doomed, has about it something genuinely prophetic. On the other hand, it could be argued that he retreated before this intuitive knowledge that society and culture, of which he himself was the delicate final flower, were already dying, and that he turned in despair to Baroque masquerade and mystical yearning because he could not bring himself to recognize, in all its raw crudity and destructiveness, what had life in it instead of death. So he clings to the tradition he represents like a man tied to the mast of a ship that is breaking up. His search for "the way into life," perhaps his main theme once his prodigious youth had gone, suggests that he knows he has put himself outside it. But he cannot be dismissed as a figure, elegant and autumnal, of Viennese charm and final melancholy; there is in him more steely strength, more depth, too, than that; unlike almost all his contemporaries, he is now gaining and not losing stature; and he is far from being merely the poet

whose words we cannot hear, above the brass and percussion of the orchestra, in *Elektra* and *Der Rosenkavalier*.

It was this artist, of whom differing estimates are still possible, who formed a partnership that created the words for which he will be longer remembered than for his independent achievements. His words *can* be heard above the brass and percussion. Strauss wished it so; the words were important to him.

Why did Hofmannsthal accept the partnership? It goes without saying that he was far more than the ordinary librettist, and he was treated by Strauss as such. Strauss recognized his worth almost immediately. He wrote to him: "Your nature is so complementary to mine! We were born for each other and we will certainly accomplish something worthwhile if you remain faithful to me." Hofmannsthal agreed: "It is more than a possibility, it is certain knowledge on my part, that we are destined together to create some, perhaps a number of works, which will be beautiful and remarkable."

Their natures *were* complementary. Hofmannsthal's Austrian refinement balanced Strauss's strong and occasionally rough Bavarian genius. Hofmannsthal did not think too much of Strauss's dramatic taste, much as he acknowledged his musical endowment. He waved aside suggestions for operatic subjects that Strauss put forth, sometimes gently and diplomatically, sometimes impatiently and brusquely; and, at least on one occasion, laid down the ultimatum that Strauss was either to stop talking about the particular plot he had in mind or he, Hofmannsthal, would give up the partnership. On the other hand, Strauss's intuition of what was possible in opera, and what was not, prevented the poet from becoming too verbose or too vague, at least in the early period of collaboration. The result is that Hofmannsthal's best plays, considered merely as plays, are the two librettos *Der Rosenkavalier* and *Ariadne auf Naxos*.

Hofmannsthal knew that in working with Strauss he had a good chance to spread his own reputation beyond national bounds. The poet is confined to his own language; the composer speaks the Esperanto of music. To raise the worth of the operatic libretto was a congenial task to the stagestruck author. Strauss encouraged him: "You are the born librettist. In my mind that is a great compliment. For I consider it much more difficult to write a good opera than a good play."

The parnership lasted for twenty-four years. The two men worked together well. But as men they never really liked each other. The correspondence throws up cold waves of politeness and occasionally of something less than politeness, only rarely waves of affectionate friendship. Perhaps it helps a creative partnership *not* to be personal friends. We know about the quarrels of Gilbert and Sullivan. Did Beaumont and Fletcher get along? One is inclined to doubt it.

More than once, however, Strauss paid a tribute to his partner as an artist, and almost always did the poet pay tribute to the musician. In 1924 Strauss wrote Hofmannsthal a charming letter on the occasion of Hofmannsthal's fiftieth birthday. Anything that he could tell him in words would be banal, "in comparison with what, as the composer of your wonderful poetry, I have already said to you in music. It was your words which drew from me the finest music that I had to give; this knowledge must fill you with deep gratification. Let therefore Chrysothemis, the Marschallin, Ariadne, Zerbinetta, the Empress, and, not least, H (Helena) 'admired much and much reproved' — join me in calling on you and thanking you for all you have dedicated to me out of your life's work, and kindled in me, and rounded to life."

Yet in many another, less festive moment, Hofmannsthal sorely tried Strauss's patience — and vice versa. In 1917, after the failure of *Le Bourgeois Gentilhomme,* Strauss, testy and nervous, lost his equanimity and angrily wrote Hofmannsthal's wife that "it really would not do to have Hugo merely brush aside my doubts with an extravagant gesture." The least he had a right to ask was that Hofmannsthal read and ponder over Strauss's suggestions. The quarrel was precipitated by Hofmannsthal's writing to Strauss that he found his suggestions for altering the work "beneath discussion . . . they demonstrated to me that your taste and mine are miles apart, at least as concerns matters of this kind. Pray let me have in due course your decision whether I am free to dispose otherwise of this Molière adaptation, of which I do not intend to alter one iota." Strauss, after being angry, gave a soft answer. "Why do you immediately become bitterly angry when I make a proposal, even if you find it not worth discussing? One ought to be able to discuss anything at all, and particularly a work for the theater. . . . I will readily admit that your taste is more cultivated than mine. . . . But kill me if you like, I do not find anything more distasteful than plays which do not draw and are written for the proverbial five perceptive spectators."

Strauss addressed the poet as "Honored Herr von Hofmannsthal." In a few letters he unbent sufficiently to call him "Dear Friend." But no more than that. They made a journey to Italy together; even this journey, which was undertaken for artistic reasons and not for pleasure, did not bring them close. As I have said, Hofmannsthal admired and respected the musician, but the man — he rather looked down on Strauss, who could be blunt and callous. Strauss could not understand Hofmannsthal's mercurial moods, the frequent headaches, the attacks of depression, the deep concern with which the poet observed Europe's political morality declining. What did Strauss care about political morality? He was interested in getting on with the work; he was always demanding, "Where is the next act? Where is the next scene?"

As Hofmannsthal grew older, his melancholy deepened and he fled into lonelier isolation. Strauss kept driving on, his appetite for work being as insatiable as when he was young. There they were, one working moodily in Austria, the other methodically in his villa in Garmisch; and the circumstances that their personal meetings were relatively few has given us their copious correspondence, letters that allow us a fascinating glimpse into the workshop.

One other circumstance may have contributed to their seeing each other infrequently: the two wives did not like each other. Once Strauss had become famous and wealthy and had moved into his own villa, his wife, Pauline, began to take on airs. She frequently referred to the fact that she belonged to a titled family. The people she liked were not musicians or poets — even if the poet had a "von" before his name — but members of society, bankers, and military celebrities. As a hostess she had now become pretentious, as a wife dictatorial. Her "Richard" was to her the good-natured genius who could earn remarkable sums of money as well as flattering renown, but all the same as a man of elegance, as a man of charm, as a dinner-table conversationalist, well, really, he wasn't in it. He needed mothering, he needed to be taken care of, watched carefully, nursed along, spared all nuisances.

But he needed also to be treated brusquely and bossed and sent about his business. "Go, Richard, go compose," she would tell him and banish him to the workroom. The more he accepted her domination, the more waspish she became. He not only accepted it but he didn't mind in the least. The German language has an expressive word for a henpecked husband: *Pantoffelheld,* "hero of the slipper." The composer of *A Hero's Life* enjoyed the role. He continued to hold Pauline in unswerving affection even after she lost most of her looks and even though her behavior must have embarrassed him. Was he an uxorious philosopher or an indolent husband? A little of both. In his attitude, loyalty combined with tolerance, love with laziness. As the years advanced, Pauline did not become easier to live with. She saw to it that the peach jam at breakfast was first-class, but the sweetness in her own personality dried up. She became parsimonious and kept everything in the house under lock and key, a bunch of keys dangling from her waist. As a *Hausfrau* she was capable even of interrupting her husband at his work. She sent him to the village to buy milk while he was composing *Elektra,* "the maid being busy washing the windows." He went.

One of Hofmannsthal's intimate friends was the remarkable Harry Graf Kessler. In heritage and fortune, looks and behavior, an aristocrat of high order, he was one of those rounded, alive, and responsive personalities whom nineteenth-century Europe knew how to breed. Though born a German, he was completely cosmopolitan in his outlook. Though born to a conservative tradition, he was strongly liberal and democratic in his political philosophy. He loved the arts and was more than a dilettante. His home was in Weimar but he was always turning up in this city or the next, in London, Paris, or Rome. Kessler knew many of the leading artists of the day. The sculptor Aristide Maillol was a close friend. So was Edvard Munch, who painted his portrait. After the First World War, he took an active though ineffectual part in the government of the Weimar Republic, his name being linked with those of Rathenau and Stresemann. When National Socialism entered Germany, Kessler immediately and voluntarily left the Third Reich. He went to Paris, never to return to Germany. From there he sent warnings against Hitler to the unheeding Germans; there he befriended the banished artists. He died in France in 1937, an almost forgotten exile.

He attended a performance of *Elektra* in Berlin under Bruno Walter. After the performance, Pauline invited him and Max Reinhardt to supper at her home:

> At the dinner table Paulinchen showed her good and bad sides; in a motherly fashion she urged everybody to eat, particularly Max, who sat next to her and whose plate she kept heaping with an egg, a slice of meat, a helping of salad. But she was also irritatingly vulgar and tactless. She would have none of *Woyzeck* (Büchner's play, not the opera): How could she take an interest in the fate of a dirty little subaltern? How did that touch her ("her," she let us read between the lines, a general's daughter)? I said, "But *Carmen* is also the story of a subaltern." Pauline: "Yes, but romantic, Spanish, Merimée." I: "It seems to me that a German subaltern is no less consequential than a Spanish one. . . . Ah well! I am just a plain democrat." Pauline: "You, a *Graf,* a democrat? Then you are befouling your own nest." I: "Beg pardon, *gnädige Frau.* Whether I befoul my own nest is a judgment which I must reserve for myself."
>
> Richard Strauss had become more and more uneasy. Now he broke into the conversation in order to terminate it, and explained to me that his wife knew nothing of politics. I was to pay no attention. . . .

Hofmannsthal would hardly have enjoyed the company of such a woman. And since Pauline was always with Strauss, it was wiser to meet as seldom as possible. Even early in their relationship Strauss had to apologize for Pauline's behavior to Hofmannsthal. He wrote: "I hope you will come again to Berlin — and I promise you that my 'original' of a wife won't throw her keys into the room." Obviously Pauline had been in a temper.

Yet whatever were Hugo's personal feelings about Richard and Pauline, the partnership endured. Perhaps we can find practical reasons as well: even before inflation and the influx of foreign royalties, Strauss made it possible to augment the poet's income. Hofmannsthal did not disdain this augmentation.

Such was the man whom Strauss first met casually in Paris in 1900 and with whom he created six operas. Such was the man who, when he died of a cerebral hemorrhage in July of 1929 — as he dressed to go to the funeral of his son, Franz, who, two days earlier, had committed suicide — left a hole as wide as a church door in Richard Strauss's life.

The Cavalier of the Rose

by
ANTHONY BURGESS

BASED ON *Der Rosenkavalier* BY
HUGO VON HOFMANNSTHAL

I.

History is always the past. We never live through history. When we are old, we discover to our surprise that we *have* lived through it. When we die we join it. A sunlit morning in Vienna, two naked lovers waking in each other's arms — what has this to do with history? But outside the great bed, the silken chamber, the magnificent house on the edge of the city with the woodlarks crying, outside in the great world, history was preparing itself for the attention of the historians. Maria Theresa, a child of Vienna, daughter of the late Emperor Karl VI, reigned as Queen of Hungary and Bohemia and Archduchess of Austria. Her consort Francis Stephen, Grand Duke of Tuscany, was her equal partner in rule, and he had touched fashionable Vienna with the refinements of Tuscany and even the Tuscan language. Soon, though, France would be inciting Prussia and Bavaria and Saxony and Naples and Sardinia to bite at Maria Theresa's territories, shouting their justification in the extinction of the male line of the Hapsburgs. The War of the Austrian Succession was still to come, seven years of struggle to end with the Peace of Aix-la-Chapelle and Maria Theresa's confirmation as ruler of her realms and the election of her husband to the imperial throne. Of the movement of history the lovers knew nothing and cared less. The movements of their own bodies were of greater interest. They had put off their nominal roles in the hierarchy of Austrian rule along with their titles. The Princess and the Count had been reduced, or elevated, to the rank of mere adulterous lovers. Articulate, as befitted their titles, they had words as well as caresses. Octavian, the young Count, spoke of the beauty of his mistress, the refinement of her sensibilities as well as the treasures of her body. Ah, who could ever measure their perfections?

She, the Princess von Werdenberg, wife of Field Marshal Prince von Werdenberg, said, wittily: "Mignon, don't grieve about the absence of a measuring rod. Do you want my perfections — your word, not mine — to be advertised in the daily courier or proclaimed in the streets?"

"Ah no, angel, angel, I'm happy enough to be the sole custodian of that knowledge." He drew the white cambric shirt of the day before on to his spare white body. He was young, younger than she, and might be thought of as more beautiful than handsome. But there was nothing epicene there: he was brave, skilled with the sword, and would be ready to ride at the head of his squadron when the War of the Succession began. Only fools heard in the high clear voice and saw in the slim body the lineaments of the effeminate. There was nothing effeminate in his love-making. "But when I say *you,*" he was saying as he dressed swiftly, "and speak of your this and that, I'm just as foolish as when I say *I.* The words have no meaning. We lose our identities in love and become one being."

"Which means," said the Princess, "that I may not say *I love you.* But I say it. I say it now."

He was a little petulant as he squinted at the bright spring morning that the uncurtained window framed. "I hate the day," he said. "When the day comes you belong to others. If I can't keep in the dark, at least let me shut out the birdsong. Voices of the world, ugh." She smiled as he rushed over to close the half-open casement. In the distance bells began tinkling softly. He saw her smile and asked why she smiled. Love, her face said, I smile with love, with the pleasure of seeing you after a night of not seeing you. Angel. Beloved. He flew to her arms. The bells tinkled again. The bells approached.

"The couriers," she said. "The outside world." She was already in the furred negligee of the morning. A woman of astounding beauty, but a beauty that had already achieved its climax. She was older than her Mignon, the Count Octavian, and she knew it. She would not grow more beautiful.

"Letters," Octavian said, "from Saurau and Hartig and the Portuguese ambassador. I won't have it, I'll keep the world out, I'm master here." There was a fumbling at the door.

"It's my morning chocolate," she said. "Quick. Hide behind that screen." He did. A little black boy entered, all in yellow, with little silver bells ajangle on his shoulder-knots, sleeves and calves. He bore steaming chocolate and Viennese whipped cream on a silver salver.

"Your esteemed and beauteous highness," someone had taught the boy to say, "I bid you good morning. Here is chocolate, hot. Here is *Schlagobers,* cold."

And there was Octavian's sword with sheath and belt lying on the candy-striped couch. "Thank you, Mahomed," she said. "On that table there." So that the black boy, who was as much of a gossip as anybody in her household, should not see her grasp the sword and thrust it into the hands of its owner behind the screen. She frowned at Octavian, an earnest of words to come. Careless idiot. The black boy placed the tray on the little table, pushed a plush-seated chair beside it, bowed with his hands joined across his breast, then, in a kind of dance step that made his bells jingle, left the chamber backwards. Octavian came out, blowing with relief.

"Careless idiot. Featherbrain. Is it the done thing for a lady of rank and fashion to have a sword lying in her bedchamber? A certain lack of breeding shows in you sometimes."

"If my lack of breeding upsets you," he said, "I could best express my love and devotion by removing my lack of breeding along with myself."

A joke, of course, but she could not help hearing in it a kind of rehearsal of farewell. She smiled tenderly, however, and said:

"Bring a chair. Drink some chocolate. Share my cup."

"No," he said. He lifted the table with its aromatic burden over to the candy-striped couch. "Here," he said. So they shared the one cup and she stroked his hair and, when the chocolate was finished, he lay with his head in her lap. He spoke her name, which was also and primarily the name of their Archduchess: Maria Theres'. Octavian. Angel. Mignon. Beloved. My own boy. Boy was right. She was in her thirties and he was a boy. Octavian said:

"Your husband the Field Marshal is hunting brown bear and black boar in the wilds of Croatia. And I lie here in the indolent flower of my youth. But what could be better? I'm so happy!"

It is always unwise, she thought, to say one is happy. Happiness is like history, something in the past. The mention of her husband cast a shadow. She said:

"Let him sleep, or hunt. I dreamed about him last night."

His head started up from her lap. "You dreamed of *him* — while you and I were —"

"I can't order my dreams as I order dinner. There's no need to look like that, Octavian. Be angry with the dream if you like, but not with me. I dreamed he was here, at home again."

"Here." He looked over at the bed and shuddered.

"There was a noise — horses clattering, the voices of men arriving. Then there he was — here. I can still hear it, that noise."

"There *is* a noise," he said, sitting up, then rising. "Men and horses. It can't be your husband, though. He's at Esseg, isn't he — that's a hundred miles away —" Horses approached, men: he could hear them. Caught, the cuckolder caught? And any door out would lead to servants. The window? "It can't be. It's someone else. Do you expect someone else?"

She seemed fearful, and this made him fearful too. No very honorable situation. "It's amazing," she said, "how fast he can travel when he wishes. Why, there was one occasion —"

"What occasion? What do you mean?" he said jealously.

"Oh, nothing. I think the horsemen are passing. Nothing at all to bother you with." She too was on her feet now.

"Despair! Despair." He had the couch to himself. He threw himself upon it. "Why do you do this to me?" It was very theatrical, a boy's behavior. He had buried his head in a cushion. He could not hear what she now heard. She heard footsteps not in the antechamber, where strangers awaited the levée, but in the closet. Servants would not keep him out, would not even delay him. She grasped at Octavian's silken collar. She said:

"The dream was right. Up, out, he's coming." Octavian had already drawn his sword. "Don't be foolish, hide. No, not the antechamber, it will be full of people. No, not there — Hide — in the bed — close the curtains."

He looked young and ridiculous, upright, sword brandished. "I stay with you. We'll have it out. We love each other."

"Oh, idiot. In there. Behind the curtains."

"And if I'm caught here —" His sword-arm looked less sure of itself. "What will happen to you, beloved?"

She stamped with impatience. "Hide!" He was undecided where to hide. That screen again? No, the suspicious husband might push it aside. The bed, then. He crawled into the mess of pillows and tumbled sheets and drew fast the thick velvet curtains. She stood, waiting, turned to the door, trying to calm her breathing. She could hear servants trying to keep out a male with a loud and importunate voice. It did not sound like her husband. Our mistress is sleeping. She is not well. She has a profound migraine. And then she recognized the voice. It was that of her cousin Baron Ochs of Lerchenau. Ochs coming here, and so early? Then she remembered something — a long long letter from Ochs delivered to her when starting off in her coach for a drive through the Vienna Woods, her Mignon snuggling beside her, the first kiss as the wheels rolled, the letter forgotten. This was a kind of corruption. And if the letter had been from her husband, saying: Liebchen, I return at once, an urgent summons, business at court? Corruption, neglect, passion driving out reason as expressed in the cool business of the well-organized day, the letters carefully read and as carefully answered. Had they already gone too far? She heard the voices coming closer.

"Perhaps if your lordship would be good enough to wait a brief while in the gallery —"

"Insolent nonsense, fellow. I am Baron Lerchenau and I wait for no one. Out of my path at once unless you prefer to be whipped out of it. Make way."

"It's Ochs," she told the hidden Octavian. "He's battering the door down. Stay there, do not move." And indeed a heavy fist, garnished with heavy rings, was already firmly rattattatting. But Octavian came out of hiding. He wore his mistress's nightcap, sufficiently like the mobcap of a servant, and his mistress's nightgown, which would serve as the daygown of a maid.

"Tell me my duties, highness," said Octavian in the high voice of a girl, curtseying clumsily. "Your highness knows that this is only my first day in your highness's service."

"Out," she said, and she ran over to kiss him. "Go on, that way. If you wish to pretend, pretend properly. Mincing little steps, head shyly down. And watch that sword. It's sticking out at the back like a tail. And give me an hour, beloved. We'll meet by the fountain in the Italian garden —"

Octavian's hand was on the doorknob at the moment that the door was flung open. Ochs, and behind him footmen expressing their regret to their mistress with hands on hearts, hands held wide, wide eyes almost tearful. Octavian's head was lowered in a show of maid's modesty. Unseeing, he butted Ochs. Confused, he curtseyed and went to the wall. The open door was full of Ochs and footmen. No way out yet. But Ochs, with a ready eye for a wench of the lower orders, said: "Pardon me, my dear, I trust I did not hurt you." Octavian curtseyed his way back toward the bed. Change the sheets, a maid's chore. "Pretty little thing," Ochs said.

"Good morning, cousin," the Princess said. "How well you look."

"There," growled Ochs at the footmen. "Welcome, you see? Expected. If you were in my employ you'd soon be out of it. Away, this is private." And he himself slammed the door on them.

II.

Baron Ochs of Lerchenau was sometimes called a Falstaff without the wit. His belly was more than Falstaffian: it denoted heavy dinners and heavy bevers before and after them. He would have looked more presentable with a Falstaffian beard, but this was an age of clean shaves and wigs. His nose was a maimed beacon: its red shine was marred by the lumps of good living and a wart on the left-hand slope that sported three filaments which waved in the breeze of his bark. His eyes of a sharp blue were couched in fat. A high noble forehead might have counteracted the meanness of the mouth, with a pouting lower lip that flared crimson, the vast jowls and cheeks, the potman's nose and the swinish eyes, but his brow was narrow and low. It was a face that might have been more acceptable if nature had placed it on his no-neck upside down. The voice was hectoring and knew no variation of tone. He was dressed in flowered silk spotted from his early breakfast. He kicked off his buckled shoes, evidently tight, without permission as he sat on an overdainty chair that grumbled quietly at its burden. He had thrown off his topcoat, and it lay like a dog on the carpet. His hat, which was panached like Cyrano's, he was slow in removing.

He sat and panted and looked around him. It was a noble room, though it was only a bedchamber. He nodded at its cream and gold and, as if deciding that it was worthy of his brief sojourn, he at last took off his hat and spun it in the direction of the couch. It did not reach the couch. "Pick it up, my dear," he told the back of the sheet-removing Octavian. "Hang it somewhere." And as Octavian obeyed he said: "Pretty little thing. No more of that, though. Done with dallying. Settling down now." And, to the Princess, "I knew you wouldn't object to my coming early. They said out there that you had a bad headache or something. Lot of nonsense, of course. You look as fresh as a rose. Rose, yes. We'll come to that later. I like the early morning. Wake up hungry these days, good thing, gets me out of bed. No," he said, in response to an invitation not given, "don't bother to order me breakfast. I had a fine haunch of boar this morning. Hung five days, marinated in red wine, a bunch of herbs. A pint of sherry. A man has to look after himself. Those days of breakfast round the bathtub, Princess Whatshername, a regular invitation, where is she now? Not so young as I was, you can see that. Pretty little thing," he said again, eyes on Octavian plumping a pillow. "Not seen her before."

"She's just come up from the country," the Princess said. "She has a lot to learn, of course. You can go now, Mariandel," she said to Octavian, wondering why she had chosen that name. Of course, her old schoolfellow, poor girl, made a terrible marriage.

"Let her stay," Ochs said, "charming little baggage." And then: "Well, what do you think of the news?"

"News?"

"Come now, the letter."

"Oh, the letter. This headache drove it clean out of my mind. Well," she said carefully, "it seemed to me to be very good news."

"Glad you think so. Thought you might be a bit surprised, though. I mean, I never thought of myself as the marrying type."

So that was what the letter was about. "And who is the fortunate lady?"

"Come now," and he barked a laugh as though at an impossibility, a letter from him, the Baron Ochs of Lerchenau, and unread, "it was all in black and white, cousin. A peach and an unripe one, something to get these teeth into." He showed his teeth, his only good feature. "Barely fifteen, by God."

"Of course. I was just saying the name to myself a minute since as you were coming in, cousin."

"Ah, no. I didn't mention the name. A peach, I tell you. A waist I can get one hand round. Fresh as a violet. Thought I'd give you the important matters first — youth, beauty and so on. Wealth, and all the rest of it. Position — well, I have to admit to a bit of doubt. Not much of a family. Faninal. You wouldn't know it, of course. Faninal." He tasted the sound of it, like some foreign dish he was not sure whether or not to like.

"A local family?"

"All too local. Viennese merchant class, that's the problem. Her Majesty's just put a *von* in his name. He was in charge of army victualing. Salt beef and flour for the troops in the Netherlands. I can see," he said, "from the set of your lips that you're not too happy about it." But the slight pout had been intended for Octavian: take the tray and get out of here: your boots were visible when you bent over the bed then: nobody takes as long as that to change sheets. "A misalliance, you may be thinking. But the girl — wait till you see her. Straight out of a convent, knows nothing of the world, voice like an angel. Such innocence."

He said the word with a growl, as though innocence were for eating. "And the old man — von Faninal, as we must call him now — owns half the bourgeois property in the city, got a fine mansion of his own, not long for this world, so his doctor told me. Heart. Heart." He tapped the Princess on the knee boldly, grunting at the effort of leaning forward to do it. "She's an only child." And he winked horribly.

"Do take that tray out, Mariandel," she said. "And those dirty sheets."

"Well," said Ochs, leaning back. "If she's taking the tray out she may as well bring another tray in. You're quite right, cousin, I am somewhat peckish," finding, as he often did, an excuse for hoggishness in others' imagined exhortations to be hoggish, "the morning air, it does indeed promote appetite, you are, as so often, perfectly correct. Not much, though. Some cold sirloin, underdone, and a new loaf perhaps. I have a passion for new bread. The bread at the inn was *not fresh.*" He glowered at her, as though it were her fault. "But I've nothing against their marinated boarflesh, nothing at all." He waited, as for a contradiction. And then, seeing Octavian going with soiled sheets and tray to the door, he levered himself up in his stockinged feet and padded toward him. "Allow me to open it for you, my dear." And then, in a breathy whisper, "You and I could be very cozy together one evening. I'll arrange it, you just leave it to me, my love." Octavian, as was expected, giggled. "Here, let somebody else do the work, one of those bone-idle footmen out there." He opened the door and cried: "Come on, come on, help the girl, will you? And fetch me some breakfast — beef, ham, new bread, butter, beer — quick, quick, get on with it." He, as it were absentmindedly, took the freed right hand of Octavian and padded back with him to the middle of the room. He said to the Princess:

"The real reason why I came was to ask you for an ambassador."

"Ambassador?"

"Yes, you know the custom, somebody to hand over the silver rose to the bride-to-be. Damned silly custom perhaps, but it's expected. Marks the aristocracy off from the riffraff of the bourgeoisie. I've brought it."

"Brought it?"

"It's down below. One of my men has it. I came with a full retinue, never do things by halves is my motto." And still he held on, as if absentmindedly, to the hand of Octavian, whose giggles were in danger of modulating to a more masculine guffaw.

"One of our kinsmen, you mean," the Princess said. "Who? Preysing? Lamberg?"

"I leave it all in your lilywhite hands, dear cousin."

"That shall be done, dear cousin. It's time for my levée. Is there anything else I'm to do for you?"

"Well," he said, "there's the matter of a marriage settlement. I'd like to see that attorney of yours, a good man, I remember. I don't retain one of my own, as you know, no use for them normally. I mean people of our rank are above the law, but this might be a bit of a tricky business, the bourgeoisie holds on to its money." And still he held on to Octavian. The Princess said:

"Very well, cousin. Mariandel, go and see if my attorney is in the anteroom, will you?" But Ochs held on and said:

"No need, leave it to me, I'll yell for him." And he opened the door with his free paw. His yell was forestalled by the entry of the Major-domo. Ochs had not expected that. He, a baron, had opened the door for a mere upper servant. The Major-domo bowed. He was a thin man and had the gray look of the ulcerated. He was ribboned and powdered and polished. The Princess said:

"Good morning, Struhan. Is my attorney there?"

"Yes, your highness, and also your steward, your *chef de cuisine,* and, ah yes, his grace the Duke of Silva commends to your highness a singer and a flautist of high accomplishment." A certain dryness entered his tone. "And, of course, there are the usual petitioners."

Ochs, meanwhile, was saying breathily to Octavian: "A nice little supper, eh, just the two of us? Have you ever had a nice little *tête-à-tête* with a gentleman?"

"Let them wait, Struhan," the Princess said. The Major-domo bowed and left. "Taking your pleasure where you find it, cousin," she said to Ochs. "I thought I heard you say something about a new life, settling down."

"Oh, your highness," Ochs said formally, "it's the atmosphere here, you know — relaxed, no Spanish affectation, friendly, I always feel I'm among friends here." But he let the hand of Octavian go.

"A man of birth and honor, newly betrothed — come, my cousin, is this any way to behave?" Her tone was only mock-severe.

"Do I have to live like a monk just because I'm going to be married?" said Ochs, padding toward her. "It's the hunting instinct in me, you know, always hot on the scent. You women, with respect, can never know the sensation. I mean, you're merely the quarry."

"There's a season for hunting," she said.

"Ah no, this is a different kind of chase, no close season when love is involved. Seriously now, in all seriousness, I seek the acquaintance of your serving wench here to a different end. I ask permission to install her in my new household, a little gift, a well-bred attendant on my baroness. What do you say?"

"Your baroness will wish to make her own choice. Besides, this girl is my special jewel. High-bred, as you say, very."

"Blue blood, I don't doubt," Ochs said, "it shines out of her. I always say a man of the blood should be surrounded by the blood, even when it flows on the wrong side of the blanket. I have a body-servant quite as well born as myself — a prince's son. He's downstairs at this moment, with the silver rose in his keeping. Whenever your highness shall deign to choose an ambassador, he'll receive the rose from the hands of a prince's son."

"Mariandel," said the Princess, "will you be so good as to —"

"Let me have her," pleaded Ochs with a low growl. "I mean, let my baroness have her."

"— bring me the miniature of the Count Octavian."

Octavian stared at her. She smiled back. Octavian went to a

small glass cupboard in the farthest corner of the chamber. Ochs drank in the mincing gait with admiration. He said:

"A prince's by-blow," and then: "Would it be a good thing to give the girl an illuminated copy of my pedigree, just to keep her reminded, you know — or perhaps the lock of the hair of the first of the Lerchenaus, that's going back a bit, the First Hereditary Grand Warden of the Domains of Carinthia?" The Princess said nothing; she took from Octavian's hands a portrait of Octavian, framed in silver, inset with small diamonds.

"Here, cousin," she said. "Here, I think, is your ambassador. What do you think of him?"

"As your highness wishes. That's settled then.

"But look. This is my young cousin, Count Octavian."

Ochs dutifully looked. He started. "My God," he said, his pig-eyes swiveling from the real to the pictured. "No wonder I thought — I was right about the blue blood —" And Octavian wondered uneasily whether his mistress was not perhaps going too far. Egad, it's the same, let's have that dress off her, by heaven, a young man in your room, the Prince shall know about this — But all Ochs said was: "Knew I was right, always had a nose for blood."

"Rofrano is the name," said the Princess. "Younger brother of the Marquis —"

"Ah, that explains this, then. I remember old Rofrano. By God, he had an eye and a hand and a — Well, blood will always out. Who cares about the the the niceties?"

"So you see perhaps, cousin, why she's precious to me. Very well, Mariandel, you may go now." Octavian curtseyed. Ochs accompanied her to the door, saying:

"Pretty child, leave everything to me. We'll have *such an evening together,*" very breathily. Octavian pitched his voice to the high limit:

"Naughty man," and then was gone, slamming the door in Ochs's nose. Ochs rubbed his nose. The door opened. Ah, she was coming back. But she was not coming back. A whole rabble started to come in.

III.

A very ill-favored old lady of the chamber came in first. The contrast with the supposed her who had gone out made Ochs retreat a couple of paces. Two footmen came in after her. They took the Princess's toilet table, placed it in the middle of the chamber, and concealed it from the entering mob with a three-faced screen. The Princess got behind it with the lady of the chamber. Then came the Princess's attorney, an old man in sour black with asthma, followed by the *chef de cuisine* and the *sous-chef,* who carried the leather-bound book of menus. A pert milliner was next, and then an evident scholar from the untidiness of his rusty black, a great tome under his arm. Small hairless dogs of a South American breed pranced in, followed by their keeper and would-be vendor, on whose left shoulder a marmoset gibbered. Then there was the Italian Valzacchi, a subtle but workless busybody, gossip, self-styled man of affairs, with a lady like a very gloomy Madonna, a great gossip-gatherer named Annina. A widow, a military one left penniless, impoverished minor aristocracy clear in her gait and profile, led in three daughters in profound but tasteful mourning. She raised her finger at the girls and they broke into a scrannel song specially composed for them:

"High-born orphans we
Who ask your charitee."

Then there came in Ochs's breakfast, on a tray borne by one of the Baron's own men, an ill-favored starveling with a faint squint. The Baron had forgotten one appetite with the stimulation of another. He pointed to a low square stool: he would pick at it later when this mob had gone. He reckoned without the prancing dogs.

The milliner praised her new confection loudly: "*Le chapeau Paméla — la poudre à la reine de Golconde.*" The animal-vendor cried his wares. There was quite a din. An Italian tenor and a flautist were personally escorted in by the Major-domo, who would doubtless get his commission if patronage were secured. The tenor sang; the flautist provided a florid obbligato. Quite a din.

"Our father died in the war
And left us very poor.
Munificent Princess,
Pray comfort our distress."

"*Le chapeau Paméla. C'est la merveille du monde!*"

The Princess's personal hairdresser, M. Hippolyte, waited with his assistant. The Princess scorned wigs, except on court occasions. She had the finest, silkiest, corn-yellow hair in abundance: to shear and hide it would be a deadly sin.

"Lap-dogs, monkeys, free from fleas,
Accompanied by guarantees
And really awesome pedigrees."

"*Di rigori armato il seno
Contro amor mi ribellai
Ma fui vinto in un baleno
In mirar due vaghi rai . . .*"

The tenor showed off his high C flat; the flautist fluted in the breathy depths. The Princess appeared. The screen was removed. All bowed. She was ready to face the public morning, all except her coiffure. The Major-domo was by her side. He held a small purse. The Princess beckoned to the tallest of the three orphans, gave her the purse, kissed her gently on the brow. Such graciousness, such generosity, such condescension. The rusty-gowned scholar stepped in with his folio. A first edition Ariosto. Priceless, but it has a price, it would adorn your highness's library — But Valzacchi sneered and proffered a news-sheet, a single black-edged page. He called himself its editor, but Annina did all the work. "All the latest scandals," he offered. "Secret information. A dead body found in a certain count's town house. A rich merchant poisoned by his wife with the help of her lover. Very new news — happened only at three this morning — hot from my private press."

"No," said the Princess.

"*Tutti quanti* — the jealously guarded *segreti* of *le beau monde*."

"No," said the Princess. The orphans withdrew with their low-curtseying mother:

"Eternal bliss attend you,
The holy heavens befriend you."

The hairdresser's coattails flew as he examined her highness from every angle. A courier in black, pink and silver entered with a deckled-edged note. The Major-domo had a silver salver ready. He handed her highness the note on its salver. She read the note. She did not like what she read. The assistant to the hairdresser handed him curling tongs. They were too hot. Some paper to cool them on. Her highness handed him the note. Bows and bows, that would do very well.

*"Ahi! Che resiste puoco
Cor di gelo a stral di fuoco . . ."*

The Princess introduced her attorney to the Baron. The Baron led him to a gilded chair in the corner. The Baron sat; the attorney, panting asthmatically, remained standing.

"I'll put it simply to you, then you can dress it up in all the legal tomfoolery. I want a separate endowment, a gift if you like, nothing to do with the dowry, do you understand me? I'll tell you precisely what I want. I want the title-deeds of that demesne that he has, Gaunersdorf, see what I mean? No encumbrances, no claims, no entails —"

"With all due respect and in all dutiful submission, your lordship does not appear to realize that the husband may give a *donatio ante nuptias* to the wife, but not the wife to the husband. Such a contract would be quite without precedent."

"But, damn it, man, this is a special case —"

"Law makes no recognition of special cases."

"Oh, doesn't it? You listen to me. I, sir, am the living head of a family of ancient power and nobility. I am condescending — mark that word — to marry a certain nobody, a Mademoiselle or Miss Faninal, whose father has nothing except money — no pedigree, no patent of nobility. Now I doubt if our Archduchess would be pleased with such a union — I wonder sometimes if heaven itself doesn't frown upon it — and yet I'm going through with it. And I demand that you find something in the law that permits me adequate compensation for —"

Three more of the Baron's men came in — body-servant, almoner, chasseur. The chasseur's livery was too small for his yokel body. The face was that of the lowest village lout. The hands, square and horny, twitched as if to wish to strangle a chicken. The almoner had the cunning leer of a lay lawyer or village abortionist. He was stunted but beefy. The body-servant was lathe-thin and had the idiot look of a long incestuous line. There was noble blood, there was no doubt about it. He held a stout leather jewel case.

"There it is," Ochs said. "The silver rose in its box, all cleaned up and ready. You see how honorably I do everything? I demand some loophole in the law — see what I mean?" The attorney thought he saw that he would be strangled like a chicken if he did not find this loophole. The flautist started a new cadenza. The tenor began a new stanza:

"Ma si caro è'l mio tormento
Dolce è si la piaga mia,
Ch'il penare è mio contento
E'l sanarmi è tirannia . . ."

"You could, of course, have a special clause put in the marriage settlement — *donatio inter vivos,* we call it —"

"No! Compensation, presented as such! Legal compensation!"

He shut up singer and flautist at once.

"This won't do, Hippolyte," said the Princess, twisting and turning before the mirror her tirewoman held. "This won't do at all."

In shock and horror the coiffeur flew round like a moth, adjusting fingers like flames. Ochs looked for his breakfast, found bread, butter and beer but no beef. Small distended dogs lay around, innocently blinking. The Baron grunted, getting absentminded, looked for his shoes. The marmoset had curled up in one of them. He sent it scampering like a fly up the wall. It dropped like a feather into the arms of its cooing master. Ochs straightened the welsh-combed locks of his body-servant. The flames of the coiffeur's fingers sank. He surveyed. "Better?"

"Much better," said the Princess, and, to her Major-domo: "Tell them all to leave."

Valzacchi said to the Baron: "Is your lordship looking for something? Can we be of any help?"

"My other shoe. Ah," to the almoner, who had found it. "Who the hell are you?" to the inclining Valzacchi.

"Discreet people ready to help, ready to be your lordship's most faithful servants. Discreet, silent —"

"Come statua di Giove," said Annina.

"Useful," said Valzacchi.

"Useful, eh? How useful?"

"We work as uncle and niece," said Annina. "We keep our eyes wide open. Supposing, now, your lordship were to marry a youthful bride —"

"How did you know about that?" Ochs was suspicious and impressed. Valzacchi was quick with:

"If your lordship had reason to be jealous, for example. *Dico per dire.* Who can ever tell? Human nature is frail, especially in the young. Every step the lady takes, every *billet doux* she receives — you understand? We are always around. It is our business. *Affare nostro.* Your lordship follows me?". He dryly flicked thumb against fingers. A little advance? A thaler or so? Ochs pretended to be above understanding the gesture. He growled:

"Let's try you out, then. Do you know a lady named Mariandel?"

"Mariandel?"

"Her highness's personal servant."

"Sai tu? Cosa vuole?"

"Niente."

"Information you wish?" said Valzacchi. "No trouble. *Niente problema.* We know what you want, I think. Trust us."

Ochs grunted and turned to the Princess. "And now, your highness, there is nothing more to do than to leave with you this — object." He clicked his fingers impatiently. "Come, Leopold, the jewel case." The body-servant awkwardly brought it forward. "See," opening it, "the silver rose." The sun caught it, frail, exquisite.

"Leave it in its case," said the Princess. "Place it on that escritoire." With ill-coordinated steps the body-servant did what was asked.

"Or perhaps," said Ochs, "if you called your servant, Whatshername, she could take it to Count Whatshisname. I could give her a trip in my coach —"

"She has other things to do. Thank you. Leave everything to

me. And now, your lordship, I must ask you to go. I fear I shall be late for church —"

He was all grunts and bows. The almoner had his plumed hat ready, the chausseur his coat. "The most gracious courtesy and assistance your highness renders me — I am overwhelmed." And he leaned over her as though it were he who was to do the overwhelming. He withdrew with his shuffling attendants. Valzacchi and Annina joined the train, quietly, obsequiously, discreetly. The last of the little dogs was scooped up. The tenor and flautist bowed: they had been heard, they had given pleasure, the Major-domo would get his cut. The Major-domo made sure the chamber was clear of visitors. He bowed his way out. The Princess was left alone.

IV.

Alone. Great ill-smelling oaf, talking of honoring an innocent girl with his hot foul breath and his bone-cracking embraces. The holy state of wedlock. Straight out of a convent into the squalor of a grunting bed. Well, had it not been like that for her, Maria Theres'? Innocence defiled. Virginity, *les neiges d'antan*. The young Theres' who, soon enough, would be the Old Princess, the Old Field Marshal's Lady, there she goes, Old Princess Tess. We all grow old, and yet what devil permits us to remain young within? Throw away all our mirrors, let us decree a special mirror-smashing day in the courtyard. And yet we can't blind the rest of the world. The mystery of growing old. Is there some moment in time from which we date our growing old, as fixed as a birthday? The first wrinkle, the first thickening of the flesh beneath the chin? We wake up one morning and hear the cracked trumpets of the revelation: your highness has grown old. But her highness feels much as she did when she left the convent.

The door opened wide without ceremony. The servants had departed. Octavian strode in in his riding boots, his riding jacket tails bouncing to his stride, his arms open. They embraced.

"You were sad about something, angel. I saw."

"Moody, if you wish. You know what I'm like — up, down, like a swing in the Prater."

"I know what it was. It was fear, wasn't it? And it wasn't fear for yourself, beloved —"

"We imagine something happening and we feel — what can I call it? The appropriate emotions, I suppose. The feelings stay with us even when the vision has passed. Suppose it had been —"

"But it wasn't. It was only that buffoon, Ochs, well named. Nothing's changed. You're still mine and always mine." He tightened his embrace.

"Don't. My old nurse used to say — what was it? — he who grasps too much holds only air."

"You're mine! Tell me that you're mine!"

"Oh, please —" She struggled, unwonted. Surprised, he freed her. "Less strength, less wildness — be gentle, be tender. Don't be like the others."

Suspicion froze him. "All the others — you speak as you spoke before — who are all these others?"

"I didn't say *all.* I was thinking of two — one came this morning — the other might have come."

"You've changed, angel of light — changed in a single hour or two — I don't like it — it frightens me." But he renewed his embrace.

"It will come even to you some day, Mignon — perhaps sooner than you think. The realization that things pass, that life is a dream — all the rest of the worn-out coins that strew the boards of the theaters. And you know why writers still jingle those worn-out coins? Because they're the metal of truth. The truth is banal and can only be spoken in clichés. We're in a banal situation — something out of a play so bad it makes the spectators yawn. The lover and the erring wife and the husband's sudden return. Our love can't have permanency in it, and so I wonder if we can call it love. What do we do — run away, you a farmhand, me a milkmaid? This will all end. I see it. You refuse to see it."

"I shall never leave you, never —"

"Oh yes. And sooner than you dream of. Oh, if only time could be reined like a horse. Sometimes, at night, while my husband snores and dreams of hunting, I get up and stop all the clocks in the house. They tick on to a future I dread. And then I wake in the morning and find that they've all been started again."

"I don't believe in time," he said. "Love — that's the one reality, and love knows nothing of time. Love can't be measured by clocks or yardsticks or —"

"Like *my perfections,*" she said sadly. "You remember, it's only an hour ago you were so eloquent about them. One of the gifts of youth — eloquence in the morning. Mignon," she said, and she turned away from him, "you'll leave me. You'll find somebody else. Innocent, young, pretty. You came to me as a pupil. This morning you spoke of being the master. You who learned will want to teach."

He looked at her with a new coldness. "I see. You're trying to drive me away. Too young, too awkward, too rough and callow and impulsive. Very well, I'll be tender, gentle, what you will. But you'll never drive me away."

"Leave that to time," she said quietly. "To change. Nothing stands still."

"You speak today like some ancient gloomy philosopher. But you're still my darling and always will be." He embraced her gently. He kissed her eyelids as though bidding her bad dreams sleep.

"Mignon, you must go. I'm already late for church, and after that I must visit my poor Uncle Greifenklau — he's very old and very ill — and lunch with him. I'll send a message to your house, Mignon, and let you know whether we can meet later. Perhaps I shall go for a drive in the Prater and, quite by accident of course, you will be riding there. Isn't that best?"

"All shall be as you command." He bowed and left.

He bowed and left. The door was scarcely closed when she realized that he had gone, or rather she had let him go, without one solitary token of — She had not kissed him, he had not kissed her. This was, really — She rang manically for a footman. The urgency of her ringing brought four running in. "Run out," she said. "After the Count. Quick. There is something I have to tell him. Very urgent. *Quick.*"

It was too late. They came back breathless. Like the wind, they said, off like the wind. They called, but he did not seem to hear. Like the wind. "Very well," she said crossly. "You may go." But then she remembered something else. "Send Mahomed to me." She heard jingling bells approaching. The little black boy entered with profound obeisances. She pointed to the case, which contained the silver rose. "Take it," she said. He took it and started to leave, backwards, bowing. "Wait, I didn't say where. Take it to the Count Octavian. You know where he lives. No message. He knows all about it. Off you go." Bows, bows, backwards out. She sat there in a melancholy which birdsong and mounting spring sun did nothing to lighten.

V.

Herr von Faninal was taking his leave of his daughter Sophia. He was old to have so young a daughter, but he had married late, at a point in his life when he felt he had accumulated enough wealth to qualify for marital alliance with the nobility. But none of the great houses of Austria seemed anxious to welcome a bourgeois son-in-law, despite the wealth. A bourgeois daughter-in-law was, of course, quite a different matter. So Faninal had decided not to abase himself further at soirées and in hunting lodges — to which, anyway, invitations were few and came only from younger sons to whom he had lent money — and to seek a bride in the higher reaches of the merchant class. After all, there was the question of an heir. The girl he married was delicate. Faninal mistook want of vitality, frailty, pallor for good breeding. She hardly survived the birth of their only child, Sophia. He did not wish to marry again. He looked for an aristocratic alliance through his daughter, with, beginning in a grandson, nobility, to which his own low blood had contributed, stretching till the crack of doom. So now, before going out, he said exultantly:

"This is a great day, child. A noble day, a holy day." As if to confirm this, bells began ringing in a nearby church. Today the token of the noble alliance would be presented. Indeed, very soon. He gave his daughter his hand to kiss, a gesture he had learned from the nobility. Marianne, Sophia's duenna, a coarse woman easily impressed by the insolence of rank, which she confused with the attributes of nobility, was looking out of the window of the great salon, impressive mainly in its vulgarity. She said:

"Joseph's outside there, sir, with the new coach and the four new horses, grays they are. All waiting for you, sir. Joseph looks lovely." And then the Major-domo came in. Without deference he said to his master:

"By your leave, sir, if I may say so, it's time you were out and off. If I may remind you, it's an unpardonable breach of etiquette for the father of the bride to be present when the bridegroom's messenger arrives. The rose, I mean. He's due about now."

"Very well." Footmen opened the door.

"Even to meet him — on the stairs, in the driveway — bad luck as well, sir, apart from the unpardonable breach of —"

"Very well. When I return it will be with the bridegroom. Be ready for him, Sophia. Don't forget to behave like a lady."

"Just think," breathed Marianne reverently. "The virtuous and noble Lord Lerchenau." Faninal left. Marianne watched from the window. "There they go. Francis and Anthony up behind, and Joseph cracking his new whip, and off they go, and everybody having a good look." But Sophia was not listening. She was distraught and she felt guilty. She did not like her bridegroom. He was fat and coarse and his manners did not seem appropriate to the kind of nobility she had read about in books in bed, with a forbidden candle, in the convent. All she could do was pray. She thanked God for raising her above her class and she begged him not to allow her to be puffed up about it. But she did not feel in the least puffed up and she did not even think that thanks were in order. But that was sinful. She prayed to be allowed, in her sinfulness, to see the greatness and the sanctity of matrimony, to feel in her heart the conviction that she was entering an estate most pleasing to God. This meant that God approved of Baron Ochs, his pawing, gluttony, belching. Truly, the ways of God were very mysterious.

From without, approaching, she heard the cry "Rofrano! Rofrano!"

"They're all crying *Rofrano,*" cried Marianne. "That's the name of the Count who's bringing the rose. The rose cavalier they call him. Can you hear? There it is — one carriage with the rose in it, and then another carriage, and a lot of servants bowing and scraping — and there he is. Awfully young he is, too. Can't be more than nineteen. Beautiful, all in silver, like the archangel Gabriel or whichever one it is that defends us in the day of battle. They're opening our front door. Get ready, child. Head up, smile, act like a lady."

But Sophia prayed, and she did not quite know for what she was praying. The prayer did not get much farther than O God O God O God.

The footmen sprang to open the great double doors at the triple rap of the mace of the Count's Major-domo. The doors opened and a breathtaking procession filed in. Octavian, the Count Rofrano, came first, bareheaded, wigless, his hair like a flame, in white and silver, carrying in his right hand the delicate rose of silver. Then his household entire, footmen and Hungarian haiduks with their swords like scimitars, couriers in white leather with green ostrich plumes, then the more drably dressed household of Faninal. Marianne curtseyed joyfully: what a day this was. Sophia just stood, her lips parted. Octavian also just stood, his lips parted. There is always confusion and wonder and even fear in the heart when the eyes confront some new sample of youth and beauty. Octavian, who had been bred at court and had as mistress the fine flower of imperial beauty and distinction, felt a kind of stage fright. He had formal words to utter and he stumbled over them. He was not used to the sight of innocence. He said stoutly:

"I am honored, fair one, to be the ambassador of the most noble lord the Baron Lerchenau and to present to you on his behalf this token of his ever-living everlasting love and devotion, the silver rose of betrothal." And he gave the rose to her. Sophia said, somewhat tonelessly:

"I thank your honor for his honorable condescension and am to your honor honorably I mean eternally indebted." So that was that. She held the rose delicately in her fingers. It was beautifully made, no doubt about it, petals hammered to a thinness most exquisite, and a scent came off it, or was that her imagination? She put it to her nostrils. "It smells like a real rose," she said.

"They do that," said Octavian. "I mean, they sprinkle a few drops of attar on it, Persian attar that is. It's what they usually do." She gave it to him to sniff. "Delightful, yes." And he looked at her pert red lips and into her solemn gray eyes set wide but not too wide. Octavian did not like what was happening to him. A new door was opening, and he had not ordered the opening of the door. Innocence, that was what it was, freshness and youth and damnable, he meant blessed, innocence. He had forgotten all about innocence. As for her, she was like Miranda seeing her first man. Caliban she knew, and a father who was more prosperous than

Prospero. O blessed Lord, she was going to marry Caliban. Her duenna came up and held out her hand. The ceremony was over. Sophia consigned the rose to Marianne, who put it back in its case. Now was the moment for a brief colloquy between rosegiver and rosegiven. This was, she knew, part of the procedure. Chairs were placed, the servants solemnly trooped out. The duenna signed to her mistress that the three of them should sit. They sat.

What Sophia said now was the truth. "I know all about you, dear *cousin,*" she said. She was to join the nobility; it was a fiction that the Austrian nobility was one great family: *cousin* was quite in order.

Octavian felt a tremor. Those innocent lips were to say something about a secret liaison that was no secret. "What do you know, *ma cousine?*" he said, trying to smile.

"There's a book I read in the convent called *The Mirror of Austrian Nobility.* I still read it, I take it to bed with me every night. I know all about the nobility — that's only right since I have to join it. I know all about the princes and dukes and counts and barons. I know exactly how old you are — eighteen years six months three days — and I know all your baptismal names — Octavian, Maria, Ehrenreich, Bonaventura, Fernand, Hyacinth —"

"You know them better than I do."

"And there's another thing I know —"

Oh my God here it came. "What is it, *chère cousine?*"

"Your friends call you Mignon. Your best friends, I mean — the great beauties of the court. Mignon — that means darling or favorite or something. A kind of pet name."

"That's right, a pet name." But who had first used that pet name?

"Will you be coming to the wedding, cousin? It won't be long now. My fiancé was asked to wait till June, but he's very impatient." Impatient, yes, he thought, and he drove away the ghastly image of that mound of blubber making the bed shake. Not merely obscene — truly sinful — and he, Octavian, the ambassador, was abetting that sin. But she was so innocent, she knew nothing, the nuns had taught her that marriage was a yoking of souls and they had failed to mention the yoking of bodies. She was saying something now about the sanctity of marriage and the duty of wifely submission and she was asking him —

"Do you think much of marriage, cousin? Or do you think yourself to be too young? Or do you want to remain a bachelor all your life? But no, you can't, can you, you have the responsibility of continuing the family line and — all the rest of it."

She was too good, too beautiful. He was abetting the casting of this real pearl into the trough of a real — He found himself, to his surprise, saying the word aloud: "Beautiful." And then, seeing her blush, "I beg your pardon." But then: "No, why should I beg pardon for speaking the truth? Your bridegroom is a lucky man." He said it growling. She said, her eyes lowered, flames on her cheeks:

"You take liberties, sir, but I suppose a man of your rank is entitled to take liberties." And then, with an innocence that nearly broke his heart: "You are beautiful too. And good, I can see that. You are the nicest and most charming man I have ever met."

"How many have you met?" he asked sadly.

"Only the Baron and his — er — friends."

"Yes, that explains it."

"Oh." She rose, aflutter. The door was opening. Octavian rose; the duenna rose. Faninal, all bows, ushered in Ochs, and even gave Ochs's servants precedence over his own. There they were, the whey-blooded body-servant, the leering almoner, the village dog who was Ochs's chasseur, two others, country louts in livery that did not fit and bore the marks of napkinless meals, and a new acquisition — a dwarfish clown with a plaster on a battered snout, sadly waving a punchinello stick with bells on it. Faninal said:

"I have the honor to present to your lordship your lordship's bride."

Baron Ochs bowed to his father-in-law elect. He went over to Sophia as though she were the wedding cake, not the bride. He said: "*Délicieuse.* My compliments, sir," as though Faninal were the chef. He kissed Sophia's hand and smacked his lips over it. "A delicate hand. A hand of a delicacy rarely found in the bourgeoisie." He tasted it again. Octavian growled quietly.

Faninal introduced Sophia's duenna, who curtseyed low thrice. Ochs said: "Yes yes yes," and waved her away. Sophia moved as far away as she could from the one to whom she was condemned to be so close. Vulgar, she thought. More vulgar than ever. Like a horse dealer who's just bought a yearling colt. But Marianne, who had joined her, said: "A real nobleman, very gracious, and very friendly with it. Your father's done well for you, dear. You should be the happiest girl alive."

Ochs was talking to Faninal. "This lad here," he said, "the one who brought the rose, he's the spitten image of a girl the Princess von Werdenberg has in her service. Charming little baggage." He nudged Faninal and nearly made him fall. "I may be engaged to be married, but that doesn't mean I have to wear blinkers, eh? No, I tell you this about him and this baggage just to remind you that aristocratic morality is a bit different from what you members of the bourgeoisie are used to. More free and, if you like, more generous. Seed spilt everywhere, regardless of class. You see that body-servant of mine, the long-legged one? Well, he's all royal blood. Interesting little case of dark secrets in a noble house, what? Forbidden relationships, do you understand me?" He nudged Faninal and nearly made him fall. "You're one of us now, Faninal. Almost. Come here, Count," he said to Octavian. "I was just saying about aristocratic morality. I knew your father the Marquis — God, talk about wild oats —" He nudged Octavian, but Octavian did not even stagger. "That little baggage the Princess has — but you wouldn't know, of course — Never mind, never mind."

Sophia stood in the corner, ignored. Octavian flashed her a signal: sympathy, regret, vicarious apology, compassion, affection — His heart flashed him a danger signal of its own.

The Major-domo ushered in a pair of servants who bore a decanter and glasses (expensive but inelegant) and a tray of canapés. At the same time he ushered off the rest of the servants, including the Baron's. These limped and slouched and wiped noses on sleeves and commenced their country-bred guffaws before they were properly out of the great vulgar salon.

"Tokay, your lordship — a good vintage. I pray you, partake."

"Well, you know what's what, I'll say that for you, Faninal." He pinged with a horny thumbnail on one of the glasses. It rang sweet and clear. To Octavian he said, while the Tokay gurgled out, too loud, too vulgarly: "You have to condescend a bit, you know. Friendly but not too much so. Let them know who's master. Let's have little Sophy over here." He whistled like an ostler and laughed to show it was all in fun. "Come, girl, come, filly." Marianne pushed her over to the glass-clinking. "Now, girl," he said, his left arm fumbling for her waist, "the time has come for you to learn what's what. There are two ways of going about things in society. There's the way of nonsense and flimflam, *mille pardons* and by your ladyship's leave and all the rest of it, and there's the other way, the one I like — free and easy, nice and friendly, open and honest, to the devil with good manners, see what I mean?" And he tried to kiss her. She resisted. His overcharged glass spilt Tokay on the turkey carpet. Octavian groaned in his very bowels.

But Faninal was thinking: "What a prize, what a promotion! A real-life baron kissing my own daughter, and there's Count Rofrano, brother to the Lord High Steward — in my house, in my own drawing room! Bliss! Rapture!"

Octavian was thinking: "Boor, lout. I'd like to poke under that blubber with my blade. I'd like to hear him squeak like the pig he is."

"I know what it is," roared Ochs. "You're shy, it's the Count here that's making you shy. Well, you'll have to learn, Sophy. The higher you go in rank the less shy you have to be. Why, I remember the time when I used to attend the Princess Whatshername in her bathroom, every morning. Steam and soap and coffee, and there she was, sponging away, not caring a fig for what your father here would call propriety. You can get away with anything. And why? It's because the aristocracy is the whatyoucall — I've forgotten the word, what's the phrase? You know it, Tavy my boy —"

"The arbiter of manners," said Octavian icily.

And Faninal was thinking: "Oh, if only these walls could change into glass and everybody see in. Seagreen with envy, the lot of them, that's what they'd be. Bliss! Rapture!"

"Manners are what we make 'em. Get rid of your bourgeois airs and graces, Sophy girl. Give me a bit of a cuddle." And he held her for a second or so. Tender young pullet. White and tender and I bet she's blushing all over. Ah, the luck of the Lerchenaus. Sophia tore herself away. Ochs waddled after her. Plucky little filly. He liked a bit of a fight. Her cheeks burning so you could warm your two thumbs on them, if she'd let you get close enough, damn her.

"Please," pleaded Sophia. Octavian found he had crushed his Tokay glass in his hand. He let the pieces drip to the carpet. No blood, but soon there would be blood if the Baron did not — Marianne came running to pick up the shards. She said:

"Lovely to see them, isn't it, your grace? Like a little boy he is with his japes and tricks. Could laugh till I cry with his goings on."

The door opened. The Major-domo came in with her highness's asthmatic attorney, accompanied by a sniffing clerk. The clerk handed to Faninal a bundle of documents. Something to do with that bend in the law that Ochs had commanded. Ochs meanwhile panted with the asthma of the chase. Sophia spoke ice and fire. She said:

"I have never in my life been so —"

"A short life, my love. Now you're starting to grow up. Come on, just one little peck." He grabbed her. She pushed. Marianne looked on contentedly. Laugh till you cry. The ways of the aristocracy. Octavian found himself grinding his teeth, a thing he'd not done since childhood, and then only in sleep.

"Real spitfire," panted Ochs. "Oh well, that's the way I like 'em. Makes me feel young again. Talk about the luck of the Lerchenaus —" And then he saw her highness's attorney. He desisted from play, drew himself up, marched toward the law, or the bending of it. On his way he whispered loudly to Octavian:

"Business now. Don't be afraid to — you know, give her the odd sheep's eye, Tavy my boy. I don't mind your breaking her in. Makes it all the easier for, you know, the eventual rider." He winked.

"If, my dear son-in-law," said Faninal, trembling with the joy of the locution, "you'd be good enough to withdraw into the ah withdrawing room — a little matter of legal business."

"Certainly, hahaha father-in-law." The door was opened. Ochs said: "Matter of precedence, might as well get used to these things. Matter of rank. Three paces behind me, if it's not too much trouble." And out he waddled, Faninal three steps behind, the agencies of the bending of the law going humbly after. Marianne curtseyed and curtseyed even after the door was closed.

"So, *ma cousine,*" trembled Octavian. "That's the thing you propose to marry?"

"I don't propose. But I won't, I won't, father can put me in a nunnery if he wishes. Oh, if only she'd leave —" She meant her hovering duenna. "If I could speak to you alone —"

"What would you tell me? What would you ask?"

"But it's no use. You're one of his own kind — oh, you know

what I mean — I mean you aristocrats have to stick together."

"Ah no. And besides, I don't know the lout. I never saw him before this morning. Stick together indeed —"

"You must help me, you must —"

At this moment the double doors flew open. One of Faninal's servant girls, a pretty little thing from Upper Austria, entered screaming, Lerchenau's body-servant followed in an ill-coordinated run. The clown with the plaster on his snout shambled after, his punchinello bells jangling with sad lust. The Major-domo entered, panting, perturbed. He panted:

"They got at the wine. They're drunk, the lot of them. Come on," to the duenna, "help the girl, can't you?" And to Sophia and Octavian he bowed in embarrassment. He had never reckoned that this sort of thing would be part of the major-domo's office —

The duenna rescued the girl, hitting out lustily. The Baron's servants they might be, but there were limits. Out, out. Octavian and Sophia were alone at last. It was most irregular.

And yet there was nothing to say. Nothing to do except take her hands and kiss them and then murmur: "Dear Sophia, let me think. There must be something." But, of course, there was only one thing. You protect a poor girl from her father's criminal folly, but what is the nature of the motive of the desire to protect? You are not a substitute father. There is only one thing you can be. There was no such thing as love at first sight, but other emotions were permitted at first sight — pity, for example. Yet pity was never enough. Moreover, what false canon permitted pity for what was wholly admirable, indeed admirably holy — youth, grace, beauty? Only love gave one the right to brave fathers and legal contracts, and how could he utter the word? He was in love with a married lady, was he not? To her he owed the protection of his sword, the shedding of his own blood if need be. It dawned upon him that he was defiled, in no state of grace. He seemed to hear a heavy cathedral bell tolling the word *adulterer*. In a single tick of the ornate clock on the wall, writhing with gilt cherubim, he put himself in a state of grace. He took Sophia in his arms and he kissed her. He murmured the forbidden word that was not, after all, forbidden.

To the shock of both of them they found they were not, after all, alone.

VI.

There were two great fireplaces in this salon, and both were covered with fire screens, and before the fire screens there were large vulgar vases filled with ferns and flowers of the season. From behind one fire screen Valzacchi appeared, from behind the other Annina. They were proving their worth to the nobleman they saw as a steady patron. They had entered early that morning as bearers of those flowers, an alleged gift from the Baron himself. In the crowd of servants they had soon been forgotten. They had hidden themselves in the empty chimneys. They both bore traces of soot, but not much: those chimneys had been well cleaned for the coming of summer. As they appeared Octavian and Sophia could do nothing but stare, but they did not loosen their embrace. But they broke the embrace when Valzacchi screamed:

"Baron Lerchenau, come quick, we found them at it!" And he tried to grasp the lithe Octavian, who was not willing to be grasped. Sophia began to make expiring noises. Annina had the door open and was yelling:

"Baron, your lordship, your wife-to-be is here with a gentleman, kissing and hugging. Come quick and see them doing it!" If she had had her way she would have had them thrust back into each other's arms, totally *in flagrante.*

The Baron was not long in coming in. He stood there, very calm, and he grinned at Octavian. After all, he had said something about breaking the girl in. Not too much of it, though — there were limits. Sophia came close to the protecting sword of Octavian. Octavian said:

"This lady has something to tell you."

"I've nothing to tell him," said Sophia. "Whatever I said, he'd never understand."

"Oh, you underestimate me, milady," said Ochs genially.

"There have been certain changes in your arrangements," Octavian said. "That is what she wishes to tell you."

"Well, then, let her speak up."

"This lady," Octavian began.

"Dumb, is she? Or she's briefing you as her attorney, is that it?"

"This lady —" And Octavian looked to Sophia to say the word. But she said:

"I can't. You speak for me."

"Yes, Mr. Attorney?" grinned Ochs.

"This lady," Octavian said firmly, "refuses to fulfill an unacceptable contract. There will be no marriage."

"Really?" said Ochs with large assumed interest. And then, with ferocity: "Come on, milady, as the world will soon be calling you, since contracts have been mentioned, you may as well come and sign now. Everything else of a legal nature has been very satisfactorily resolved. So let's close the matter, milady."

"No," cried Sophia, hiding behind Octavian.

"Yes!" and he roughly tugged at her arm.

"You," said Octavian, "are an ill-mannered buffoon, a cheat, a dowry-hunter, a boor, a bore, a scoundrel, a lecher. Leave this lady and leave this house, or you'll feel the sharp end of my sword."

"Orders, eh? Your house, is it? We'll see what the master of the house says about that. As for your offer of violence, you effeminate puppy —" He put two fingers in his mouth and whistled, as for a pack of dogs. The pack of dogs appeared promptly enough, and they all looked drunk. While they were shambling in Ochs said: "You Viennese boys had better start learning where the true authority lies. The backbone of this country is the country barony. Her grace the Archduchess knows that if you don't, whippersnapper. Lay your fingers on me and you'll soon know all about it. Now get away from my affianced bride and out of my presence. One more whistle from me and you'll learn something else — what it's like to have your beauty spoiled by a couple of broken teeth. Now get out." And he reached out a paw for Sophia. Octavian drew. He cried:

"Come on, let's have you, you lout. Draw!" Sophia cried on God and heaven.

The Baron stepped back. "Showing a sword in a lady's presence?" he said feebly. "Are you mad?"

"Yes," said Octavian, and he lunged. Ochs drew too late. Octavian pinked him in the upper right arm. The sword's point ran deep enough under the fat to draw blood. The Baron yelled murder and dropped his sword. The rabble of servants growled and lurched toward their master's assailant. Octavian sent his sword whizzing among them. They growled their way to a wall, huddling. Ochs's almoner, assisted by Valzacchi and Annina, helped his lordship into a chair. His lordship cried:

"Look at the blood! Fetch a doctor! I'm dying! Put him under arrest! Call the police!"

His servants mumbled dirty words but kept their distance from that sword. The whole Faninal household streamed in, from Major-domo to third under-gardener. Valzacchi and Annina ripped the Baron's coat off. A thin trickle of dark red blood showed that a vein had been pierced. The Baron screamed that he was dying. One of Ochs's men made a drunken grab at the maid from Upper Austria. A free-for-all, all said and done. The maid hit back. The maid's sweetheart, the house carpenter and clockman, hit out. There was a lot of hitting out, but not at Octavian. The Baron groaned. Octavian put an arm round Sophia and said: "Dearest one." And then Faninal walked in. Ochs was quick with his complaints.

"All these damned servants of yours, Faninal, and not one can fetch a surgeon or a basin or a bandage. Oh, the sight of blood — it makes me ill when it's my own." The duenna wrung her hands and wept. "Don't stand there whining," yelled Ochs. "Do something. Your mistress there is going to be married to a corpse if you don't — Oh, the agony, look at the blood!"

Annina got in quick with an explanation to Faninal: "That gentleman there with the sword out, no, he's putting it in now, he was kissing and hugging your daughter here. We were watching, following his lordship's *istruzioni*. That *spiega tutto*."

"Oh," cried Faninal in terrible distress, "oh, my dear son-in-law, to think such a thing should happen under my roof. You lot there, yes, you" — he meant his entire household — "to horse, ride my thoroughbreds to death till you find a doctor. Wait," he added. "Let this be a lesson to all of you. Easy wages, eh? Easy pickings? No sense of responsibility. I feed the lot of you on the fat of the land, capons and cream, by God, and this is what happens. Go on, out, what are you waiting for?" Then he turned to Octavian. This was difficult: deference tugging at fury. "You, sir. I should have thought that a gentleman of your rank and breeding —"

"I beg forgiveness, sir," said Octavian quietly. "I cannot express my regret with sufficient humility or grief. But, believe me, it had to be. What was done was not done wantonly or frivolously. At a later time I would be glad to explain —"

"He acted like a gentleman of honor, Father," put in Sophia. "And that man over there did not. He treated me like, like —"

"You are speaking of my future son-in-law?" said her father. "You have the effrontery to suggest that my future son-in-law —"

"If you wish him to be your future son-in-law," said Sophia with unwonted boldness, "then you must find another daughter."

The father could not, of course, believe his somewhat hairy ears. He spluttered. Sophia said:

"Naturally, I must humbly beg your pardon."

A doctor was brought in. He lived across the way. He had heard screams. He had no very large practice. He examined the patient. Faninal cried: "She begs my pardon. She stands under the protective arm of this this this schoolboy here, if he will permit the expression." In a burst of agony he howled: "Ruined!" Meaning the scandal of his daughter's refusal to ennoble his house, the noble bridegroom dying for all he knew, the sneers and laughs of his bourgeois circle, the juicy story that would already be spreading about the neighborhood. "By God," he cried, "you will do as I say." And to Octavian, "You will leave instanter, sir. In all dutiful humility and deference to your rank, I order you never to darken —" He saw the melodramatic absurdity of the expression, he was no fool, he let it hang in the air uncompleted.

Octavian looked for his hat. The holding of the hat had been in the charge of one of his own servants, but he had previously arranged for those servants to go home after depositing him here, since it had been his intention to visit his mistress the Princess immediately after the brief ceremony he had envisaged. The ceremony had expanded itself into a brawl, and, almost casually, the whole world had changed. He would not now visit the Princess. He would write her a letter. A maidservant brought his hat, curtseying. Profoundly cynical obeisances were exchanged between himself and Faninal. The door was opened for him. But he could not go yet. His beloved was in distress. There was a distressing exchange going on between her and her father.

"I won't marry him! I'll die first!"

"You'll stay in your room till you learn right obedience and good behavior."

"I'll lock myself in. I'll starve to death rather than —"

"You'll be dragged out, miss, and be forced to do as I say."

"I'll kill myself."

"You'll do no such thing. You'll marry his lordship if I have to drag you to the altar myself."

"You can't make me say yes. I'll say no no no no —"

"Take your choice — marriage or a nunnery. Locked up in a cell, penitence and bread and water for the rest of your days."

At the sound of the word *water* the Baron cried: "I'm dying of thirst. It's all the blood that I've lost." The doctor indicated that the bleeding had stopped, the patient would live.

"My dear son-in-law, such a relief." Faninal embraced him. The Baron howled with the pain of it: Faninal's fingers had gone straight to the throbbing wound. "A convent, you hear?" Faninal thundered at Sophia. Octavian whispered words like: Beloved, dearest, have no fear. Leave everything to me. Octavian felt a plan stirring.

"What will you drink, dear son-in-law? Wine? Beer? Hippocras with ginger in it?"

"Wine, wine, gallons of it. I die of desiccation."

Faninal clapped his hands as though applauding. Servants rushed to fetch wine. Octavian gave Sophia one last squeeze of the hand. Valzacchi and Annina hovered round their patron, not too sure now of his patronage. Things had not gone quite as expected. Ochs glared at them. "Made a delightful mess of things, haven't you? Out of my sight."

"*Signore mio* —"

"*Non era la nostra colpa* —"

Octavian left. Valzacchi and Annina watched him leave, watched his discreet kissing of the fingertips toward Sophia as he left. They looked at each other. Transference of allegiance? If the young lord could be brought to understand that it was a mere trade, no hard feelings — Octavian had left.

Outside the salon Octavian saw the attorney and his assistant waiting. They were impassive. They had heard enough cries of agony in their time. Octavian approached them. He begged a sheet of paper and a pen.

"There is this small writing-room here, your lordship. A desk, ink, see — a newly sharpened quill —"

"For the signing of the marriage contract, I presume?"

"For that."

Octavian wrote. Valzacchi and Annina hovered at the door of the little writing-room. "Your esteemed lordship," whined Valzacchi, "I trust you will not hold it against us that we were merely practicing our profession. We regret, both of us, that we chose the wrong — er — patron. We are not lacking in a sense of morality. After all, we are both Florentines. We are, if I may be permitted so to presume, always on the side of true love." Annina nodded. Valzacchi had spoken in his native tongue. He took it for granted that his young lordship would understand. Octavian understood very well. He took some thalers from his purse. He explained very briefly what he wished them to do.

VII.

Ochs lay on a sofa with a pint of wine in his fist. He was alone. He had requested solitude. He proposed to doze a little, quieten the beating of his heart. The bloodletting had, in fact, done him more good than harm. His wound had been bandaged and his arm rested in a silken sling. He'd got the better of the young puppy after all. Tail between his legs. A willing or an unwilling bride — where was the difference? Marriage was essentially a financial arrangement. Still, he anticipated with pleasure the struggles of the wedding night. In an hour or so he would eat something — something that combined daintiness with bulkiness. This Faninal, father-in-law hahaha, kept a good table.

He sniffed the scent of a woman. That Italian bitch was there behind his reposing head. "We regret so much," she said, "my uncle and I. One last opportunity to show our worth. This we beg."

"Out, out."

"You remember you asked us to perform a particular service. It is to do with a young lady."

"Lady?"

"I have here a note, see. Scented."

"Give it me." He was very alert now. He handed her his wine mug and tried to open the letter with his free hand. "Damn. Need my spectacles. Read it out."

"But perhaps it is very intimate, your lordship."

"Read it out."

"It says: 'Most honorable sir. Tomorrow evening I am free of my duties to her highness —' "

"Her! She! What's her name now?"

" '— You were so gracious as to find me pleasing to your lordship. But I was not able to respond because her highness kept looking at us. I am only young, you see, and not used to the ways of the great world. If your lordship would care to arrange what he suggested — *tête-à-tête* is, I think, the word you used — I should be pleased and honored to accept. Pray grant me the pleasure of a note in your lordship's own hand and send it to me through the kind Italian lady who brings you this. Your devoted Mariandel.' "

"Mariandel — that was the name. Remember her all right, sweet little baggage — couldn't recall her name. Well, well, talk about the luck of the Lerchenaus —"

"She wants a reply, your lordship."

"I know she wants a reply. Can you write?"

"Of course, your lordship. Has your lordship forgiven us?"

"I'll think about it. Get pen, ink, paper. Quick, now." As she hastened off, shaking a fist at him that he did not see, he picked up his wine mug, grinned, then drank to the luck of the Lerchenaus.

VIII.

All was ready. Octavian's transvestite disguise was not, as before, a mere improvisation. He had taken trouble with it. He had procured a fine blond wig, had shaved with extra care, had made up his face with paint, powder, and an eyeliner, and was clad in a demure evening gown of salmon-pink. Beneath the disguise, however, he was garbed like a man, even to the riding boots, though he had removed the spurs. When he entered the private room of the White Horse Inn, neither Valzacchi nor Annina recognized him — not, that was, till he lifted his skirt to get at his pocket. From the pocket he drew a purse, and this he threw with grace at Valzacchi. Valzacchi, past-master at purse-catching, caught it deftly. Valzacchi and Annina ran to him and kissed his hands. "Everything ready?" asked Octavian.

Yes, everything ready. Annina herself was in a kind of disguise.

She was dressed in mourning, her eyes were outlined with kohl, she wore a veil. Valzacchi was as he usually was — discreetly dapper. He pointed out to Octavian the recess with the curtain before it that hid a bed. The trapdoor, see. The men? The — ? All was ready. Mariandel's duenna? The thing must be done properly. A decent old lady entered at Valzacchi's summons. A church clock struck the half-hour. Was that hoofs they heard, the rolling of the wheels of a coach? Valzacchi clapped his hands. They all left, except for Valzacchi.

When Ochs came in, arm still in its sling, he had Octavian with him. He beamed satisfaction. Valzacchi, who had opened the door, bowed and bowed. The landlord appeared, rubbing his hands dryly together. Waiters hovered. "Is this as your lordship wishes?" asked the landlord. "More candles? Or perhaps your lordship would prefer a more commodious apartment?"

"This will do," Ochs said graciously. "Too much light, though. This isn't a court ball. A little intimacy." Candles were hastily snuffed. "Where's that music coming from?"

"Oh, the musicians regularly play in the next room," said the landlord. "If your lordship would prefer that they come in here and provide whatever program your lordship deigns to request —"

"I see, and pay for the privilege? No, let them stay where they are. What's that up there?" He pointed to a window.

"A window, your lordship."

"I know it's a damned window, idiot. I don't want any fool looking in when I'm — eating. It puts me off my food. Privacy is what I'm paying for."

"That's what they call a blind window, your lordship. It looks out on to a wall. May supper now be served?" The waiters stood to a kind of attention.

"What do those grinning apes there intend to do?"

"To wait on your lordship."

"I don't want them. Shoo, shoo, off. Where's my man? Ah, there he is." The whey-blooded spindly body-servant had stalked up to him. "He'll do all the serving necessary. And you can leave it to me to pour out the wine. All right, let's have the privacy I'm paying for. Sit down, my dear." Valzacchi was the last to leave. "See here, you," Ochs said, "do your best to keep the bill low. You know these places, they charge the earth if they can get away with it. I'll make it worth your while." Valzacchi bowed and bowed and went out.

"Better, eh?" leered Ochs. "Just you and me, sweetheart. A little of this wine, eh?" He started to pour.

Octavian adjusted his vocal cords. "I don't drink," he trilled.

"Oh, come now. Wine of the country, blood of the earth. It will put ink in your pen." Got that wrong; it was himself he meant. He sat next to her and ventured a cuddle.

"Oh, sir," cried Octavian.

"No, not *sir*. No ceremony. Forget that I'm aristocracy and you're only what you are. A man and a maid sitting down to a cozy supper — that's all *we* are. How about a kiss?" Octavian coquettishly turned his head away. With a great horny paw Ochs grasped Octavian's chin and jerked the sweet little face round to the kissing position. Then he saw not a sweet little face but the face of the dastardly young swine who had dared to — oh no. "Haunts me," he growled. "Keep on seeing him — the vicious blackguardly young dog —"

At that moment the trapdoor by the table jerked open and the head of a man peered up. Octavian saw. Ochs was trying to kiss his ear and did not see. "Not yet!" mouthed Octavian. Ochs now thought he saw the face of a man down there on the floor. Then he saw that he did not see. Or did he?

"Did you," he said somewhat tremulously, "see something — ?"

"Something?"

"A man?"

"Is your honor feeling all right?"

Ochs filled himself more wine. "Lost blood," he said. "Affects the brain."

"What did your lordship say?"

"Never mind." The door opened and let in a gush of music so loud it made Ochs gush sweat. "Shut that blasted —" It was the body-servant serving soup. "All right. Now get out. *Out*. Better."

"Your lordship is very fidgety. Does your honor feel not too well perhaps? Perhaps I had better go home. Some other evening perhaps?"

"No no no no no!" He took his wig off as though preparing for bed. He loosened his collar. "Warm, that's all. A bit close in here." And then he saw —

There was a face at the window the innkeeper had called blind. Blind or not, a couple of sad dark eyes looked at him from it. And then the upper half of somebody, some woman or other, filled the window, its arms stretched into the room. The figure was in mourning. A sepulchral voice filled the room:

"My husband! That's my long-lost husband!"

Ochs's dithering hand upset his soup plate. Soup all over his sleeve, he tremoloed: "Who was that? Did you see that?"

"See what, your lordship?"

The window was blind again. "Nothing, nothing. I lost blood, you know. See this sling on my arm? Attacked by a ruffian."

"Blood, your honor?"

"Affects the —"

And then the door was flung open. Valzacchi, the innkeeper and three waiters were trying to hold somebody back. A woman, in deep mourning, the same one —

"I am his wife, I tell you. This is my long-lost husband. I swear before Almighty God. I demand justice. Restore him to my suffering arms —"

"Is this a madhouse?" wavered Ochs. He needed more light. Why was there not more light? Of course, it was he himself who had demanded the intimacy of darkness. He put a soup-dripping hand to his brow. He waddled toward the group to see if it was really there. The woman cried his name:

"Leopold Anton of Lerchenau! Why did you desert me?"

"I know you," said Ochs, peering. "Seen you before. God, does everybody have a double?" He blinked at Octavian-Mariandel.

"Of course you know me! Your discarded wife! God is just, Leopold! He looks down on you now!"

At that moment four children came running in yelling: "Papa!"

A bit too soon, Annina was thinking. She forgot her lines. Then she remembered them:

"Do you not see the fruits of our love? Your children and mine, Leopold!"

The children, their ages graduated from a lisping four to a yelling eleven, clutched at him, crying: "Papa!" Ochs hit out at them with a napkin. Octavian whispered to Valzacchi:

"Did the messenger go to Faninal's house?"

"He'll be here, fear not."

"Get all this lot out of here," cried Ochs to the landlord.

"I don't have that kind of authority, your lordship. I have no right to interfere in family matters."

"Family matters! Never saw them before in my life, never touched that hag there even with my walking-stick. These brats are not mine."

"So your lordship says."

"All right," said Ochs. "I'll have the police in. Get the police."

"Is that wise, your lordship? A matter of desertion. Very heavy penalties —"

Ochs strode shakily over to the door. He noticed an open window near it. Not seen that before, who opened it? It gave on to the street. He bawled out to the street:

"Police! Fetch the police! A nobleman is being assaulted! A member of the aristocracy is in great danger!"

The cry of "Police!" was being taken up out there. Good. A little entertainment. We villagers lead a dull life. "Poliiiiice!"

Ochs ought to have been surprised by the prompt entry of a Police Inspector and a couple of Constables. The Inspector looked like a man who, like Ochs, had been interrupted at supper. He was buttoning his tunic as he frowned at everybody but particularly at Ochs.

"What's all this, then?"

"Ah," said Ochs. "Get this rabble out, will you, Sergeant? If a man of quality can't take his supper in peace —"

"The rank is Inspector," the Inspector said. "Is this your house? No, evidently not. So you keep out of it. Now, who's lodging the complaint?"

"Well," said the innkeeper, "I'm the innkeeper here. There's been a bit of trouble, Inspector. His lordship, that one over there —" And he jerked his shoulder at Ochs, who was looking for his wig.

"That fat man without a wig, yes. Calls himself a lord, does he? That's bad."

"Look here," Ochs spluttered. "I'm not used to this sort of treatment —"

"No, sir? Well, there's time to learn. Who do you say you are?"

"*Say* I am? Damn it, man, I *am* the Baron Lerchenau —"

"Can you prove it?"

"Prove it? *Prove it?*"

"Yes. Any witnesses?" The Inspector sat down at the table. His two Constables took up their positions behind him.

"Witnesses? *I need witnesses?*" And he looked around blazing for witnesses. "You," he said to Valzacchi, "you know who I am, damn your eyes. Tell this policeman here."

"*Non lo so*," shrugged Valzacchi. "He may be who he says he is, and he may not be. I know nothing about him."

"You lying Italian scoundrel, you filthy foreign scum, tell the Sergeant here —"

"Inspector. And keep a civil tongue in your head, sir. Hm. Things are beginning to look pretty bad, I'd say —"

Octavian let out a loud falsetto wail. "Oh, I'm ruined — oh, my reputation —"

"And who's she, then?" the Inspector asked.

"She — ? She — why, she's someone under my er personal protection — A kind of — A sort of —"

"Protection, eh? Looks to me as if you're the one in need of protection. Who is she? Come on, speak."

"She she," spluttered Ochs, "is young Mistress Faninal, Sophia Anna Barbara, that is, daughter to — damn it all, you'll be hearing from me about this, Inspector as you call yourself — I'm not accustomed to this insolent interrogation — Her father's Faninal — he's well known around here —"

The room was crammed now like a court of law. The man who now entered had to push his way through. "Yes, tolerably well known," said Faninal. "You sent for me, I gather. Why?" He sniffed a strange sort of place for a man of Ochs's rank to be in. A common alehouse, I'd call it. "I was in bed when your message came. Urgent I was told. Well, would you be good enough to —"

Ochs forgot for a moment that here was not only a prospective father-in-law but a man who admired, deferred, would help. He interrupted him coarsely. "Who the hell told you to shove your interfering snout into my affairs?"

"Come," Faninal said severely. "Your messenger comes battering on my door, shouting about your being in grave danger — I see now what kind of danger. But, of course, we members of the merchant class are not, as you are, *above the law* —"

"One moment," the Inspector said. "I demand to know what all this is about. This is a friend of yours, is it?"

"I hardly know him," Ochs said, still looking for his wig. "Just seen him around, that's all."

"Your name, sir?"

"Friedrich von Faninal. My address —"

"Never mind, sir. And you know this man?"

"Yes, my son-in-law — in a prospective sense, that is."

"And this young lady is your daughter?"

Faninal squinted at Octavian. "No, this is not my daughter."

"This er gentleman here says she is."

"I see. Well, as my daughter is waiting outside in a sedan chair, this problem of identity can soon be resolved. You, sir," he frowned at Ochs. "I see now what you mean by the special morality reserved to the upper classes. You'll hear more of this."

"Where's my damned wig? You, landlord, find the damned thing. For God's sake; to qualify as your son-in-law a man has to be a blasted eunuch. My wig, damn it." He pushed the four children aside in his search for it. Automatically they started their "Papa! Papa!" chorus.

Faninal recoiled in horror. "Whose — are — these — chil——"

"Nobody's. That woman there who says she's my wife, she's a damned liar. Never set eyes on her before now."

"Oh, Leopold, how could you?" And Annina wept.

Sophia entered, hatted and cloaked. Ochs's first thought was of his unwigged bald pate. He found his feathered hat and shoved it on. Hatting himself on the appearance of a lady.

"I heard all this noise, Father — Oh, Father —"

For Faninal, whose doctors had not lied to the inquiring Baron, was near to collapse. A chair, brandy — Ochs had found his wig. He doffed hat, donned it, felt slightly more in control of the — He said, jauntily:

"Well, so much for all that. I've eaten nothing so I pay nothing. Oh, the wine, yes —" He prepared to throw some small coin at the landlord. "You," he said to Octavian. "Come with me, girl. We'll find somewhere select, really private. Damned madhouse."

But Octavian ignored him and went over to the recess where the bed stood. Ochs watched with his mouth open as he closed the curtain. His mouth opened wider as he saw lady's clothes — gown, petticoat, false bosom — thrown through and onto the floor. The landlord rushed in to cry:

"Ladies and gentlemen — her highness the Princess of Werdenberg!"

And, to the surprise of everyone, the Princess's retinue filed in. Then the lady herself, a vision of beauty, formally dressed, with train. This last the little black boy, bells ajangle, carried. Ochs showed not only surprise but pleasure. He waddled toward her, bowing and bowing.

"Your highness — cousin — this is truly overwhelming. How did you — Who told you?"

"This servant of the royal blood, as you call him —" She nodded toward the spindly whey-faced smirking scion of princely irregularities.

"This, your highness, cousin, is a token of true friendship. Now you can put this minion of the law in his place. For the Austrian aristocracy to have to submit to — Well —"

But the Inspector was at attention and saluting.

"Your highness, I am an officer of the commissariat for the district of —"

"I think," said the Princess, "we know each other."

"Indeed, your highness. I had the privilege of serving as orderly to his highness the Field Marshal." Octavian put his head through the curtain of the recess. Ochs saw the head and waved it away. Faninal had recovered from his faintness. He said:

"If your highness will permit —" He stood, bowed, tottered. "A little unwell — If you, dear child —" And Sophia helped him out of the room. Who, wondered the Princess, was that almost excessively pretty girl? Then she knew. She showed no surprise though she felt it when Octavian, no longer Mariandel, came out from the curtained recess. He greeted her with a somewhat timid smile. A lot of explaining to do. Sophia came back in. She curtseyed to the Princess. Then she addressed Ochs:

"My father is not well enough to tell you himself, but he charged me with the task of ordering you to keep away from our house. Keep away, he said. You will be hearing from him." And she prepared to leave again.

"*Corpo di Bacco!*" the Italian expletive was proper for the princessly presence and his own muted assertiveness. "You, miss, you will not speak to me in that manner, do you hear?"

"Less than you deserve," said Sophia. She left with dignity.

"And that young lady — ?" said the Princess to Octavian.

"The lady for whom I was made chevalier of the rose."

"That I know now, idiot. I see your hand in all this. Well, not only yours. Didn't I tell you that — sooner than you expected —"

"I wrote you a letter. I wrote it many times. I couldn't find the right words."

"Now then," said Ochs, puffing toward Octavian. "We've had enough nonsense for one evening. Put your proper clothes on —" And then: "Oh. Yes. Your highness — I was trying to persuade Mariandel here to join — Yes, of course — that's all over. What I mean is —" He looked at Octavian more closely. "By the living God, it's you — you young — It's you. Draw!" But he was not carrying his sword, and his sword arm was in a sling.

"*Withdraw* is the word," said the Princess. "Leave while you still have some dignity left."

"Somebody has to suffer," grumbled the Baron. "It strikes me that there's been a sort of conspiracy going on."

"The luck of the Lerchenaus," suggested Octavian. He clicked his fingers. Annina took off her mourning veil. She said to the children:

"Say goodbye to your father."

"Papa! Papa! Papa!"

Ochs hit at them with his hat. The innkeeper came in with a bill. Candles, food ordered though uneaten, hire of coach — It was a long one.

"The luck of the Lerchenaus," said the Baron bitterly.

IX.

Sophia saw her father, somewhat better, brandy and smelling salts had restored him, go off alone in his coach. The sedan chair she would no longer need. Her duenna, to whom it would have done good to be stripped of her illusions about the aristocracy, she instructed to wait. She would go back to that room alone. She knew that Octavian would be there.

But she had expected to find him there alone. She stood outside the door and listened. Another woman. The Princess.

"Now that the mob has departed," the Princess was saying, "at least grant us a little real privacy. Close the door."

And it was coming to close the door that Octavian found his

new beloved in the shadows. "Sophia," he said, more sternly than lovingly, "you'd better come in."

"She said she wanted to be private with you."

"Come in." And he led her in by the hand. She was shy, confused. "You have not been formally presented to her highness," he said. "May I, your highness, beg leave to present —"

"I know. You're very pretty, my dear, and very young. And I congratulate you on your escape. Straight from the convent into the arms of — I know all about it, my dear. Not all girls are so lucky."

"I owe my escape to, to —"

"To Mignon, yes. And now Mignon shall leave us for a little while. Go on, drink some wine with the roisterers in the taproom, my lord Count Octavian. Return in ten minutes."

"But, your highness —"

"Fifteen minutes."

Octavian left rather sulkily. At the door he turned back to give Sophia a glance fraught with various meanings — love, warning, dubiety, chiefly warning. The Princess was a strong-minded and clever woman. Sophia kept her face blank, but there was a little fear in it. The Princess saw the fear.

"Perhaps," Sophia faltered, "I ought to go home, see how my father is."

"Your father will be well enough. I know your father."

"You know him?"

"My husband the Prince is a Field Marshal. Your father has lately specialized in victualing the army. Your father is a man who knows his business. A feigned heart attack is a useful device of commerce."

"Oh, but that's not true, that's not fair."

"Soon, when we've had our talk, I'll fetch him back here. The night's business may as well as end where it seems to have started. His heart will seem sound enough when he hears the news."

"What news?" The Princess heard the hope in her voice.

"Tell me, child, how long did it take you to fall in love with Mignon?"

"I see. It's you who christened him Mignon."

"Yes. Darling of the court. Everybody's favorite. The name seemed appropriate. How long had you known him before you decided you were in love?"

She kept her head down. "It was he who said it first. But when he said it — well, I knew —"

"My dear, Octavian's very young. This darling of the court has been more loved than loving. Don't think you've fallen in love with — well, a precocious libertine. You're better matched than you think. And he's more innocent than he believes."

"You," gulped Sophia, "you're one of the ones who love him?"

"How could I fail? Youth's a fine thing. I grow old, child. There was a time when I thought I'd recover my youth by tasting his. A common illusion. In his presence I feel my age."

"Then you don't — He doesn't —"

"Love me? Oh, he admires me, of course —" Sophia smiled a little at the *of course:* who could fail? "But I'm a married woman, with duties, responsibilities — and a husband who, when he's not at war, is hunting inedible animals. I'm also a lady of rank and influence. I think it will take me about five minutes to persuade your father to give his blessing. I'll go now. I know the house. It belonged to the impoverished Duke of Sauerstadt. Have you a servant outside?"

"A duenna, as they call them —"

"She won't be happy at what's going to take place now. A boy and a girl alone together, and not even betrothed. Very well, come in, Octavian." For she knew Octavian was waiting outside the door: she could almost hear his agitated breathing. So Octavian came in, and she left, saying: "Be discreet. Soon you'll be free of the need for discretion. But not too soon. Things have been happening rather quickly."

Sophia and Octavian stood a yard or so from each other. Octavian gulped. "What did she tell you?"

"That once she thought she was in love with you, but then she decided she had better not be in love with you. She said also that I'm in love with you."

"She knows everything. She's never wrong. Angel!"

"Did you call her angel?"

"Never!" He would be at confession first thing in the morning. He would cleanse his soul. "You're my one angel, for ever and ever."

But, being a woman, even if only fifteen, she knew better. That lady had taken something from him, and so she would never have him all. But what she had she loved. "And you," she said, "are my —" She knew nothing of the language of love: she lacked his education. "I love you," she said.

"Angel!" And then they were in each other's arms.

They were not in each other's arms twenty minutes later. They sat at the table, hands clasped, talking eagerly about their future together: it was all roses and excluded the War of the Austrian Succession. They did not notice her father and his former love come in. They did not come in very far. It was enough for her father to see them. Enough for the Princess. But they stood, quickly, clumsily, bowed one, curtseyed the other.

"It's late," her father said. "The coach is outside. I'll be waiting there." And to the Princess: "Youth, eh? Youth, youth."

"Ah yes," said the Princess. She would not be waiting.

The lovers kissed. And then, knowing how many tomorrows they had, they were willing to part. Dreams are part of young love, and dreams are best dreamed alone. They ran out together. Sophia dropped her handkerchief, a spotted one. In love as she was, she still had the makings of a thrifty housekeeper. Or so it seemed, for the Princess's own little black boy, Mahomed, came into the room, looking for it. He found it and ran out with a jubilant tinkling of his little bells.

In time, when he grew up, Mahomed left the old Princess's service and joined a troupe of actors. He specialized in the part of Othello, to whom the finding of a spotted handkerchief spells disaster not jubilation. Octavian lost a leg and an eye in the War of the Austrian Succession. Sophia died bearing her second child. The widowed Princess entered a nunnery. Baron Ochs married the richest heiress of all Austria and died at ninety-one in his bed. Or, if you wish, none of these things happened. The nature of a story is that it has no future in it. And there is no past in it either; we leave the past to history. So the young lovers are always young and live in an eternal present. Mahomed's bells will always be jingling. You can tell the story again, and it will be the same as before.

"It would," Sophia's father sometimes said, "have made rather a good comic opera."

LIBRETTO

Der Rosenkavalier

(The Rose-Bearer)

COMEDY FOR MUSIC IN THREE ACTS

by

HUGO VON HOFMANNSTHAL

ENGLISH VERSION BY ALFRED KALISCH

Summary

by

John Cox

The scene is set in Vienna.

Act I

The Princess's Bedchamber at the Werdenberg Palace.

Octavian, the seventeen-year-old Count Rofrano, has spent the night with Marie Therese, whose husband, Prince von Werdenberg, the Field Marshal, is away on a hunting expedition.

Dawn signals no reduction in the Count's ardor, although for the moment it is sublimated in abstract philosophizing about the uniqueness of their love. Octavian resents the time the Marschallin must devote to public duty, to the daily routine which is already beginning.

They breakfast together, affectionately using nicknames for each other: hers "Bichette," his "Mignon," but this mood is shattered when the Marschallin casually mentions that last night she dreamed of her husband.

She lets slip that on a previous occasion, presumably while she was with another lover, her husband came home unexpectedly, as in last night's dream.

Voices outside make it seem that the dream is about to come true. Octavian hides in a closet. There he finds a maid's uniform, which he puts on, intending to slip away unrecognized.. However, the danger is diminished when the unexpected intruder turns out to be the Marschallin's cousin, Baron Ochs of Lerchenau.

Octavian's escape is thwarted by Ochs, to whom anything in a skirt is fair game. He makes himself at home, shamelessly ogling the "maid," and preventing "her" from leaving. The Marschallin hurriedly gives the transformed Octavian the name Mariandel.

The business of the Baron's visit is his imminent betrothal. In particular, he is looking for a young nobleman to present the traditional silver rose to his bride-to-be, Sophie von Faninal.

Sophie is the only child of a newly ennobled merchant anxious to be connected to an established aristocrat. Ochs expresses humorous contempt for Faninal's *parvenu* snobbery and means to make him pay dearly for it.

The Marschallin promises her help and attempts to dismiss Ochs, but he asks first for the services of her lawyer. While she makes the arrangements for this, he offers "Mariandel" an assignation. The Marschallin, amused as much by his mistake as by the bravura of Octavian's performance, rashly pushes the masquerade to the limit by suggesting Octavian, Count Rofrano, as the bearer of the silver rose and shows Ochs his portrait.

Ochs is astounded by the resemblance to Mariandel, which the Marschallin explains away by describing "her" as an illegitimate daughter of Octavian's father. Ochs boasts that he, too, has sired a natural son whom he employs as body-servant.

The Marschallin holds her daily levée, at which she receives petitioners, messengers, tributes and tradesmen during the completion of her toilette. Baron Ochs takes the opportunity of conferring with her lawyer.

With Ochs present, the levée does not lack incident. Reinforced by the intrusion of his own retinue, he presses the reluctant lawyer to make preposterous demands on Faninal.

Others present include Valzacchi and Annina, gossips from a low news-sheet, who ingratiate themselves with Ochs, whose son Leopold hands over the silver rose to the Marschallin.

The Marschallin dismisses the levée. Alone for the first time that day, she gives expression to her troubled feelings.

The Baron's callow selfishness, with its easy assumption of social and masculine superiority, has reminded her of her own arranged marriage, loveless, straight from the convent. She sees her whole life in one clear glimpse, the young bride giving way to the old Princess.

Octavian's return does not cheer her up, a fact which upsets and baffles him, since he cannot accept that his love is not enough to make the Princess completely happy.

She warns him not to rely on physical love to solve all problems, wounding his pride by likening him to other men. He cannot comprehend her obsession with the passage of time, and when she insists that he will soon leave her for someone his own age he is crushed.

Offering him a rendezvous, later perhaps, beside her carriage in the park, the Marschallin dismisses Octavian. Too late, she remembers she has failed to kiss him goodbye. She quickly sends a messenger after him with the silver rose.

Act II

The Reception Room of Faninal's Town House.

The duenna breathlessly reports that the presentation of the silver rose is about to take place.

Sophie, in whose honor the entire ceremony is to be given, prays to God to make her worthy but not proud.

The silver rose is presented to Sophie von Faninal on behalf of Baron Ochs by Octavian, Count Rofrano. He falls in love with her at first sight. She is deeply affected by him, but naively supposes that Ochs, whom she has never met, must be even more beautiful. But when Faninal introduces her to her bridegroom, she is sharply and totally disillusioned.

Ochs's behavior, while entirely good-natured, is in style more suited to a horse fair. Octavian, too, is offended by Ochs's gross familiarity. But any injury he may feel on his own account is soon engulfed in the helpless horror he feels at what is happening to Sophie, now being mauled by Ochs as if she were a peasant.

Ochs's excessive attentions are curbed by the arrival of the lawyer to discuss the marriage contract. The Baron commits Sophie to the care of Octavian, with the confidential injunction to "loosen her up a bit."

Sophie, who realizes that she is in love with Octavian, puts herself totally in his hands to extricate her from this marriage. Octavian explains that he can help only if she will be resolute on her own behalf, so that they can resist it together.

Valzacchi and Annina intrude upon their embraces and call the Baron. Ochs laughs it off at first, but loses patience when Sophie refuses to sign the marriage contract. Octavian draws his sword to protect her. The situation rapidly deteriorates, and Ochs is wounded.

The wound is no more than a scratch, but it causes a great outcry.

Faninal brushes aside Octavian's apology and demands his instant departure. As he leaves, Octavian is intercepted by Annina and Valzacchi. The three of them plot against Ochs.

Sophie flings defiance at her father. Faninal tries desperately to save the marriage, but succeeds only in aggravating Ochs further.

Octavian's plot is set in motion. Annina brings a note purporting to be from the maid Mariandel, informing Ochs that tomorrow she has an evening off. He is delighted, and the disastrous course of the present is completely forgotten in the joyful anticipation of tomorrow's night of dalliance. Truly, the luck of the Lerchenaus!

Act III

A Private Room at an Inn.

With the help of Annina and Octavian, again disguised as Mariandel, Valzacchi completes his plans for the humiliation of Baron Ochs.

Ochs is appalled at the cost of this adventure — he dismisses the waiters, announces that Leopold alone will serve the food, he himself the wine.

Ochs and Mariandel sit down to supper. "She" refuses wine, but Ochs insists, giving Octavian the opportunity to feign inebriation. When Ochs eagerly offers to loosen "her" bodice, Octavian gives the signal. Valzacchi's plan goes into full swing.

Chief among the intruders is Annina, disguised, claiming that Ochs is the father of her children. When the innkeeper refuses to throw her out, Ochs summons the police; but the Inspector, alas, does not accept his bona fides and is about to prefer morals charges. Ochs claims Mariandel is his fiancée and that her name is Sophie von Faninal. But at this moment Faninal arrives, hotly denies that Mariandel is his daughter, and sends for Sophie herself to prove it. He promptly has a seizure and has to be helped from the room.

Events are interrupted by the arrival of the Marschallin. She lightly but firmly assumes control of the situation and saves Ochs from being arrested.

The Princess soon senses the relationship between Octavian and Sophie, but as the masquerade is revealed and Mariandel reappears as Octavian, Ochs is just as perspicacious in assessing Octavian's relationship with the Marschallin. She reveals her own moral misdemeanor in exposing his.

Ochs is still intent on rescuing the match with Sophie, but the Marschallin orders him sternly to desist and depart.

The isolated Ochs is beset by the inn staff, who attempt the final humiliation with the presentation of their bills.

The Marschallin, realizing that Octavian's hour of decision has come, and that he must inevitably choose Sophie, helps him to do so. Stoically relinquishing all claims to him, she ensures that Faninal will consent to what is, after all, an even better match. With order and dignity restored, the Princess leaves. The two lovers, ecstatic, remain behind to contemplate alone their future happiness.

Characters

Princess von Werdenberg (*Wife of Field Marshal Prince von Werdenberg*)	*Soprano*
Baron Ochs of Lerchenau	*Bass*
Octavian (*called Mignon — a Young Gentleman of Noble Family*)	*Mezzo-Soprano*
Herr von Faninal (*a Rich Merchant, Newly Ennobled*)	*High Baritone*
Sophia (*His Daughter*)	*High Soprano*
Mistress Marianne Leitmetzer (*Duenna*)	*High Soprano*
Valzacchi (*a Man of Affairs*)	*Tenor*
Annina (*His Partner*)	*Alto*
A Commissary of Police	*Bass*
Major-domo of the Princess	*Tenor*
Major-domo of Faninal	*Tenor*
The Princess's Attorney	*Bass*
Innkeeper	*Tenor*
A Singer	*High-Tenor*
A Scholar	
A Flute-Player	
A Hairdresser	
His Assistant	
A Widow of Noble Family	
Three Orphans of Noble Family	*Soprano* *Mezzo-Soprano* *Alto*
A Milliner	*Soprano*
A Vendor of Animals	*Tenor*
Four Footmen of the Princess	*Two Tenor* *Two Bass*
Four Waiters	*One Tenor* *Three Bass*

A Little Blackamoor, Footmen, Couriers, Heyducks, Cookboys, Guests, Musicians, Two Watchmen, Four Little Children, Various Personages of suspicious appearance.

Place of Action

Vienna, in the early years of the reign of Maria Theresa.

[This libretto is offered as a basic guide to *Der Rosenkavalier*. It should be noted, however, that productions of the opera vary widely and that selected passages are sometimes omitted or emended in performance. With regard to the English translation by Alfred Kalisch, the version which appears here was completed at the time of the first performances of *Der Rosenkavalier* in England and in the United States, and has been left more or less intact in the pages that follow. The complexities of Hofmannsthal's German (particularly the inclusion of various Viennese dialects and the overall flavor of eighteenth-century formalities), which are well known and which make the choice between more "stylized" or more "modern" renderings especially difficult, led to the decision to edit only those passages where idiomatic expressions no longer in use in English needed to be reworded and brought closer to their intended meaning. — Ed.]

1. Costume sketch, Octavian. By Alfred Roller for original production of *Der Rosenkavalier,* Dresden, 1911. (COURTESY OF BOOSEY AND HAWKES, LTD.)

2. Act I, opening scene. Teresa Zylis-Gara as the Marschallin, Tatiana Troyanos as Octavian, Metropolitan Opera, 1976. (PHOTO: JAMES HEFFERNAN, METROPOLITAN OPERA)

3. Act II set design. Sketch by Robert O'Hearn. (COURTESY OF THE EDUCATION DEPARTMENT, METROPOLITAN OPERA GUILD)

4. Act III set design. Sketch by Robert O'Hearn. (COURTESY OF THE EDUCATION DEPARTMENT, METROPOLITAN OPERA GUILD)

5. Act II, Metropolitan Opera, current production. (PHOTO: JAMES HEFFERNAN, METROPOLITAN OPERA)

6.
Costume design, the Marschallin, Act III. Original sketch by Robert O'Hearn. (COURTESY OF ROBERT O'HEARN)

Prop photographs, Act I, *Der Rosenkavalier,* Metropolitan Opera, current production. (PHOTOS: JAMES HEFFERNAN, METROPOLITAN OPERA)

7. The Marschallin's dressing table.

8. The silver rose.

9. Yvonne Minton as Octavian, Metropolitan Opera, 1977. (PHOTO: JAMES HEFFERNAN, METROPOLITAN OPERA)

10. Luciano Pavarotti as the Italian Singer, Metropolitan Opera, 1976. (PHOTO: JAMES HEFFERNAN, METROPOLITAN OPERA)

11. Gwyneth Jones as the Marschallin, Metropolitan Opera, 1977. (PHOTO: JAMES HEFFERNAN, METROPOLITAN OPERA)

ACT ONE

The bedroom of the Princess. In the alcove to the left the large, tent-shaped four-poster. Next to the bed a threefold screen, behind which clothes are scattered to the ground. A small table, chairs, etc. To the right, folding doors leading to the bedchamber. In the center, scarcely visible, a little door let into the wall. No other doors. Between the alcove and the small door, a toilet table and some armchairs against the wall. The curtains of the bed are half drawn. Through the half-open window the morning sun streams in. From the garden sounds the song of birds. Octavian kneels on a footstool, half embracing the Princess who is reclining in the bed. Her face is hidden; only her beautiful hand is seen, and her arm peeping from out the sleeve of her nightgown of lace.

OCTAVIAN
(rapturously)

Wie du warst! Wie du bist! Das weiss niemand, das ahnt keiner!	All thy soul, all thy heart — None can measure their perfection.

PRINCESS
(raises herself on her pillow)

Beklagt Er sich über das, Quinquin? Möcht' Er, dass viele das wüssten?	Why grieve so sorely at that, Mignon? Should it be known on the housetops?

OCTAVIAN
(passionately)

Engel! Nein! Selig bin ich, dass ich der Einzige bin, der weiss, wie du bist. Keiner ahnt es! Niemand weiss es! Du, du, du! was heisst das "Du"? Was "du und ich"? Hat denn das einen Sinn? Das sind Wörter, blosse Wörter, nicht? Du sag'! Aber dennoch: Es ist etwas in ihnen; ein Schwindeln, ein Ziehen, ein Sehnen und Drängen, ein Schmachten und Brennen: Wie jetzt meine Hand zu deiner Hand kommt, das Zudirwollen, das Dichumklammern, Das bin ich, das will zu dir; aber das Ich vergeht in dem "Du" . . . Ich bin dein Bub', aber wenn mir dann Hören und Sehen vergeht — wo ist dann dein Bub'?	Angel! No! Blessed am I That it is I alone who know their secrets. Who can measure such perfection? Thou, thou, thou! What means that "Thou"? This "Thou and I"? Have they meaning or sense? They are merely empty nothings. What? O say! But there's something, yes, something is in them; A craving, a longing, an urging, A fainting and yearning: To thee now my hand has found its way. And this quest for thee, and this clinging — It is I who seek thee out, Mingling with thee and lost in that "Thou" . . . I am thy Boy; but when reft of all senses I lie in thy arms. Where then is thy Boy?

PRINCESS
(softly)

Du bist mein Bub', du bist mein Schatz! Ich hab' dich lieb!	You are my Boy, you are my love! I love you so!

OCTAVIAN
(starts up):

Warum ist Tag? Ich will nicht den Tag! Für was ist der Tag!
Da haben dich alle! Finster soll sein!

Why dawns the day? How hateful is day. For what is the day!
Then all men can see thee. Let it be dark!

(He rushes to the window and closes it. The distinct tinkling of a bell is heard. The Princess laughs to herself.)

OCTAVIAN

Lachst du mich aus?

Smil'st thou at me?

PRINCESS
(tenderly)

Lach' ich dich aus?

Smile I at thee?

OCTAVIAN

Engel!

Angel!

PRINCESS

Schatz du, mein junger Schatz!

Dearest, my sweetest love!

(again a discreet tinkling)

Horch!

Hark!

OCTAVIAN

Ich will nicht.

I will not!

PRINCESS

Still, pass auf!

Hush! Beware!

OCTAVIAN

Ich will nichts hören! Was wird's denn sein?

Deaf and blind am I. What can it be?

(The tinkling grows more distinct.)

Sind's leicht Laufer mit Briefen und Komplimenten?
Vom Saurau, vom Hartig, vom portugieser Envoyé?
Hier kommt mir keiner herein. Hier bin ich der Herr!

Is it couriers with letters and declarations?
From Saurau and Hartig or the Portuguese ambassador?
I hold the door against the world. I am master here!

(The little door in the center is opened and a small blackamoor in yellow, with silver bells, carrying a silver salver with chocolate, enters with mincing steps. The door is closed behind him by unseen hands.)

PRINCESS

Schnell, da versteck' Er sich! Das Frühstück ist's.

Quick! Go conceal yourself. My chocolate!

(Octavian steps behind the screen.)

PRINCESS

Schmeiss' Er doch Seinen Degen hinters Bett.

Foolish boy! Hide your sword behind the bed.

(Octavian reaches after the sword and hides it. The boy puts the salver on one of the small tables, moves it to the front of the stage and places the sofa next to it, bows to the Princess with his hands crossed over his breast, then dances away backward with his face always toward his mistress; at the door he bows again and disappears. The Princess appears from behind the curtains of the bed. She has wrapped around her a light dressing gown trimmed with fur. Octavian reappears from behind the screen.)

PRINCESS

Er Katzenkopf, Er Unvorsichtiger!
Lässt man in einer Dame Schlafzimmer seinen Degen herumliegen?
Hat Er keine besseren Gepflogenheiten?

You featherhead! You careless good-for-nothing!
Is it allowed to leave a sword lying in the bedroom of a lady of fashion?
Where have you learnt to show such lack of breeding?

OCTAVIAN

Wenn Ihr zu dumm ist, wie ich mich benehm',
und wenn Ihr abgeht, dass ich kein Geübter in solchem Sachen bin,
dann weiss ich überhaupt nicht, was Sie an mir hat!

Well, if my breeding is not to your taste,
If it displease you that in things like this my skill is far to seek,
Then truly it were better to bid you farewell.

PRINCESS
(tenderly, from the sofa)

Philosophier' Er nicht, Herr Schatz, und komm Er her.
Jetzt wird gefrühstückt. Jedes Ding hat seine Zeit.

Cease your philosophizing, my love, and come to me.
Now let us breakfast. Everything in its own time.

(Octavian seats himself close to her. They breakfast. He puts his head on her lap; she strokes his hair.)

OCTAVIAN

Marie Theres'!

Marie Theres'!

PRINCESS

Octavian!

Octavian!

OCTAVIAN

Bichette!

Bichette!

PRINCESS

Quinquin!

Mignon!

OCTAVIAN

Mein Schatz!

My beloved!

PRINCESS

Mein Bub'!

My boy!

(They continue breakfast.)

OCTAVIAN

(merrily)

Der Feldmarschall sitz im krowatischen Wald und jagt auf Bären und Luchsen. Und ich, ich setz' hier, ich junges Blut, und jag' auf was? Ich hab' ein Glück, ich hab' ein Glück!	The Field Marshal stays in the far Croatian wilds, hunting for brown bears and black boars. And I, in the flower of my youth, stay here — hunting for what? Blessed is my lot! How blessed is my lot!

PRINCESS

(a shadow passing over her face):

Lass Er den Feldmarschall in Ruh'! Mir hat von ihm geträumt.	Hush! Leave the Field Marshal in peace. I dreamed a dream of him.

OCTAVIAN

Heut Nacht hat dir von ihm geträumt? Heut Nacht?	Last night you dreamed a dream of him? Last night?

PRINCESS

Ich schaff' mir meine Träume nicht an.	My dreams are not mine to command.

OCTAVIAN

Heut Nacht hat dir von deinem Mann geträumt? Heut Nacht?	What? You dreamed a dream last night of him? Last night?

PRINCESS

Mach' Er nicht solche Augen. Ich kann nichts dafür. Er war auf einmal wieder zu Haus.	Why look so sad and angry? 'Tis no fault of mine . . . My husband was at home again.

OCTAVIAN

(softly)

Der Feldmarschall?	The Field Marshal?

PRINCESS

Es war ein Lärm im Hof von Pferd' und Leut' und er war da, Vor Schreck war ich auf einmal wach, nein, schau' nur, schau' nur, wie kindisch ich bin: ich hör' noch immer den Rumor im Hof. Ich bring's nicht aus dem Ohr. Hörst du leicht auch was?	There was a noise below of horse and hound — and he was here. In fright I started up in haste. Now look, look what a child I am — still I can hear it, all the noise below. 'Tis ringing in my ears. Do you not hear it?

OCTAVIAN

Ja freilich hör' ich was, aber muss es denn dein Mann sein!? Denk' dir doch, wo der ist: im Raitzenland, noch hinterwärts von Esseg.	Yes, truly, sounds I hear: but why so sure it is your husband? Think but where he's hunting: far away, At Esseg or a score of leagues beyond.

PRINCESS

Ist das sicher sehr weit?	You think he is so far?

Na, dann wird's halt was anders sein. Dann ist's ja gut.	Then what we hear is something else, and all is well.

OCTAVIAN

Du schaust so ängstlich drein, Theres'.	You look so full of fear, Theres'.

PRINCESS

Weiss Er, Quinquin — wenn es auch weit ist —	But see, Mignon — though it be distant,
Der Feldmarschall ist halt sehr geschwind. Einmal —	The Prince at times travels wonderous fast. For once —

OCTAVIAN

(*jealous*)

Was war einmal?	What did he, once?

(*She pauses.*)

Was war einmal? Bichette!	What did he, once? Bichette!
Bichette! Was war einmal?	Bichette! What did he, once?

PRINCESS

Ach sei Er gut, Er muss nicht alles wissen.	Oh, let him be — why must I tell you all these things?

OCTAVIAN

(*throws himself in despair onto the sofa*)

So spielt Sie sich mit mir!	See how she trifles with me!
Ich bin ein unglücklicher Mensch!	Why will you drive me to despair?

PRINCESS

(*listens*)

Jetzt trotz' Er nicht. Jetzt gilt's: es ist der Feldmarschall.	Take hold of yourself. 'Tis true. It is the Field Marshal.
Wenn es ein Fremder wär', so wär der Lärm da draussen in meinen Vorzimmer.	For were a stranger here, the noise would surely be there in the antechamber.
Es muss mein Mann sein, der durch die Garderob' herein will	It is my husband. I hear his footsteps on the private staircase,
Und mit den Lakaien disputiert.	And forcing the footmen to make way.
Quinquin, es ist mein Mann!	Mignon, it is the Prince!

(*Octavian draws his sword and runs to the right.*)

Nicht dort, dort ist das Vorzimmer.	Not there; that is the antechamber.
Da sitzen meine Lieferanten und ein halbes Dutzend Lakaien.	There for sure, a crowd with wares to offer and a score of lackeys are waiting.
Da!	There!

(*Octavian runs to the small door.*)

Zu spät! Sie sind schon in der Garderob'!	Too late! I hear them in the private passage!
Jetzt bleibt nur eins!	Now there's but one chance!
Versteck' Er sich!	Hide yourself!

(*After a brief pause of helplessness.*)

Dort!	There!

OCTAVIAN

Ich spring' ihm in den Weg! Ich bleib' bei dir.	I will not let him pass: I stay with you!

PRINCESS

Dort hinters Bett! Dort in der Vorhäng! Und rühr' dich nicht!	There — by the bed. There in the curtains! And do not move!

OCTAVIAN

(hesitating)

Wenn er mich dort erwischt, was wird aus dir,	Should I be caught by him, what fate is yours,
Theres'?	Theres'?

PRINCESS

(pleading)

Versteck' Er sich, mein Schatz.	Hide quickly now, beloved.

(Stamping her foot impatiently.)

OCTAVIAN

(by the screen)

Theres'!	Theres'!

PRINCESS

Sei Er ganz still!	Quick now, be still!

(With flashing eyes)

Das möcht' ich sehn,	Now let me see
Ob einer sich dort hinüber traut, wenn ich hier steh'.	who dares move one inch toward the door while I am here.
Ich bin kein napolitanischer General: wo ich steh', steh' ich.	I'm no faint-hearted Italian brigadier: where I stand, stand I.

(She walks energetically toward the little door and listens.)

Sind brave Kerl'n, meine Lakaien, wollen ihn nich herein lassen,	They're worthy fellows, keeping guard out there, vowing they won't make way for him,
sagen, dass ich schlaf'. Sehr brave Kerl'n!	Saying I'm asleep — most worthy fellows —

(The noise in the anteroom grows louder.)

Die Stimm'!	That voice!

(Listening)

Das ist ja gar nicht die Stimm' vom Feldmarschall!	That is not, surely not, my husband's voice.
Sie sagen "Herr Baron" zu ihm! Das ist ein Fremder.	'Tis "Baron" that they're calling him! It is a stranger!

(Gaily)

Quinquin, es ist ein Besuch.	Mignon, it is someone else.

(She laughs.)

Fahr' Er schnell in seine Kleider,	Soon escape will be quite easy.
aber bleib' Er versteckt,	But remain in hiding
dass die Lakaien Ihn nicht seh'n.	So that the footmen do not see you.
Die blöde grosse Stimm' müsste ich doch kennen.	That loutish, foolish voice, surely it is familiar —
Wer ist denn das? Herrogott, das ist der Ochs.	Who is it then? Mon Dieu! 'tis Ochs.
Das ist mein Vetter, der Lerchenau, der Ochs auf Lerchenau,	I do protest, my cousin of Lerchenau. 'Tis Ochs of Lerchenau.
Was will denn der? Jesus Maria!	What can he want? Heavens above us!

(She laughs.)

Quinquin, hört Er,	Listen, Mignon, you cannot have forgot

(Going a few steps toward the left.)

Quinquin, erinnert Er sich nicht?	The league-long letter that they brought
Vor fünf oder sechs Tagen — den Brief —	When I was in my coach (you were with me) —
Wir sind im Wagen gesessen,	
und einen Brief haben sie mir an den Wagenschlag gebracht.	Some five days ago, and I scarcely looked at it. Now do you know?
Das war der Brief vom Ochs.	That letter came from Ochs.
Und ich hab' keine Ahnung, was drin gestanden ist.	And now I have no inkling what my cousin said.

(laughs)

Daran ist Er allein schuld, Quinquin!	See to what evil ways, Mignon, you lead me!

VOICE OF THE MAJOR-DOMO

(without)

Belieben Euer Gnaden in der Galerie zu warten!	Will your lordship be pleased to wait in the gallery?

VOICE OF THE BARON

(without)

Wo hat Er seine Manieren gelernt?	Who taught you to treat a nobleman so?
Der Baron Lerchenau antichambriert nicht.	The Baron Lerchenau cannot be waiting.

PRINCESS

Quinquin, was treibt Er denn? Wo steckt Er denn?	Mignon, where are you hid? What tricks are these?

OCTAVIAN

(in a skirt and a short jacket, with his hair tied with a kerchief and ribbon to look like a cap, comes from behind the screen and curtseys)

Befehl'n fürstli' Gnad'n,	An't please you, your highness,
i bin halt noch nit recht lang in fürstli'n Dienst.	I've not long been of your highness's household here.

PRINCESS

Du, Schatz!	You, Beloved!
Und nicht einmal mehr als ein Busserl kann ich dir geben.	And only one kiss may I give you. One only, my dearest.

(Kisses him quickly. More noise without.)

Er bricht mir ja die Tür ein, der Herr Vetter.	My noble kinsman's battering all the doors down.
Mach' Er, dass Er hinauskomm'.	
Schleich Er frech durch die Lakaien durch.	Now as quickly as can be
Er ist ein blitzgescheiter Lump! Und komm' Er wieder, Schatz,	March boldly past the footman there. 'Tis sport for brazen rogues like you! And come back soon, beloved,
aber in Mannskleidern und durch die vordre Tür, wenn's Ihm beliebt.	In your own habit, and through the main door, as a gentleman should.

(The Princess sits down with her back to the door and begins to sip her chocolate. Octavian goes quickly toward the little door and tries to go out, but at that moment the door is flung

open, and Baron Ochs, whom the footmen vainly try to keep back, forces his way in. Octavian, who attempts to escape, hiding his face, runs into him. Then, in confusion, he stands aside against the wall, to the left of the door. Three footmen enter with the Baron and stand, undecided.)

BARON

(*pompously to the footmen*)

Selbstverständlich empfängt mich Ihre Gnaden.

Why, it is certain her highness will receive me.

(*He goes to the front; the footmen on his left try to bar his passage. To Octavian, with interest:*)

Pardon, mein hübsches Kind!

Forgive me, my pretty child.

(*With gracious condescension.*)

Ich sag': Pardon, mein hübsches Kind.

I said, forgive me, my pretty child.

(*The Princess looks over her shoulder, rises, and goes to meet the Baron.*)

BARON

(*gallantly to Octavian*)

Ich hab' Ihr doch nicht ernstlich weh getan?

I hope I did not inconvenience you too much.

THE FOOTMEN

(*nudging the Baron, softly*)

Ihre fürstlichen Gnaden!

See, your lordship, her highness.

(*The Baron makes an obeisance in the French manner and repeats it twice.*)

PRINCESS

Euer Liebden sehen vortrefflich aus.

My dear cousin, you look well today.

BARON

(*Bows again, then to the footmen*)

Sieht Er jetzt wohl, dass Ihre Gnaden entzückt ist, mich zu sehn.

Did I not say to you, her highness would most surely welcome me?

(*Goes to the Princess with the grace of a man of the world, offers her his hand and leads her to her chair.*)

Und wie sollten Euer Gnaden nicht!
Was tut die frühe Stunde unter Personen von Stand?
Hab' ich nicht seinerzeit wahrhaftig Tag für Tag
unserer Fürstin Brioche meine Aufwartung gemacht,
da sie im Bad gesessen ist,
mit nichts als einem kleinen Wandschirm zwischen ihr und mir.

And, of course, your highness will receive me.
We of rank take no account of early hours.
Did I not, every morning without fail, repair
To the Princess Brioche you know of? Did I not pay my respects
As in her bath she took her ease?
And there was nothing to divide us but a tiny screen?

(*Octavian has made his way along the wall toward the alcove and is busying himself, trying to escape observation, by the bed. In obedience to a sign from the Princess, the footmen carry a little sofa and an armchair to the front and retire.*)

BARON

Ich muss mich wundern,	Indeed I wonder
(Looking around angrily.)	
Wenn Euer Gnaden Livree —	that any lackey should have dared.

PRINCESS

Verzeihen Sie!	Forgive them, coz.
Man hat sich betragen, wie es befohlen war.	They did but obey me — 'twas I that bade them,
(Seats herself on the sofa, after offering the Baron the armchair.)	
Ich hatte diesen Morgen die Migräne.	I suffered much this morning from a migraine.

(The Baron tries to sit and is much distracted by the presence of the pretty waiting maid.)

BARON
(to himself)

Ein hübsches Ding! Ein gutes saub'res Kinderl!	A pretty wench, egad! She's vastly pleasing.

PRINCESS
(rising and again ceremoniously offering a seat to the Baron)

Ich bin auch jetzt noch nicht ganz wohl.	And even now I'm not quite well.

(The Baron takes his seat with hesitation and tries his utmost not to turn his back on the pretty maid.)

Der Vetter wird darum vielleicht die Gnade haben —	So, dear cousin, Bear me no ill will that I deny myself . . .

BARON

Natürlich.	Naturally!
(He turns round, so as to look at Octavian.)	

PRINCESS

Meine Kammerzofe, ein junges Ding vom Land.	My own chambermaid . . . come freshly from the country,
Ich muss fürchten, sie inkommodiert Euer Liebden.	And I fear that her rough ways cause you displeasure.

BARON

Ganz allerliebst!	Charming, I vow . . .
Wie? Nicht im geringsten! Mich? Im Gegenteil!	Displeasure? Do not think it. Me? I like such ways.
(Makes a sign to Octavian, then says to the Princess:)	
Euer Gnaden werden vielleicht verwundert sein, dass ich als Bräutigam.	But your highness may have been surprised to learn that I'm to be a bridegroom.
(Turns round.)	
indes — inzwischen —	But yet, the reason . . .

PRINCESS

Als Bräutigam?	A bridegroom?

BARON

Ja, wie Euer Gnaden denn doch wohl aus meinem Brief genugsam —	As your highness doubtless discovered from my recent letter . . .
Ein Grasaff', appetitlich, keine fünfzehn Jahr!	A novice . . . how enticing — barely fifteen years!

PRINCESS
(relieved)

Der Brief, natürlich, ja, der Brief, wer ist denn nur die Glückliche?	Yes, you wrote, why surely . . . And who has been so fortunate?
Ich hab' den Namen auf der Zunge.	The name was on my tongue this instant.

BARON

Wie?	How?

(Over his shoulder.)

Pudeljung! Gesund! Gewaschen! Allerliebst!	And how fresh! egad! how dainty! What a prize!

PRINCESS

Wer ist nur schnell die Braut?	Pray tell me who's the bride?

BARON

Das Fräulein Faninal.	Young Mistress Faninal.

(With slight vexation.)

Ich habe Euer Gnaden den Namen nicht verheimlicht.	Of her name and station I made no secret.

PRINCESS

Natürlich! Wo hab' ich meinen Kopf?	Forgive me. My memory plays me false.
Bloss die Famili ist mir nicht bekannt. Sind's keine Hiesigen?	What of her family, pray, is it native here?

(Octavian busies himself with the tray and gradually tries to get behind the Baron.)

BARON

Jawohl, Euer Gnaden, es sind Hiesige.	Yes, indeed, your highness, it is native here.
Ein durch die Gnade Ihrer Majestät Geadelter.	One which Her Majesty of late has raised to the nobility.
Er hat die Lieferung für die Armee, die in den Niederlanden steht.	The whole provisioning of all the armies in the Netherlands is in his hands.

(The Princess impatiently makes signs to Octavian that he should withdraw. The Baron completely misunderstands the Princess's expression.)

Ich seh', Euer Gnaden runzeln Dero schöne Stirn ob der Mesalliance.	I see your highness's lovely lips express disdain at such a misalliance.
Allein dass ich sag', das Mädchen ist für einen Engel hübsch genug.	But yet, although I say it, the girl is pretty as an angel and as good,
Kommt frischweg aus dem Kloster. Ist das eingize Kind.	Comes straight from a convent, is an only child.

(More emphatically.)

Dem Mann gehören zwölf Häuser auf der Wied'n nebst dem Palais am Hof.
The man has twelve houses in the city and has a mansion too.

Und seine Gesundheit
His health is failing,

(Chuckles.)

soll nicht die beste sein.
so the physicians say.

PRINCESS

Mein lieber Vetter, ich kapier' schon, wieviel's geschlagen hat.
My dear cousin, I see already which way the wind blows.

(Repeats her signs to Octavian to retire. Octavian tries to back to the door with the tray.)

BARON

Warum hinaus die Schokolade?
Why leave the chocolate unfinished?

(To Octavian, who stands undecided with averted face.)

Geruhen nur! Da! Pst, wieso denn!
Hey! Pst! Pst! What ails you?

PRINCESS

Fort, geh' Sie nur!
Quick, get you gone!

BARON

Wenn ich Euer Gnaden gesteh',
dass ich noch so gut wie nüchtern bin.
Grant me permission, your highness,
To say that I am faint for food.

PRINCESS

(resigned)

Mariandel, komm' Sie her. Servier' Sie Seiner Liebden.
Mariandel, bring it back and wait upon his lordship.

BARON

So gut wie nüchtern, Euer Gnaden, Sitz' im Reisewagen seit fünf Uhr früh.
As good as fasting, my dear cousin — sitting in my postchaise since early dawn.

(Octavian brings the tray to the Baron, who takes a cup and fills it.)

Recht ein gestelltes Ding!
Gad, what a strapping wench!

(To Octavian.)

Bleib' Sie dahier, mein Herz.
Ich hab' Ihr was zu sagen.
Stay here, my dear,
There's something I would tell you.

(To the Princess.)

Meine ganze Livree, Stallpagen, Jäger, alles —
All my livery I have brought — footmen and grooms and couriers —

(Eats voraciously.)

Alles unten im Hof zusamt meinen Almosenier.
They are all down below together with my almoner.

PRINCESS

(to Octavian)

Geh' Sie nur.
You may go.

BARON

(to Octavian)

Hat Sie noch ein Biskoterl? Bleib' Sie doch!
Have you another biscuit? Do not go —

(Aside.)	
Sie ist ein süsser Engelschatz, ein saubrer.	She is the daintiest morsel, sweet, adorable.
(To the Princess.)	
Sind auf dem Wege zum "Weissen Rosse," wo wir logieren, heisst bis übermorgen —	I halted here, but we are lodging at an inn, the White Horse,
(Softly to Octavian.)	
Ich gäb' was Schönes drum, mit Ihr —	I'd pay a heavy price to court you.
(To the Princess, very loud.)	
bis übermórgen —	But only until tomorrow.
(Quickly to Octavian.)	
unter vier Augen zu scharmutzieren! Wie?	When there is no one around to spoil our pleasure. What?
(The Princess cannot refrain from laughing at Octavian's impudent playacting.)	
Dann ziehn wir ins Palais von Faninal.	Then I and mine will be the guests of Faninal.
Natürlich muss ich vorher den Bräutigamsaufführer —	But first, I must dispatch a bridegroom's ambassador,
(Angrily to Octavian.)	
will Sie denn nicht warten? —	(Will you not have patience?)
an die wohlgeborne Jungfer Braut deputieren,	To my highly-born and beauteous bride, one who shall bring to her
Der die silberne Rosen überbringt	As a pledge of love a silver rose,
nach der hochadeligen Gepflogenheit.	As is the custom in all noble families.

PRINCESS

Und wen von der Verwandtschaft haben Euer Liebden	And on whom of all our kinsmen has your lordship's choice
für dieses Ehrenamt ausersehn?	Fallen for this grave embassy?

BARON

Die Begierde, darüber Euer Gnaden Ratschlag einzuhohlen,	It was merely because I so desired your highness's guidance on this matter
hat mich so kühn gemacht, in Reisekleidern bei Dero heutigem Lever . . .	That I did venture to intrude upon your levée today in travel clothes.

PRINCESS

Von mir?	My guidance?

BARON

. . . gemäss brieflich in aller Devotion getaner Bitte.	May be, your highness will remember that in my letter
Ich bin doch nicht so unglücklich, mit dieser devotesten Supplik Dero Missfallen . . .	I made so bold as to beg her to help me, and I should be distressed beyond words if . . .
(Leaning backwards, to Octavian.)	
Sie könnte aus mir machen, was Sie wollte.	I'd give you, my wench, anything you asked for;
Sie hat das Zeug dazu!	She's bewitched me quite!

PRINCESS

Wie denn, natürlich!	Why then, naturally!

Einen Aufführer für Euer Liebden ersten Bräutigamsbesuch aus der Verwandschaft —
wen denn nur?
den Vetter Preysing? Wie? Den Vetter Lambert?
Ich werde —

An ambassador from you to your betrothed, from among the family —
Who is fit?
Our cousin Preysing? Or cousin Lambert?
I'll tell you . . .

BARON

Dies liegt in Euer Gnaden allerschönsten Händen.

All this I gladly leave in your sweet hands, your highness.

PRINCESS

Ganz gut. Will Er mit mir zu Abend essen, Vetter?
Sagen wir morgen, will Er? Dann proponier' ich Ihm einen.

'Tis well. Will you not sup with me tonight, dear cousin?
Or else tomorrow? I'll be prepared with proposals.

BARON

Euer Gnaden sind die Herablassung selber.

Your highness's condescension overwhelms me.

PRINCESS
(*rising*)

Indes —

O yes . . .

BARON
(*aside, to Octavian*)

Das Sie mir wiederkommt! Ich geh' nicht eher fort!

You must come back again. I'll stay here till you come!

PRINCESS
(*aside*)

Oho!

Oho!

(*Aloud.*)

Bleib' Sie nur da! Kann ich dem Vetter
für jetzt noch dienlich sein?

Stay where you are! Do but command me
For any of your other needs, dear cousin.

BARON

Ich schäme mich bereits:
An Euer Gnaden Notari eine Rekommandation wär mir lieb.
Es handelt sich um den Eh'vertrag.

Truly, I'm ashamed: but I would crave
A word or two to commend me to your highness's attorney.
I would confer, touching settlements.

PRINCESS

Mein Notari kommt öfters des Morgens. Schau' Sie doch, Mariandel,
ob er nicht in der Antichambre ist und wartet.

My attorney is often here early. Go see, Mariandel,
If he's by chance yet in the anteroom in waiting.

BARON

Wozu das Kammerzofel?
Euer Gnaden beraubt sich der Bedienung
um meinetwillen.

Why send your chambermaid?
Your highness might be needing her help —
'Tis too much kindness.

(*Holds Octavian back.*)

PRINCESS

Lass Er doch, Vetter, Sie mag ruhig gehen.

Let her go, cousin, she's not needed here.

BARON

(*eagerly*)

Das geb' ich nicht zu, bleib' Sie hier zu Ihrer Gnaden Wink.
Es kommt gleich wer von der Livree herein.
Ich liess ein solches Goldkind, meiner Seel',
nicht unter das infame Lakaienvolk.

That I'll not allow. Stay you here, at her highness's beck and call,
'Twill not be long before a footman comes.
I should not let this sweet child, on my soul,
Go mix with all the scurvy men below.

(*Stroking her.*)

PRINCESS

Euer Liebden sind allzu besorgt.

There's no need for such fear, my dear coz.

(*Enter the Major-domo.*)

BARON

Da, hab' ich's nicht gesagt?
Er wird Euer Gnaden zu melden haben.

There, is it not as I said?
He comes with some news that concerns your highness.

PRINCESS

(*To the Major-domo*)

Struhan, hab' ich meinen Notari in her Vorkammer warten?

Struhan, tell me, is my attorney waiting in the anteroom?

MAJOR-DOMO

Fürstliche Gnaden haben den Notari,
dann den Verwalter, dann den Kuchelchef,
dann von Excellenz Silva hergeschickt
ein Sänger mit einem Flötisten.

Yes, the attorney waits without, your highness,
Then there's the steward, next the head cook —
Then, the Duke of Silva commends
To your highness a singer and a flute-player,

(*Dryly.*)

Ansonsten das gewöhnliche Bagagi.

And lastly all the usual petitioners.

BARON

(*The Baron pushes his chair behind the broad back of the Major-domo and tenderly takes the hand of the "chambermaid."*)

Hat sie schon einmal
mit einem Kavalier im tête-à-tête
zu Abend gegessen?

Say, have you ever,
with any gentleman been tête-à-tête
to supper?

(*Octavian simulates embarrassment.*)

Nein? Da wird Sie Augen machen. Will Sie?

No? It will open your eyes, I warrant. Will you?

OCTAVIAN

(softly, confused)

I weiss halt nit, i dös derf.	I don't know whether I can.

(The Princess listens inattentively to the Major-domo, while watching the Baron and Octavian with much amusement.)

PRINCESS

(laughing, to the Major-domo)

Warten lassen.	Let them wait then.

(Exit Major-Domo. To the Baron, who tries to regain his composure.)

Der Vetter ist, ich seh', kein Kostverächter.	My cousin takes his pleasures where he finds them.

BARON

(relieved)

Mit Euer Gnaden	Your highness puts me at my ease at once.
ist man frei daran. Da gibt's keine Flausen, keine Etikette,	With you there's no nonsense, no Spanish affectations.
keine spanische Tuerei!	No airs, no buckram, no compliments.

(Kissing her hand.)

PRINCESS

(amused)

Aber wo Er doch ein Bräutigam ist?	But a man of birth, who's just betrothed . . .

BARON

(half rising, leaning towards her)

Macht das einen lahmen Esel aus mir?	Must I, because of that, live like a monk?
Bin ich da nicht wie ein guter Hund auf einer guten Fährte?	Do I not well, like a hound of breed, keen on the quarry ever,
Und doppelt scharf auf jedes Wild: nach links, nach rechts?	To follow hot-foot every scent to right or left?

PRINCESS

Ich seh', Euer Liebden betreiben es als Profession.	I see now that my cousin pursues his sport quite seriously.

BARON

Das will ich meinen.	Why deny it?
Wüsste nicht, welche mir besser behagen könnte.	For what sport more becomes a man of birth and breeding?
Ich muss Euer Gnaden sehr bedauern,	I vow, I do condole with you sincerely
dass Euer Gnaden nur — wie drück ich mich aus —	That you can only know — 'tis hard to express —
die verteidigenden Erfahrungen besitzen.	From experience the feelings of a defender —
Parole d'honneur! Es geht nichts über die von der anderen Seite.	Parole d'honneur — nothing can equal those which inspire an aggressor.

PRINCESS

Ich glaube Ihm, dass die sehr mannigfaltig sind.	I doubt not that they are very various.

BARON

Soviel Zeiten das Jahr, soviel Stunden der Tag, da ist keine —

Though the months of the year, though the hours and the minutes be countless . . .

PRINCESS

Keine?

Countless?

BARON

Wo nicht —

There's none . . .

PRINCESS

Wo nicht —

There's none?

BARON

Wo nicht dem Knaben Cupido
ein Geschenkerl abzulisten wär!

In which sly Master Cupido
Will not smile upon him who woos him aright.

(*Always very quickly and distinctly*)

Dafür ist man kein Auerhahn und kein Hirsch,
sondern man ist Herr der Schöpfung,
dass man nicht nach dem Kalender forciert ist, halten zu Gnaden!
Zum Exempel der Mai ist recht lieb für's verliebte Geschaft,
das weiss jedes Kind,
aber ich sage:
Schöner ist Juni, Juli, August.
Da hat's Nächte.
Da ist bei uns da droben so ein Zuzug
von jungen Mägden aus dem Böhmischen herüber:
Ihrer zweie, dreie halt ich oft
bis im November mir im Haus.
Dann erst schick' ich sie heim.
Zur Ernte kommen sie und sind auch ansonsten anstellig und gut —

But then we are not birds of air and not stags,
but we are the Lords of Creation:
therefore the calendar rules not our mating — saving your presence!
Now the season of May is propitious for lovers' designs;
as every child knows.
But I say truly:
I prefer August, June or July.
What nights those are!
To us at home in summer comes an army
Of girls from Bohemia; in a swarm they cross the border:
And it's pleasant sometimes to induce
Just two or three to stay with me
till the autum falls.
They come at harvest time, nor do they refuse to work whatever task.

(*Chuckling*)

dann erst schick' ich sie heim!
Und wie sich das mischt,
das junge, runde böhmische Völkel, schwer und süss,
mit denen im Wald, und denen im Stall,
dem deutschen Schlag, scharf und herb
wie ein Retzer Wein —
wie sich das mischen tut!
Und überall steht was und lauert und schielt durch den Gattern,
und schleicht zu einander, und liegt bei einander,
und überall singt was
und schupft sich in den Hüften,

When it's done, they go home!
And how they agree,
the active, lissom folk of Bohemia, sad and sweet —
With those of our land, of true German stock,
so different, sharp and sour
like a Northern wine —
Yet they agree so well!
And everywhere lovers are waiting and seeking each other,
And whisp'ring sweet nothings in tenderest accents,
And ev'rywhere all day
And night joyfully singing

und melkt was
und mäht was
und plantscht, und plätschert was im Bach und in der Pferdeschwemm.

And milking
And reaping with a will,
And splashing in the brook and in the horse pond.

PRINCESS
(*Much diverted*)

Und Er ist überall dahinter her?

And you are ev'rywhere keeping watch?

BARON

Wollt, ich könnt sein wie Jupiter selig in tausend Gestalten!
Wär Verwendung für jede.

Would I could be, like Jupiter, happy in endless disguises!
There is room for so many.

PRINCESS

Wie, auch für den Stier?
So grob will Er sein?
Oder möchte Er die Wolken spielen und daher gesäuselt kommen
als ein Streiferl nasse Luft?

What, e'en for the bull?
Fie, fie. How coarse a jest!
'Twould be prettier in heav'n to gambol, like a fleecy coudlet,
Wafted by an am'rous breeze of spring.

BARON
(*Very gaily*)

Je nachdem, all's je nachdem.
Das Frauenzimmer hat gar vielerlei Arten, wie es will genommen sein.
Da ist die demütige Magd.
Und da: die trotzige Teufelskreatur,
haut dir die schwere Stalltür an den Schädel —
Und da ist die kichernd und schluchzend den Kopf verliert,
die hab ich gern
und jener wieder, der sitzt im Auge ein kalter, rechnender Satan.
Aber es kommt eine Stunde,
da flackert dieses lauernde Auge
und der Satan,
indem er ersterbende Blicke dazwischen schiesst,

That depends, yes, that depends.
For woman, look you, must be wheedled or captured in a hundred diff'rent ways.
The one is all humility.
The next a limb of the Devil, a very shrew,
Beats you about the headpiece with a pitchfork —
Then the third, who giggling and sobbing will lose her head —
That one I like —
And then another — look in her eyes — there's a devil, cold and repelling,
Bide but your time — sure 'twill come —
You'll discover how that devil is yielding,
And relenting.
And when her last venomous glances she darts at me,

(*With gusto*)

der würzt mir die Mahlzeit unvergleichlich.

that flavors the banquet past believing.

PRINCESS

Er selber ist einer, meiner Seel'!

'Tis you that's a devil, on my soul!

BARON

Und wär eine — haben die Gnad' — die keiner anschaut:
Im schmutzigen Kittel schlumpt sie her,
hockt in der Asche hinterm Herd —

Yet another — pray give me leave — whom none will look at:
In tatters and rags she slinks along,
crouches 'mid ashes by the hearth —

die, wo du sie angehst zum richtigen Stündl —
die, hat's in sich!
Ein solches Staunen —
gar nicht begreifen können
und Angst und Scham;
und auf die letzt so eine rasende Seligkeit,
dass sich der Herr,
der gnädige Herr
herabgelassen gar zu ihrer Niedrigkeit.

She, if the right hour have but struck for your wooing,
She's not wanting!
A wild amazement —
stunned and bewildered, halting
Twixt fear and shame —
At last she yields, like one distraught with excess of joy,
To think that he,
The master and lord
So far descends to look upon her lowliness.

PRINCESS

Er weiss mehr als das A-B-C!

You know more than your A-B-C's!

BARON

Da gibt es welche die wollen beschlichen sein,
sanft, wie der Wind das frisch–gemähte Heu beschleicht.

Then there are others, won only be stratagem,
Soft as the breeze that sighs over new mown hay in June.

(*Aloud*)

Und welche — da gilt's,
wie ein Luchs hinterm Rücken heran,
und den Melkstuhl gepackt,
dass sie taumelt und hinschlägt.

And others, look you, "Quick as lightning" is the watchword for those —
Before she knows you've attacked,
she is sprawling defenseless —

(*chuckling complacently*)

Muss halt ein Heu in der Nähe dabei sein.

But when she falls, see that she does herself no harm.

(*Octavian bursts out laughing*)

PRINCESS

Nein! Er agiert mir gar zu gut!
Lasst Er mir doch das Kind.

No! What a man! What victories!
Leave the child alone, I say.

BARON

(*To Octavian, without embarrassment*)

Weiss mich ins engste Versteck zu bequemen,
weiss im Alkoven galant mich zu benehmen.
Hätte Verwendung für tausend Gestalten,
tausend Jungfern festzuhalten.
Wäre mir keine zu junge zu herbe,
keine zu niedrige, keine zu derbe!
Tät mich für keinem Versteck nicht schämen,
seh ich was Lieb's,
ich muss mir's nehmen.

Meanest of attics can never disarm me,
The most splendid boudoir will never alarm me.
How I would like to clothe myself in scores of disguises,
For as many enterprises.
None comes amiss whether simple or cunning,
Luring me on,
or my company shunning.
The most splendid boudoir will never alarm me,
All are for me, nothing can disarm me.

Octavian

(Instantly playing his role again)

Na, zu dem Herrn, da ging i net,	No, I won't go courtin' with you,
da hätt i an Respect,	I do not think it right,
na was mir da passieren könnt,	Mercy, what would my mother say!
da wir i gar zu g'schreckt.	For sure, I should die of fright.
I wass net, was er meint,	I don't know what you say,
i wass net, was er will	I don't know why I should.
Aber was z'viel is, das ist zuviel.	One thing I know is, it's for no good.
Na was mir da passieren könnt.	Mercy! What would my mother say!
Das is ja net zum sagen,	I'd be too scared for fun,
zu so an Herrn da ging i net,	You look too bold and cunning,
mir tat's die Red' verschlagen.	I'd be too scared for fun.
Da tät sich unsereins mutwillig schaden:	Such sport leads many a poor girl to her ruin!

(to the Princess)

Ich hab solce Angst vor him, fürstliche Gnaden.	I'm afraid of him, your highness!

Princess

Nein, Er agiert gar zu gut!	No! What a man! What victories!
Er ist ein Rechter! Er is der Wahre!	What a hero! What a hero!
Lass Er mir doch das Kind.	Leave that child alone, I say.
Er ist ganz wie die andern dreiviertel sind.	But of every hundred I see each day,
Wie ich Ihn so sehe, so seh' ich hübsch viele.	There are ninety like him; it's still the same story,
Das sind halt die Spiele, die euch convenieren!	They find there's one glory,
Und wir, Herr Gott! Wir leiden den Schaden,	In all that's unseemly!
wir leiden den Spott,	And we, Heaven knows, we feel all the sorrow,
und wir haben's halt auch net anders verdient.	We bear the hard blows.
Und jetzt sakerlott,	But perhaps women sin more deeply than men.
	What manners are those!

(with feigned severity)

jetzt lass Er das Kind!	Now let the child be!

Baron

(suddenly resumes his dignified bearing)

Geben mir Euer Gnaden den Grasaff' da	Pray will your highness permit me to take this wench
zu meiner künftigen Frau Gemahlin Bedienung.	To be my baroness's chosen attendant!

Princess

Wie, meine Kleine da? Was sollte die?	What, my favorite girl? What would you gain?
Die Fräulein Braut wird schon versehen sein	And, sure, your bride will have no need of her,
und nicht anstehn auf Euer Liebden Auswahl.	Such a choice she would wish to make unaided.

BARON

Das ist ein feines Ding! Kreuzsakerlott! Da ist ein Tropfen guten Bluts dabei!	That is a splendid wench, Gadzooks, she is! I dare be sworn, she has blue blood in her.

OCTAVIAN

(*aside*)

Ein Tropfen guten Bluts!	Yes, blue blood indeed!

PRINCESS

Euer Liebden haben ein scharfes Auge!	What keen discernment is yours, my cousin.

BARON

Geziemt sich.	'Tis needful.

(*Confidentially.*)

Find' in der Ordnung, dass Personen von Stand in solcher Weise von adeligem Blut bedient werden. Führ' selbst ein Kind meiner Laune mit mir.	Is it not right that a man of birth Should have those about his person Who also are of pedigree unblemished? I have a lackey as well-born as I.

OCTAVIAN

(*still much amused*)

Ein Kind Seiner Laune?	As well-born as he is!

PRINCESS

Wie? Gar ein Mädel? Das will ich nicht hoffen.	What? Is it a girl? I hope not!

BARON

Nein, einen Sohn. Trägt lerchenauisches Gepräge im Gesicht. Halt' ihn als Leiblakai.	No, a son. So like the Lerchenaus that none can mistake him. He is my body-servant.

PRINCESS AND OCTAVIAN

(*laughing*)

Als Leiblakai!	His body-servant!

BARON

Wenn Euer Gnaden dann werden befehlen, dass ich die silberne Rosen darf Dero Händen übergeben, wird er es sein, der sie herauf bringt.	Whenever your highness shall deign to command me To give to your keeping the rose of silver 'Twill be from him that it shall be brought.

PRINCESS

Soll mich recht freuen. Aber wart' Er einmal.	I understand — but one moment I beg.

(*Beckoning Octavian.*)

Mariandel!	Mariandel!

BARON

Geben mir Euer Gnaden das Zofel! Ich lass nicht locker.	Once more I beg your highness — your chambermaid for my lady!

PRINCESS

Ei!

Ah!

(To Octavian.)

Geh' Sie und bring' Sie das Medaillon her.

Go bring the miniature set in jewels.

OCTAVIAN

(softly)

Theres! Theres, gib acht!

Therese, Therese, beware!

PRINCESS

(the same)

Bring's nur schnell! Ich weiss schon, was ich tu.

Bring it quick! I am caution itself, never fear.

(Exit Octavian.)

BARON

(looking after Octavian)

Könnt' eine junge Fürstin sein.

Gad, she might be a young princess!

(To the Princess.)

Hab' vor, meiner Braut eine getreue Kopie
meines Stammbaumes zu spendieren —
nebst einer Locke vom Ahnherrn Lerchenau, der ein grosser Klosterstifter war
und Oberst-Erblandhofmeister in Kärnten
und in der winischen Mark.

Think you it would be well if to my bride I gave
My pedigree, fairly copied —
Or even a lock of the first Lord Lerchenau — a pious founder of convents he
And first hereditary Grand Warden
of the Carinthian Marches?

(Octavian brings the medallion.)

PRINCESS

Wollen Euer Gnaden leicht den jungen Herrn da als
Bräutigamsaufführer haben?

Would your lordship choose to have this gentleman
To take the rose of silver to your mistress?

(All in an easy tone of conversation.)

BARON

Bin ungeschauter einverstanden!

Without a glance I trust your highness.

PRINCESS

(hesitating)

Mein junger Vetter, der Graf Octavian.

'Tis my young cousin, the Count Octavian.

BARON

(still very courteous)

Wüsste keinen vornehmeren zu wünschen!
Wär in Devotion dem jungen Herrn sehr verbunden!

Who could wish for a nobler or more gallant envoy?
Surely, I should be vastly in the debt of your kinsman.

PRINCESS

(quickly)

Seh' Er ihn an!

Look at him well!

(Shows him the miniature.)

BARON

Die Ähnlichkeit!

'Tis wonderful.

(Looking first at the portrait, then at Octavian.)

PRINCESS

Ja, ja.

Yes, yes!

BARON

Aus dem Gesicht geschnitten!

Like two copies from one model!

PRINCESS

Hab' mir auch schon Gedanken gemacht.

It has caused me myself some surprise.

(Pointing to the portrait.)

Rofrano, des Herrn Marchese zweiter Bruder.

Rofrano, the younger brother of the Marquis.

BARON

Octavian Rofrano! Da ist man wer, wenn man aus solchem Haus,

Octavian? Rofrano? 'Tis no small thing, such a relationship.

(Pointing to Octavian.)

Und wär's auch bei der Domestikentür'!

Even if it be not quite . . . canonical.

PRINCESS

Darum halt' ich sie auch wie was Besonderes.

For that reason have I advanced her over all the rest.

BARON

Geziemt sich.

'Tis fitting.

PRINCESS

Immer um meine Person.

Always in waiting on me.

BARON

Sehr wohl.

'Tis well.

PRINCESS

Jetzt aber geh' Sie, Mariandel, mach' Sie fort.

Now get you gone, Mariandel, on your way.

(Octavian goes toward the folding door on the right.)

BARON

Wie denn? Sie kommt doch wieder.

How now? Come back, I beg you!

PRINCESS

(purposely not noticing the Baron)

Und lasss Sie die Antichambre herein.

Admit all who are waiting outside.

BARON
(following him)

Mein schönstes Kind!	My sweetest child!

OCTAVIAN
(by the door on the right)

Derft's eina geh'!	You may come in!

(Runs to the other door.)

BARON

Ich bin Ihr Serviteur! Geb' Sie doch einen Augenblick Audienz!	I am your most obedient, humble servant — only let me speak.

OCTAVIAN
(slams the door in the Baron's face)

I komm' glei.	Yes, one moment!

(At this moment an old tirewoman enters by the same door. The Baron starts back disappointed. Two footmen enter from the right and bring a screen from the recess. The Princess steps behind the screen, attended by her tirewoman. The toilet table is moved to the center. The footmen open the folding doors through which enter the attorney, the head cook, followed by an assistant, carrying the book of menus. Then a milliner, a scholar, carrying a ponderous folio, and the vendor of animals with tiny lap-dogs and a small monkey. Valzacchi and Annina, slipping in behind the last-named, take their places on the extreme left. The noble mother with her three daughters all in deepest mourning take position on the right wing. The Major-domo leads the tenor and the flute player to the front. The Baron, in the background beckons to a footman, gives him an order, pointing "Here through the small door.")

THE THREE NOBLE ORPHANS
(shrilly)

Drei arme adelige Waisen —	Three poor and highborn orphan children —

(Their mother makes signs to them to kneel and not to sing so loudly.)

THE THREE ORPHANS
(kneeling)

Drei arme adelige Waisen erflehen Dero hohen Schutz!	Three poor and highborn orphan children, Implore your grace to grant our prayer.

THE MILLINER
(loudly)

Le chapeau Paméla! La poudre à la reine de Golconde!	Le chapeau Paméla! — La poudre à la reine de Golconde!

THE VENDOR OF ANIMALS

Schöne Affen, wenn Durchlaucht schaffen, auch Vögel hab' ich da aus Afrika.	For your pleasure In hours of leisure Of tricksy apes a score From Afric's shore.

THE THREE ORPHANS

Der Vater ist jung auf dem Felde der Ehre gefallen, ihm dieses nachzutun, ist unser Herzenszeil.

Our father in youth died a glorious death for his country, 'Tis our hearts' one desire to be his worthy children.

THE MILLINER

Le chapeau Paméla! C'est la merveille du monde!

Le chapeau Paméla! C'est la merveille du monde!

THE VENDOR

Papageien hätt' ich da,
aus Indien und Afrika.
Hunderln, so klein
und schon zimmerrein.

Parrots too of plumage gay
From India and Africay.
Lap-dogs so wise
Very small in size.

(*The Princess appears. All bow low. The Baron, on the left, steps forward.*)

PRINCESS

(*to the Baron*)

Ich präsentier' Euer Liebden hier den Notar.

I present to you, dear cousin, my attorney.

(*The attorney, with many obeisances toward the toilet table at which the Princess has seated herself, advances to the Baron on the right. The Princess signals to the youngest of the three orphans to approach her, and takes a purse from the Major-domo and gives it to the girl, whom she kisses on the forehead. The scholar attempts to approach the Princess and hand her his volumes, but Valzacchi rushes forward and pushes him aside.*)

VALZACCHI

(*drawing from his pocket a black-edged news-sheet*)

Die swarze Seitung! Fürstlike Gnade:
Alles 'ier ge'eim gesrieben!
Nur für 'ohe Persönlikeite.
Die swarze Seitung!
Eine Leikname in 'Interkammer
von eine gräflike Palais!
Eine Bürgersfrau mit der amante
vergiften der Hehemann
diese Nackt um dreie Huhr!

Ze latest scandals to please your highness!
Learnt from secret information!
Meant only for those of quality!
Ze newest scandals!
A dead body in a secret chamber
In ze town 'ouse of a prince!
A rich merchant's wife poisons 'er 'usband
Viz ze 'elp of her lover
Soon after zree o'clock zis night!

PRINCESS

Lass er mich mit dem Tratsch in Ruh'!

Trash! Let me hear no more of it!

VALZACCHI

In Gnaden:
Tutte quante Vertraulikeite
aus die grosse Welt!

Your pardon, your 'ighness:
Tutte quante. Ze hidden secrets
Of ze elegant world!

PRINCESS

Ich will nix wissen! Lass er mich mit dem Tratsch in Ruh'!

What is that to me? Let me be with your vulgar talk!

(Valzacchi retires with a deprecatory bow. The three orphans prepare to withdraw, after they and their mother have kissed the Princess's hand.)

THE THREE ORPHANS

(whining)

Glück und Segen allerwegen Euer Gnaden hohem Sinn!	May Heav'n joy send you, may bliss attend you wheresoever you may be.
Eingegraben steht erhaben er in unsern Herzen drin.	We shall praise ever, forgetting never your great generosity!

(The orphans exit with their mother. The hairdresser hurriedly steps forward, his assistant follows him with flying coattails. The hairdresser gazes at the Princess, looks solemn and steps back a few paces, the better to study her appearance. In the meantime the assistant unpacks his paraphernalia at the toilet table. The hairdresser pushes several persons back, so as to make more room for himself.

The flute-player now steps forward and begins his cadenza. Some footmen have taken up positions at the front to the right. Others remain in the background.

After brief deliberation, the hairdresser has made up his mind and with an air of determination goes to the Princess and begins to dress her hair. A courier in a livery of pink, black and silver enters carrying a note. The Major-domo is quickly at hand with a silver salver and presents it to the Princess. The hairdresser pauses to allow her to read. The assistant hands him a fresh pair of curling tongs. The hairdresser waves them: they are too hot. The assistant gives him, after a questioning glance at the Princess, who nods assent, the note, which he smilingly uses for cooling the tongs. The singer has taken up his position.)

THE TENOR

(reading from a sheet of music)

Di rigori armato il seno	Di rigori armato il seno
Contro amor mi ribellai,	Contro amor mi ribellai,
Ma fui vinto in un baleno	Ma fui vinto in un baleno
In mirar due vaghi rai.	In mirar due vaghi rai.
Ahi! che resiste puoco	Ahi! Che resiste puoco
A stral di fuoco	A stral di fuoco
Cor di gelo di fuoco a stral.	Cor di gelo di fuoco a stral.

(The hairdresser hands the tongs to his assistant and applauds the singer. Then he continues to work at the coiffure of the Princess. In the meantime a footman has admitted through the small door the body-servant, the almoner and the chasseur of the Baron. They are three strange apparitions. The body-servant is a tall young fellow of foolish, insolent mien. He carries under his arm a leather jewel case. The almoner is an unkempt village councillor, a stunted but strong and bold-looking imp. The chasseur looks as if, before being thrust into his ill-fitting livery, he had worked on the farm. The almoner and the body-servant seem to be fighting for precedence, and trip each other up. They steer a course to the left, towards their master, in whose vicinity they come to a halt.)

BARON

(seated, by the attorney, who stands before him, taking his instructions)

Als Morgengabe — ganz separatim jedoch —	By way of compensation, as a separate gift,
und vor der Mitgift — bin ich verstanden, Herr Notar? —	Before the dowry, Master Attorney, understand,

kehrt Schloss und Herrschaft Gaunersdorf an mich zurück!
Von Lasten frei und ungemindert an Privilegien,
so wie mein Vater selig sie besessen hat.

I shall receive the title-deeds of Gaunersdorf,
Released from all encumbrances and all claims whatsoever,
With privileges intact, just as my father held them.

ATTORNEY

(*asthmatic*)

Gestatten hochfreiherrliche Gnaden die submisseste Belehrung,
dass eine Morgengabe wohl vom Gatten an die Gattin,
nicht aber von der Gattin an den Gatten

Your lordship — with dutiful submission — has, I am afraid, forgotten
That a *donatio ante nuptias* may be given by the husband
But cannot ever come from wife to husband —

(*With a deep breath.*)

bestellet oder stipuliert zu werden, fähig ist.

Such contracts are quite unprecedented in our law.

BARON

Das mag wohl sein.

That may be so.

ATTORNEY

Dem ist so —

It is so.

BARON

Aber im besondern Fall —

But here, in this special case —

ATTORNEY

Die Formen und die Präskriptionen kennen keinen Unterschied.

The statutes are precise; no way is known of circumventing them.

BARON

(*shouts*)

Haben ihn aber zu kennen!

But I insist that you shall find one!

ATTORNEY

(*alarmed*)

In Gnaden!

Your pardon!

BARON

Wenn eines hochadeligen Blutes blühender Spross sich herablässt
im Ehebette einer so gut als bürgerlichen Mamsell Faninal
— bin ich verstanden? — acte de présence zu machen
vor Gott und der Welt und sozusagen
angesichts kaiserlicher Majestät —

But, do you see, when a noble race's scion condescends to a union
With such a person as Mistress Faninal,
Whose father has no pedigree — upon whose patent of nobility
The ink is scarcely dry — if then I choose in the face of God and all men
And of the Empress thus to honor her —

(*The flute-player begins another prelude.*)

Da wird, corpo di Bacco! von Morgengabe
als geziemendem Geschenk dankbarer Devotion

I think, corpo di Bacco, that such is clearly
A case where an exception can be made, and where the bride

für die Hingab' so hohen Blutes
sehr wohl die Rede sein!

Should have leave to show her gratitude
For the honor done to her.

(The singer makes as if he would begin again, but waits till the Baron is quiet.)

ATTORNEY
(to the Baron, softly)

Vielleicht, dass man die Sache separatim —

Perhaps by means of purchase and conveyance . . .

BARON
(in a low voice)

Er ist ein schmählicher Pedant: als Morgengabe will ich das Gütel!

The wretched pettifogging fool! As compensation I must have it!

ATTORNEY
(as before)

Als einen wohl verklausulierten Teil der Mitgift —

Or in the marriage settlement, with special clauses . . .

BARON
(a little louder)

Als Morgengabe! Geht das nicht in Seinen Schädel!

No — compensation. Can you not get that into your thick skull?

ATTORNEY

Als eine Schenkung inter vivos oder —

Or as a *donatio inter vivos* — or else —

BARON
(in a fury, thumping the table, shouts)

Als Morgengabe!

No, compensation!

THE TENOR
(during this conversation)

Ma si caro è'l mio tormento
Dolce è si la piaga mia,
Ch'il penare è mio contento
E'l sanarmi è tirannia.
Ahi! Che resiste puoco —
Cor . . .

Ma si caro è'l mio tormento
Dolce è si la piaga mia,
Ch'il penare è mio contento
E'l sanarmi è tirannia.
Ahi! Che resiste puoco —
Cor . . .

(At this point the Baron raises his voice so that the singer ends abruptly, likewise the flute-player. The Princess beckons the singer and gives him her hand to kiss. The singer and the flute-player retire with deep obeisances. The attorney withdraws into a corner in alarm. The Baron acts as if nothing had happened, and makes a sign of condescending approval to the singer, then goes across to his servants: straightens the tousled hair of his body-servant; then goes, as if looking for somebody, to the small door, opens it, peers out, is annoyed, looks by the bed, shakes his head and comes forward again.)

PRINCESS
(looking at herself in a hand mirror, aside)

Mein lieber Hippolyte,

My good friend Hippolyte, this will not do,

Heut haben Sie ein altes Weib aus mir gemacht:	You've made me look quite middle-aged!

(The hairdresser in consternation falls on the Princess's headdress with feverish energy and changes it again. The Princess continues to wear a pensive expression. Valzacchi, followed by Annina, has behind the back of everybody else slunk to the other side of the stage, and they present themselves to the Baron with exaggerated obsequiousness.)

PRINCESS

(over her shoulder to the Major-domo)

Abtreten die Leut'!	They are all dismissed!

(The footmen, taking hands, push them all out by the door, which they then close. Only the scholar, whom the Major-domo presents to the Princess, remains in conversation with her till the close of the episode between the Baron, Valzacchi and Annina.)

VALZACCHI

(to the Baron)

Ihre Gnade sukt etwas. Ik seh, Ihr Gnade at eine Bedürfnis. Ik kann dienen. Ik kann besorgen.	Can I be of service, sir? I see zat your lords'ip Is looking for something. I can help you, I can be useful.

BARON

(drawing back)

Wer ist Er, was weiss Er?	And, pray, who may you be?

VALZACCHI

Ihr Gnade Gesikt sprikt ohne Sunge. Wie eine Hantike . . .	Zough your lords'ip say nozzing Ve understand from your lords'ip's expression . . .

ANNINA

Wie eine Hantike . . .	Ve guess vat your lords'ip wishes . . .

VALZACCHI

Come statua di Giove.	Come statua di Giove.

BARON

Das ist ein besserer Mensch.	This is an excellent man.

VALZACCHI AND ANNINA

(kneeling)

Erlaukte Gnade, attachieren uns an Sein Gefolge.	May't please your lords'ip, we declare ourselves your 'umble servants.

BARON

Euch?	You?

VALZACCHI AND ANNINA

Onkel und Nikte, Su sweien maken alles besser.	Uncle and niece, In couples all our vork is easier.

Per esempio: Ihre Gnade at eine junge Frau —	Per esempio: 'As your lords'ip married a youzful bride . . .

BARON

Woher weiss Er denn das, Er Teufel Er?	How come you to know so much, you devils?

VALZACCHI AND ANNINA

(*eagerly*)

Ihre Gnade ist in Eifersukt: dico per dire! Eut oder morgen könnte sein. Affare nostro! Jede Sritt die Dame sie tut, jede Wagen die Dame steigt, jede Brief die Dame bekommt — wir sind da! An die Ecke, in die Kamin, 'inter die Bette — in eine Schranke, unter die Dache, wir sind da!	'As your lords'ip cause for jealousy? Dico per dire! Now or tomorrow? Who can tell? Affare nostro! Every step ze lady may take, Every coach zat ze lady 'ires, Every billet doux zat she 'as — Ve are zere! In ze corner, or by ze fire Or in a cupboard, or in ze attic, Or by ze bedside, under ze table, Ve are zere!

ANNINA

Ihre Gnaden wird nicht bedauern.	Surely your lords'ip vill not regret it.

(*They hold out their hands as if for money. The Baron pretends not to notice them.*)

BARON

(*in a whisper*)

Hm: Was es alles gibt in diesem Wien? Zur Probe nur: kennt Sie die Jungfer Mariandel?	Hm! What things we see and hear in this great town! To try your skill, do you perchance know Mariandel?

ANNINA

(*in a whisper*)

Mariandel?	Mariandel?

BARON

Das Zofel hier im Haus bei Ihrer Gnaden?	Her highness's maid that's always with her!

VALZACCHI

(*aside to Annina*)

Sai tu, cosa vuole?	Sai tu? Cosa vuole?

ANNINA

(*the same*)

Niente!	Niente.

VALZACCHI
(to the Baron)

Sicker! Sicker! Mein nickte wird besorgen.	Trust us, trust us: ve vill soon 'ave information —
Seien sicker, Ihre Gnade! Wir sind da!	Put your trust in us, your lords'ip — ve are zere!

BARON
(leaving the two Italians, to the Princess)

Darf ich das Gegenstück	May I now introduce
zu Dero sauberm Kammerzofel präsentieren?	The counterpart of your young servant to your highness?

(Complacently.)

Die Ähnlichkeit soll, hör' ich, unverkennbar sein.	The likeness is wonderful, my friends all tell me.
Leopold, das Futteral.	Leopold, the jewel case!

PRINCESS
(nods)

Ich gratulier' Euer Liebden sehr.	He does great honor to his ancestry.

(The young body-servant awkwardly hands over the jewel case.)

BARON
(taking his seat and making a sign to the young man to withdraw)

Und da ist nun die silberne Rosen!	And now, here is the Silver Rose!

(Opening it.)

PRINCESS

Lassen nur drinnen.	Do not disturb it.
Haben die Gnad' und stellen's dort hin.	Pray, place it yonder. I'll be obliged.

BARON

Vielleicht das Zofel soll's übernehmen?	Or shall I call your chambermaid
Ruft man ihr?	And give it to her — ?

PRINCESS

Nein, lassen nur. Die hat jetzt keine Zeit.	No, not to her. She is occupied now.
Doch sei Er sicher: den Grafin Octavian bitt' ich ihm auf,	But this I promise — I will at once make your wish known to the Count,
er wird's mir zulieb schon tun	For me he will consent, I know —
und als Euer Liebden Kavalier	And with all proper usages observing,
vorfahren mit der Rosen bei der Jungfer Braut.	Duly bear to your bride the rose of silver.

(Indifferently.)

Stellen indes nur hin.	Meanwhile, leave it there.
Und jetzt, Herr Vetter, sag' ich Ihm Adieu.	And now, your lordship, I bid you adieu —
Man retiriert sich jetzt von hier:	It is high time that I should go
Ich werd' jetzt in die Kirchen gehn.	Else I shall be too late for church —

(The footmen open the folding doors.)

BARON

Euer Gnaden haben heut durch unversiegte Huld mich tiefst beschämt.	The gracious courtesy your highness renders me Overwhelms me quite —

(He makes an obeisance and ceremoniously withdraws. At a sign from him, the attorney follows; and after him the Baron's three servants shuffle out awkwardly. The two Italians silently and obsequiously join the train without his observing them. The Major-domo withdraws. The footmen close the door. The Princess is left alone.)

PRINCESS

(alone)

Da geht er hin, der aufgeblasene schlechte Kerl,	Now go your way — Go, vain pretentious profligate!
und kriegt das hübsche junge Ding und einen Pinkel Geld dazu.	And what is your reward? An ample dowry and a pretty bride —
Als musst's so sein.	He takes it all, and thinks it's but his due —
Und bildet sich noch ein, dass er es ist, der sich was vergibt.	And boasts that he greatly honors her.

(Sighs.)

Was erzürn' ich mich denn? Ist doch der Lauf der Welt.	But why trouble myself? The world will have its way.
Kann mich auch an ein Mädel erinnern,	I remember a girl, just like this one,
die frisch aus dem Kloster ist in den heiligen Ehestand kommandiert word'n.	Who straight from the convent was marched off to the holy estate of wedlock.

(Takes a hand mirror.)

Wo ist die jetzt? Ja,	Where is she now! Yes.

(Sighs.)

such' dir den Schnee vom vergangenen Jahr:	Go, seek the snows of yesteryear!
Das sag' ich so:	But can it be — can it be though I say it so,
Aber wie kann das wirklich sein,	That I was that young Tess of long ago
dass ich die kleine Resi war	And that I shall be called, ere long, "the old Princess . . ."
und dass ich auch einmal die alte Frau sein werd'.	"The old Field Marshal's lady!" — "Look you,
Die alte Frau, die alte Marschallin!	
"Siegst es, da geht's die alte Fürstin Resi!"	"There goes the old Princess Therese!"
Wie kann denn das geschehen?	How can it come to pass?
Wie macht denn das der liebe Gott?	How can the powers decree it so?
Wo ich doch immer die gleiche bin.	For I am still I, and never change.

(Gaily.)

Und wenn er's schon so machen muss,	And if indeed it must be so,
warum lässt er mich denn zuschaun dabei	Why then must I sit here, looking on,
mit gar so klarem Sinn! Warum versteckt er's nicht vor mir?	And see it all and grieve? Were it not better we were blind?
Das alles ist geheim, so viel geheim.	These things are still a mystery, such a mystery.
Und man ist dazu da, dass man's ertragt.	And we are here below to bear it all.

(Sighs.)

Und in dem "Wie"	But how? but "how?"

(Very quietly.)

da liegt der ganze Unterschied —	In that lies all the difference.

(Enter Octavian, from the right, in riding dress with riding boots.)

PRINCESS
(quietly, half smiling)

Ach, du bist wieder da!	Ah! You are back again!

OCTAVIAN
(tenderly)

Und du bist traurig!	And you are pensive!

PRINCESS

Es ist ja schon vorbei. Du weisst ja, wie ich bin. Ein halb Mal lustig, ein halb Mal traurig. Ich kann halt meinen Gedanken nicht kommandier'n.	The mood has flown again. You know me, how I am — A brief while merry — a brief while mournful — My thoughts fly here and there, I know not how.

OCTAVIAN

Ich weiss, warum du traurig bist, mein Schatz. Weil du erschrocken bist und Angst gehabt hast. Hab' ich nicht recht? Gesteh' mir nur: du hast Angst gehabt, du Süsse, du Liebe, um mich, um mich!	I know why you have been so sad, belov'd, You were beside yourself with fear for us both. Is it not so? Confess to me. You were afraid, My angel, my dearest, For me — for me!

PRINCESS

Ein bissel vielleicht, aber ich hab' mich erfangen und hab' mir vorgesagt: Es wird schön nich dafür stehn. Und wär's dafür gestanden?	A little at first, But soon my courage had come back, and to myself I said — "It cannot be — 'Tis not yet." And if it had been fated?

OCTAVIAN
(gaily)

Und es war kein Feldmarschall, nur ein spassiger Herr Vetter, und du gehörst mir, du gehörst mir!	And it was no prince at all, but only a foolish clown, your cousin. And you are my own! You are my own!

PRINCESS
(pushing him aside)

Taverl, umarm' Er nicht zu viel. Wer allzuviel umarmt, der hält nichts fest.	Dearest, embrace me not so much! He who tries to grasp too much, holds nothing fast.

OCTAVIAN
(passionately)

Sag' dass du mir gehörst! Mir!	Tell me that you are mine — mine!

PRINCESS

Oh, sei Er jetzt sanft, sei Er gescheit und sanft und gut.	Oh, be not so wild! Be gentle and tender and kind.

17. Risë Stevens, well known as Octavian at the Metropolitan Opera from the late thirties until the end of the fifties. (COURTESY OF *Opera News*)

18. Eleanor Steber as Sophie, 1940. (COURTESY OF THE METROPOLITAN OPERA ARCHIVES)

19. Jarmila Novotna as Octavian, 1942. (COURTESY OF THE METROPOLITAN OPERA ARCHIVES)

Der Rosenkavalier decor sketches
for a revised production at the Metropolitan Opera
by Rolf Gérard, season of 1955–1956
(COURTESY OF THE METROPOLITAN OPERA ARCHIVES)

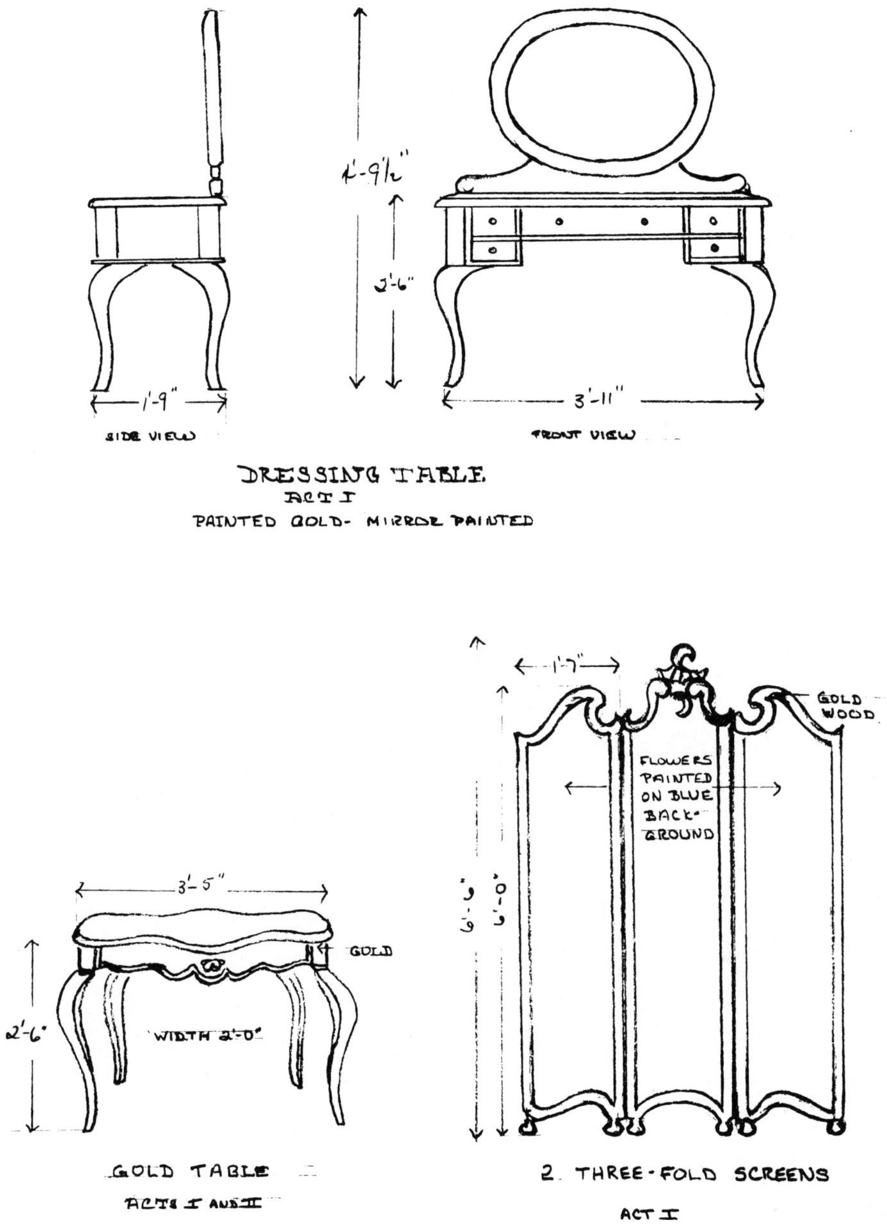

21.

22.

23.

21. Régine Crespin as the Marschallin and Hertha Töpper as Octavian, Metropolitan Opera, 1962. (PHOTO: LOUIS MÉLANÇON. COURTESY OF THE METROPOLITAN OPERA ARCHIVES)

22. For decades considered one of the best interpreters of Strauss, Elisabeth Schwarzkopf made her Metropolitan Opera debut in 1964 — an historic Marschallin, with Lisa Della Casa as Octavian and Otto Edelmann as Baron Ochs. (COURTESY OF THE METROPOLITAN OPERA ARCHIVES)

23. Elisabeth Schwarzkopf, earlier in London as the Marschallin in the 1959 revival of *Der Rosenkavalier* at the Royal Opera House, Covent Garden. (PHOTO: HOUSTON ROGERS. COURTESY OF THE THEATRE MUSEUM/VICTORIA AND ALBERT MUSEUM, LONDON)

24.

25.

26.

24. *Der Rosenkavalier* continues to be staged often in opera houses throughout the world. The Salzburg Festival Hall reopened in 1960 with a lavish new production directed by Rudolf Hartmann. Act II: Sena Jurinac as Octavian presents the rose to Hilde Gueden as Sophie. The production was filmed "live" by Rank Films and distributed widely in Europe and the United States. (COURTESY OF THE SALZBURG FESTIVAL PRESS BUREAU)

25. Italian film director Luchino Visconti created an "art nouveau" *Der Rosenkavalier* at the Royal Opera House, Covent Garden in 1966. Act III: Sena Jurinac as the Marschallin, Josephine Veasey as Octavian, Michael Langdon as Baron Ochs, Joan Carlyle as Sophie, and Robert Bowman as the Innkeeper. (PHOTO: HOUSTON ROGERS. COURTESY OF THE THEATRE MUSEUM/VICTORIA AND ALBERT MUSEUM, LONDON)

26. The Glyndebourne Festival Opera invited Erté to design its new 1980 production of *Der Rosenkavalier*. John Cox directed, with Rachel Yakar as the Marschallin. Act I: the Levée. (PHOTO: GUY GRAVETT. COURTESY OF GLYNDEBOURNE FESTIVAL OPERA)

27. Tatiana Troyanos as Octavian and Judith Blegen as Sophie, Metropolitan Opera, current production. (PHOTO: JAMES HEFFERNAN, METROPOLITAN OPERA)

Nein, bitt' schön,	No, I ask you now —
(Octavian is about to answer excitedly.)	
sei Er nicht, wie alle Männer sind!	Do not be like all the other men.

OCTAVIAN
(suspiciously)

Wie alle Männer?	Like all the others?

PRINCESS
(quickly recovering herself)

Wie der Feldmarschall und der Vetter Ochs.	As the Marshal is, and as my cousin Ochs.

OCTAVIAN
(still dissatisfied)

Bichette!	Bichette!

PRINCESS
(emphatically)

Sei Er nur nicht, wie alle Männer sind.	No — do not be like all the other men.

OCTAVIAN
(angrily)

Ich weiss nicht, wie alle Männer sind.	The others? How can I know what they are —
(With sudden tenderness.)	
Weiss nur, dass ich dich lieb hab',	Only I know I love you.
Bichette, sie haben mir dich ausgetauscht.	Bichette, there surely is some changeling here.
Bichette, wo ist Sie denn!	Bichette, it is not you.

PRINCESS

Sie ist wohl da, Herr Schatz.	No, it's still me, my dear.

OCTAVIAN

Ja, ist Sie da? Dann will ich Sie halten,	Yes, it is you? Closer will I clasp you,
dass Sie mir nicht wieder entkommt!	That you'll never, never escape me,
(Passionately.)	
Packen will ich Sie, packen, dass	I will cling to you tightly,
Sie es spürt, zu wem Sie gehört —	That you will know, in truth, whose you are.
zu mir: Denn ich bin Ihr und Sie ist mein!	You are mine. For I am yours and you are mine!

PRINCESS
(freeing herself from him)

Oh, sei Er gut, Quinquin. Mir ist zumut,	Oh, be kind, Mignon. I feel I know
dass ich die Schwäche von allem Zeitlichen recht spüren muss,	That all things earthly are but vanity, but empty dreams —
bis in mein Herz hinein,	Deep in my heart I know
wie man nichts halten soll,	How we should grasp at naught,
wie man nichts packen kann,	How we can cling to naught,
wie alles zerlauft zwischen den Fingern,	How the world's joys cheat and elude us —
alles sich auflöst, wonach wir greifen,	How shadowy all things are that we deem precious,

alles zergeht wie Dunst und Traum.	All things must pass, like mists — like dreams.

OCTAVIAN

Mein Gott, wie Sie das sagt.	Oh Heav'n! Why so distraught?
Sie will mir doch nur zeigen, dass Sie nicht an mir hängt.	Do you want to tell me that you no longer love me?

(*Weeps.*)

PRINCESS

Sei Er doch gut, Quinquin!	Be not so sad, Mignon.

(*Octavian weeps more bitterly. Quietly.*)

Jetzt muss ich noch den Buben dafür trösten,	And now I must console him —
Dass er mich über kurz oder lang wird sitzen lassen.	And for what? Because — sooner or later — one day he'll leave me.

(*Strokes his hair.*)

OCTAVIAN

Über kurz oder lang?	I will leave you one day?

(*Angrily.*)

Wer legt Ihr heut die Wörter in den Mund, Bichette?	Who is it prompted you to talk of this, Bichette?

PRINCESS

Das Ihn das Wort so kränkt!	Do my words hurt you so?
Die Zeit im Grund, Quinquin.	What's fated must come, Mignon.

(*Octavian stops his ears.*)

Die Zeit, die ändert doch nichts an den Sachen.	Time — what matter if it be sooner or later?
	Time — how strangely does it go its ways —
Die Zeit, die ist ein sonderbar Ding.	First we are heedless — Lo! 'tis as nothing!
Wenn man so hinlebt, ist sie rein gar nichts.	Then a sudden waking, and we feel nothing else but it,
Aber dann auf einmal, da spürt man nichts als sie.	All the world tells of it, all our souls are filled with it,
Sie ist um uns herum, sie ist auch in uns drinnen.	No face but shows the mark of it,
In den Gesichtern rieselt sie,	No mirror but shows it to us —
im Spiegel da rieselt sie,	All my veins feel its throbbing,
in meinen Schläfen fliesst sie.	And there — 'twixt you and me —
Und zwischen mir und dir	It flows in silence,
da fliesst sie wieder, lautlos, wie eine Sanduhr.	Trickling — like the sand in an hour-glass —

(*Earnestly.*)

Oh, Quinquin!	Oh! Mignon!
Manchmal hör' ich sie fliessen —	But sometimes I hear it flowing
unaufhaltsam.	Ceaselessly.

(*Softly.*)

Manchmal steh' ich auf mitten in der Nacht	Sometimes I arise in the dead of night
und lass die Uhren alle, alle stehn.	And take the clocks and stop them every one —
Allein man muss sich auch vor ihr nicht fürchten.	And yet — to be afraid of it — what profit is it?
Auch sie ist ein Geschöpf des Vaters, der uns alle erschaffen hat.	For Heaven, mindful of all its creatures, in its wisdom ordains it so.

Octavian

(quietly and tenderly)

Mein schöner Schatz, will Sie sich traurig machen mit Gewalt?
Wo Sie mich da hat,
wo ich meine Finger in Ihre Finger schlinge,
wo ich mit meinen Augen Ihre Augen suche,
wo sie mich hat —
gerade da ist Ihr so zumut?

And why let such dark forebodings cloud your soul, belov'd?
Now that I am here,
With my fingers like tendrils round your fingers twining,
Now that my eyes are plunged in yours and blaze with rapture,
Now that I am here,
At such time can you think of grief?

Princess

(very serious)

Quinquin, heut oder morgen geht Er hin
und gibt mich auf um einer andern willen,

(Hesitates.)

die schöner oder jünger als ich.

Mignon, now or tomorrow, surely,
You will go from me, leave me and choose another.

(Hesitates.)

One younger or prettier than I.

Octavian

Willst du mit Worten mich von dir stossen,
weil dir die Hände den Dienst nicht tun?

Is it with words you would dismiss me,
Thinking your hands will not serve your turn?

Princess

(quietly)

Der Tag kommt ganz von selber.
Heut oder morgen kommt der Tag, Octavian.

The day will come unbidden —
Now or tomorrow it must come, Octavian.

Octavian

Nicht heut, nicht morgen! ich hab dich lieb.
Nicht heut, nicht morgen!
Wenn's so einen Tag geben muss, ich denk' ihn nicht!
So einen hässlichen Tag!
Ich will den Tag nicht sehn

(With growing passion.)

Ich will den Tag nicht denken.
Was quälst du dich und mich, Theres'?

Not now, not tomorrow — 'twill never come, because I love you!
Though Fate has decreed it must come, I will not think of
Nor see such a day,
I will not think of such a day,

(With growing passion.)

I will not see nor think of it!
Why torture me and yourself, Theres'?

Princess

Heut oder morgen oder den übernächsten Tag.
Nicht quälen will ich dich, mein Schatz.
Ich sag' was wahr ist, sag's zu mir so gut als zu dir.
Leicht will ich's machen dir und mir.
Leicht muss man sein,
mit lechtem Herz und leichten Händen
halten und nehmen, halten und lassen . . .

Now or tomorrow — if not tomorrow, very soon —
'Tis not to torture you, my dearest,
'Tis truth that I'm speaking — to myself no less than to you.
Let us then lightly meet our fate.
Light must we be,
With spirits light, with touch light-fingered,
Hold all our pleasures — hold them and leave them . . .

Die nicht so sind, die straft das Leben, und Gott erbarmt sich ihrer nicht.	If not, much pain, much grief await us, and none in Heaven or earth will pity us.

OCTAVIAN

Sie spricht ja heute wie ein Pater. Soll dass heissen, dass ich Sie nie mehr werd' küssen dürfen, bis Ihr der Atem ausgeht?	You speak today like a confessor — Does it mean that never again — no, never, I shall kiss you — kiss you in endless rapture?

PRINCESS

Quinquin, Er soll jetzt gehn, Er soll mich lassen. Ich werd' jetzt in die Kirchen gehn, und später fahr' ich zum Onkel Greifenklau, der alt und gelähmt ist, und ess' mit ihm: das freut den alten Mann. Und Nachmittag werd' ich Ihm einen Laufer schicken, Quinquin, und sagen lassen, ob ich in den Prater fahr'. Und wenn ich fahr' und Er hat Lust, so wird Er auch in den Prater kommen und neben meinem Wagen reiten. Jetzt sei Er gut und folg' Er mir.	Mignon, you must go now. 'Tis time to leave me. I now must go to church, and then Visit my dear uncle Greifenklau, Who's old and bedridden, And dine with him: 'twill please the old man much. In the afternoon I'll send a courier to your house, Mignon, and he will tell you Whether I shall take the air; And if I drive, And if you please, You will meet me in the Prater riding And stay awhile beside my carriage . . . Do what I ask — and be not rash.

OCTAVIAN

(*softly*)

Wie Sie befiehlt, Bichette.	As you command, Bichette.

(*He goes. A pause. The Princess starts up violently.*)

PRINCESS

Ich hab' Ihn nicht einmal geküsst.	He has gone, and not one kiss!

(*She rings violently. Footmen enter hurriedly from the right.*)

Lauft's dem Herrn Grafen nach und bittet's ihn noch auf ein Wort herauf.	Run and overtake the Count And say I beg a word with him.

(*Exeunt footmen quickly.*)

Ich hab' ihn fortgehn lassen und ihn nicht einmal geküsst.	I have let him go from me. No farewell — not one kiss!

(*The four footmen enter breathless.*)

FIRST FOOTMAN

Der Herr Graf sind auf und davon.	The young Count is off and away.

SECOND FOOTMAN

Gleich beim Tor sind aufgesessen.	At the door he mounted quickly.

THIRD FOOTMAN

Reitknecht hat gewartet.	Servants had been waiting —

FOURTH FOOTMAN

Gleich beim Tor sind aufgesessen wie der Wind.

At the gate he mounted like the wind —

FIRST FOOTMAN

Waren um die Ecken wie der Wind.

Galloped round the corner like the wind —

SECOND FOOTMAN

Sind nachgelaufen.

We all ran after —

THIRD FOOTMAN

Wie haben wir geschrien.

We cried ourselves hoarse —

FOURTH FOOTMAN

War umsonst.

'Twas too late.

FIRST FOOTMAN

Waren um die Ecken wie der Wind.

Galloped round the corner like the wind —

PRINCESS

Es ist gut, geht's nur wieder.

Very well. You may leave.

(The footmen withdraw.)

PRINCESS

(calling after them)

Den Mohammed!

Send Mahomet.

(Enter the blackamoor, with tinkling bells. Bows.)

Das da trag'.

Carry that —

(The boy quickly takes the jewel case.)

Weisst ja nicht wohin. Zum Grafen Octavian.
Gib's ab und sag':
Da drin ist die silberne Ros'n.
Der Herr Graf weiss ohnehin.

Stop, till I say where — to Count Octavian
And say he'll find
Within it the silver rose.
'Tis enough — the Count will know.

(The blackamoor runs off. The Princess leans her head on her hand and remains deep in thought — till the curtain falls.)

ACT TWO

A room in the house of Herr von Faninal. Center door leading to the antechamber. Doors right and left. To the right a large window. At either side of the center door chairs against the wall. In the rounded corners at either side are large fireplaces.

HERR VON FANINAL

(saying goodbye to Sophia)

Ein ernster Tag, ein grosser Tag!
Ein Ehrentag, ein heiliger Tag!

A solemn day, a day of note,
A festive day, a sacred day!

(Sophia kisses his hand.)

Marianne

Der Josef fahrt vor mit der neuen Kaross',
hat himmelblaue Vorhäng',
vier Apfelschimmel sind dran.

There's Joseph at the door with the new carriage.
It has curtains of blue satin.
And four fine grays to draw it.

Major-domo

(confidentially to Faninal)

Ist höchste Zeit, dass Euer Gnaden fahren.
Der hochadelige Bräutigamsvater,
sagt die Schicklichkeit,
muss ausgefahren sein
bevor der silberne Rosenkavalier vorfahrt.
Wär nicht geziemend,
dass sie sich vor der Tür begegneten.

Now by your leave, sir, 'tis high time for starting.
For the most noble father of the bride —
So etiquette prescribes —
Must not be found within,
When the bridegroom's messenger appears who brings the Silver Rose.
'Twould be unseemly
If at the door you should encounter him.

(Footmen open the doors.)

Faninal

In Gottes Namen. Wenn ich wiederkomm',
so führ' ich deinen Herrn Zukünftigen bei der Hand.

Well then, so be it. When I return again,
I'll be bringing your bridegroom with me, holding him by the hand.

Marianne

Den edlen und gestrengen Herrn von Lerchenau!

The virtuous and noble Lord of Lerchenau!

(Exit Faninal. Sophia advances to the front by herself, while Marianne is at the window.)

Marianne

Jetzt steigt er ein. Der Xaver und der Anton springen hinten auf.
Der Stallpag' reicht dem Josef seine Peitsch'n.
Alle Fenster sind voller Leut'.

Now he's getting in. Now Antony and Francis have climbed up behind,
Now Joseph cracks his whip and now they've started,
All the windows are full of folk.

Sophia

In dieser feierlichen Stunde der Prüfung,
da du mich, o mein Schöpfer, über mein Verdienst erhöhen
und in den heiligen Ehestand führen willst,

In this most sacred hour, my God, O my Creator,
When Thy great blessings lift me high above my worth, I thank Thee,
That to the Holy Estate by Thy will I am led.

(She controls herself with difficulty.)

opfere ich dir in Demut, mein Herz in Demut auf.
Die Demut in mir zu erwecken,
muss ich mich demütigen.

A contrite heart unto Thy Throne — Thy Throne — I bring.
Oh! Grant that the sin of vainglory
May ever be far from my soul.

Marianne

(very excited)

Die halbe Stadt ist auf die Füss'.

Half the town is now afoot!

SOPHIA

(collects her thoughts with difficulty)

Demütigen und recht bedenken: die Sünde, die
Schuld, die Niedrigkeit, die Verlassenheit, die Anfechtung!

Be far from me . . .
From all temptations, Lord, preserve me, and of pomp and vanities
In this world here below by Thy great mercy —

MARIANNE

Aus dem Seminari schaun die Hochwürdigen von die Balkoner.
Ein alter Mann sitzt oben auf der Latern'.

From the seminary all the reverend men look on dumbfounded,
And high up on a streetlamp there is one old man.

SOPHIA

Die Mutter ist tot und ich bin ganz allein.
Für mich selbst steh' ich ein.
Aber die Ehe ist ein heiliger Stand.

My Mother is dead and all alone am I.
There's none to plead for me but I alone,
But wedlock is in truth a holy estate.

MARIANNE

(crying out delighted)

Er kommt, er kommt in zwei Karossen.
Die erste ist vierspännig, die ist leer. In der zweiten, sechsspännigen,
sitzt er selber, der Rosenkavalier.

He's here! He's here! I see two coaches.
The first one has four horses — it is empty. In the second, (six horses it has)
I see him, the Cavalier of the Rose.

SOPHIA

Ich will mich niemals meines neuen Standes überheben —

Let me not be puffed up unduly with pride by the honors,

(The servants, followed by three couriers, who are running after Octavian's carriage, cry in the street below: "Rofrano! Rofrano!")

— mich überheben.

Of my new station.

(She loses her self-control.)

Was rufen denn die?

What is it they cry?

MARIANNE

Den Namen vom Rosenkavalier und alle Namen
von deiner neuen fürstlich'n und gräflich'n Verwandtschaft rufen's aus.

They're shouting the name of him that's come and all the titles
Of this your highborn new relation and his noble names.

(With excited gestures.)

Jetzt rangieren sich die Bedienten.
Die Lakaien springen rückwärts ab!

Look! Now our footmen take position,
And all his servants have alighted now!

(The voices of the couriers, drawing nearer: "Rofrano! Rofrano!")

SOPHIA

Werden sie mein' Bräutigam sein Namen
auch so ausrufen, wenn er angefahren kommt!?

And when my future husband comes, pray tell me,
Will they call out then? Will his name be shouted too?

(The voices of the couriers immediately under the window: "Rofrano! Rofrano!")

MARIANNE

(enthusiastically)

Sie reissen den Schlag auf! Er steigt aus! Ganz in Silberstück' ist er angelegt, von Kopf zu Fuss. Wie ein heil'ger Engel schaut er aus.	They open the door now! He alights! All in silver he glitters from head to foot, A holy angel might he be —

SOPHIA

Herrgott im Himmel! Ich weiss, der Stolz ist eine schwere Sünd'. Aber jetzt kann ich mich nicht demütigen. Jetzt seht's halt nicht! Denn das ist ja so schön, so schön!	Dear God in Heaven! I know that pride is a most deadly sin; But today all my prayers are vain — I cannot Be duly meek — For it is all so fair! So fair!

(The footmen quickly open the center doors. Enter Octavian bare-headed, dressed all in white and silver, carrying the Silver Rose in his hand. Behind him his servants in his colors — white and pale green — the footmen, the Heyducks, with their crooked Hungarian swords at their side; the couriers in white leather with green ostrich plumes. Immediately behind Octavian a black servant carrying his hat, and another footman carrying the case of the Silver Rose in both hands. Behind these, Faninal's servants. Octavian, taking the rose in his right hand, advances with highborn grace toward Sophia; but his youthful features bear traces of embarrassment and he blushes. Sophia turns pale with excitement at his splendid appearance. They stand opposite each other — each disconcerted by the confusion and beauty of the other.)

OCTAVIAN

(with slight hesitation)

Mir ist die Ehre widerfahren, dass ich der hoch- und wohlgeborenen Jungfer Braut, in meines Herrn Vetters Namen, dessen zu Lerchenau Namen, die Rose seiner Liebe überreichen darf.	I am much honored by my mission To say to you, most noble lady, highborn bride, That my dear kinsman, whose ambassador I am, Baron Lerchenau, begs you To take from me, as token of his love, this rose.

SOPHIA

(taking the rose)

Ich bin Euer Liebden sehr verbunden — Ich bin Euer Liebden in aller Ewigkeit verbunden —	I am to your honor much indebted — I am to your honor for all eternity indebted —

(A short pause of confusion. Sophia smells the rose.)

Hat einen starken Geruch wie Rosen, wie lebendige.	'Tis a most powerful fragrance — like roses — yes, like living ones . . .

OCTAVIAN

Ja, ist ein Tropfen persischen Rosenöls darein getan.	Yes — some few drops of Persian attar have been poured on it.

SOPHIA

Wie himmlische, nicht irdische, wie Rosen
vom hochheiligen Paradies.
Ist Ihm nicht auch?

A celestial flower, not of earth it seems.
A blossom from the sacred groves of Paradise.
Think you not so?

(Octavian bends over the rose, which she holds out to him; then raises his head and gazes at her lips.)

Ist wie ein Gruss vom Himmel. Ist bereits zu stark, als dass
man's ertragen kann.

'Tis like a heavenly message. Oh, how strong the scent,
I scarce can suffer it.

(Softly.)

Zieht einen nach, als lägen Stricke um das Herz.

Drawing me on — like something tugging at my heart.

SOPHIA AND OCTAVIAN

(as in a reverie — still more softly)

Wo war ich schon einmal
und war so selig?

Where did I taste before
Such heavenly rapture?

SOPHIA

(with expression)

Dahin muss ich zurück! und müsst ich völlig sterben auf dem Weg!
Allein ich sterb' ja nicht.
Das ist ja weit. Ist Zeit und Ewigkeit
in einem sel'gen Augenblick,
den will ich nie vergessen bis an meinen Tod.

Though death await me there, to that fair scene I must take myself once again.
But yet, why think of death?
'Tis far from hence!
In one blessed moment dwells all life and all eternity —
Never may its holy memory fade — till death, till death.

OCTAVIAN

Ich war ein Bub',
da hab ich' die noch nicht gekannt.
Wer bin denn ich?
Wie komm' denn ich zu ihr?
Wie kommt denn sie zu mir?
Wär' ich kein Mann, die Sinne möchten mir vergehn.
Das ist ein seliger Augenblick,
den will ich nie vergessen bis an meinen Tod.

I was a child
Until I saw her fair face this day!
But who am I?
What fate brings her to me?
What fate brings me to her?
Feeling and sense would leave me, were I not a man.
Day blessed to all eternity —
Never may its holy memory fade — till death, till death.

(During this, Octavian's servants have taken up their position on the left at the back, Faninal's with the Major-domo to the right. Octavian's footman hands the jewel case to Marianne. Sophia wakes from her reverie and gives the rose to Marianne, who places it in the case. The footman with the hat approaches Octavian and gives it to him. Octavian's servants then withdraw, and at the same time Faninal's servants carry three chairs to the center, two for Sophia and Octavian, and one for Marianne farther back, at the side. Faninal's Major-domo carries the jewel case with the rose through the door to the right. The other servants immediately withdraw through the center door. Sophia and Octavian stand opposite each other almost restored to the everyday world — but still a little embarrassed. At a sign from

Sophia, both seat themselves, and the duenna does likewise at the same moment as the door on the right is locked from without.)

	SOPHIA
Ich kenn' Ihn schon recht wohl, mon cousin!	You're quite well known to me, *mon cousin.*
	OCTAVIAN
Sie kennt mich, ma cousine?	You know me, *ma cousine?*
	SOPHIA
Ja, aus dem Buch, wo die Stammbäumer drin sind, Dem Ehrenspiegel Österreichs. Das nehm' ich immer abends mit ins Bett und such' mir meine zukünftige, gräflich' und fürstlich Verwandtschaft drin zusammen.	Yes, of your House I have read in a book, "The Mirror of Nobility." I take it of an evening to my room, And look for all the princes, dukes and counts who are to be my kinsfolk.
	OCTAVIAN
Tut Sie das, ma cousine?	Is it so, *ma cousine?*
	SOPHIA
Ich weiss, wie alt Euer Liebden sind: Siebzehn Jahr' und zwei Monat'. Ich weiss all Ihre Taufnamen: Octavian, Maria, Ehrenreich, Bonaventura, Ferdinand, Hyacinth.	I know how old to a week you are: Seventeen years and a quarter. I know all your baptismal names: Octavian, Maria, Ehrenreich Bonaventura, Ferdinand, Hyacinth.
	OCTAVIAN
So gut weiss ich sie selber nicht einmal.	In truth, I have never known them half as well.
	SOPHIA
Ich weiss noch was.	I know also —
	(*She blushes.*)
	OCTAVIAN
Was weiss Sie noch, sag' Sie mir's, ma cousine?	And what is it you know besides, *ma cousine?*
	SOPHIA
	(*without looking at him*)
Quinquin.	Mignon.
	OCTAVIAN
	(*laughing*)
Weiss Sie den Namen auch?	Do you know that name too?
	SOPHIA
So nennen Ihn halt seine guten Freund' und schöne Damen, denk' ich mir, mit denen er recht gut ist.	So all your best friends are allowed to call you, Court beauties also, more than one, Who are most friendly with you.

(A short pause. Naively:)

Ich freu' mich aufs heiraten! Freut er sich auch darauf?
Oder hat Er leicht noch gar nicht dran gedacht, mon cousin?
Denk' Er: Ist doch was andres als der ledige Stand.

I'm glad I shall marry soon!
Will you not like it too
When you shall find a bride? Have you not thought of it, *mon cousin?*
But think, how very lonely all you bachelors are!

OCTAVIAN
(softly)

Wie schön sie ist!

How fair she is!

SOPHIA

Freilich, Er ist ein Mann, da ist Er, was Er bleibt.
Ich aber brauch' erst einen Mann, dass ich was bin.
Dafür bin ich dem Mann dann auch gar sehr verschuldet.

Truly, you are a man, and men are what they are.
But till a husband is her guide, a woman's nothing.
For these things to my husband I'll be much indebted.

OCTAVIAN
(deeply moved — softly)

Mein Gott, wie schön und gut sie ist.
Sie macht mich ganz verwirrt.

My God, how fair and good she is.
She quite confuses me.

SOPHIA

Ich werd' ihm keine Schand nicht machen
und meinen Rang und Vortritt.

I never will, for sure, disgrace him —
And as for rank and position

(Very eagerly.)

Täte eine, die sich besser dünkt als ich,
ihn mir bestreiten
bei einer Kindstauf' oder Leich',
so will ich, wenn es sein muss,
mit Ohrfeigen ihr beweisen,
dass ich die vornehmere bin
und lieber alles hinnehme
wie Kränkung oder Ungebühr.

If haply another woman ever should
Dare to dispute it,
At christenings or funerals,
I'll show her very quickly,
If it must be, with a slapping,
That I am better bred than she,
And rather will bear anything
Than such o'erweening impudence.

OCTAVIAN
(eagerly)

Wie kann Sie denn nur denken,
dass man Ihr mit Ungebühr begegnen wird,
da Sie doch immer die Schönste, die Allerschönste sein wird.

No, do not think there's anyone
So graceless as to slight you.
For you will still be the fairest, always the crown you will bear.

SOPHIA

Lacht er mich aus, mon cousin?

Do not mock me so, *mon cousin* —

OCTAVIAN

Wie, glaubt Sie das von mir?

What, you think that of me?

SOPHIA

Er darf mich auslachen, wenn Er will.
Von Ihm lass ich alles mir gerne geschehen,
weil mir nie noch ein junger Kavalier . . .
von Nähe oder Weitem also wohlgefallen hat wie Er.
Jetzt aber kommt mein Herr Zukünftiger.

You are allowed to laugh if you will,
From you I will gladly take all that you choose.
For, truthfully, no gentleman I've seen
Or met with has been able yet to please me half as well as you.
But now here comes my future husband.

(The door at the back is thrown open. All three rise and step to the right. Faninal ceremoniously conducts the Baron over the threshold toward Sophia, giving him precedence. The servants of Lerchenau follow in his footsteps, first the almoner, then the body-servant. Next follows the chasseur, with a clown of the same kidney, who has a plaster over his battered nose, and two others no less uncouth, looking as if they had stepped straight from the fields into their liveries. All, like their master, carry sprigs of myrtle. The servants of Faninal remain in the background.)

FANINAL

Ich präsentiere Euer Gnaden Dero Zukünftige.

I have the honor, your lordship, to present your bride.

BARON

(bows — then to Faninal)

Deliziös! Mach' Ihm mein Kompliment.

Délicieuse! I compliment you, sir.

(He kisses Sophia's hand as though examining it.)

Ein feines Handgelenk. Darauf halt' ich gar viel.
Ist unter Bürgerlichen eine seltne Distinktion.

A hand so delicate is a thing I much admire.
'Tis an attraction rarely found among the bourgeoisie.

OCTAVIAN

(to himself)

Es wird mir heiss und kalt.

Can I restrain myself?

FANINAL

Gestatten dass ich die getreue Jungfer
Marianne Leitmetzerin —

Permit me my most faithful friend and servant —
Marianne Leitmetzer

(Presenting Marianne, who makes three deep curtseys.)

BARON

(with a gesture of vexation)

Lass Er das weg.

Pray, spare me that.

(After having almost knocked Sophia over, Lerchenau's servants come to a standstill, and then withdraw a few paces.)

Begrüss Er jetzt mit mir meinen Herrn Rosenkavalier.

Now greet the Count, and thank him for being my ambassador.

(They go towards Octavian, bowing. He returns the compliment.)

SOPHIA

(standing at the back with Marianne, to herself)

Was sind das für Manieren? Ist er leicht ein Rosstauscher

How vulgar his behavior. He is like a horse-dealer

und kommt ihm vor, er hätt' mich eingekauft?

Who thinks he's bought me like a yearling colt.

MARIANNE

Ein Kavalier hat halt ein ungezwungenes,
leutseliges Betragen.
Sag' dir vor, wer er ist
und zu was er dich macht,
so werden dir die Faxen gleich vergehn.

Oh what a cavalier! How free from affectation, how full of grace is his behavior!
Tell yourself who he is,
What he helps you to be,
And soon your silly whimsies will be gone.

BARON

(*to Faninal*)

Ist gar zum Staunen, wie der junge Herr jemand Gewissem ähnlich sieht.
Hat ein Bastardl, recht ein saubres, zur Schwester.

I can but wonder, when I see his face, how like he is to someone else.
He has a sister — a young little bastard.

(*Coarsely confidential.*)

Ist kein Geheimnis unter Personen von Stand.
Hab's aus der Fürstin eignem Mund,

These are no secrets among persons of our rank,
It was her highness who told me so,

(*Genially.*)

und weil der Faninal sozusagen jetzo
zu der Verwandtschaft gehört!
Mach' dir kein Depit, darum Rofrano,
dass dein Vater ein Streichmacher war,
befindet sich dabei in guter Kompagnie,

And since you, Faninal, may be considered almost as being one of us.
There is no need to be ashamed, Rofrano,
That once your father chose to sow his wild oats —
I warrant you he was in noble company,

(*Laughing.*)

der selige Marchese.
Ich selber exkludier' mich nicht.

The late lamented Marquis.
I count myself among it, too.

SOPHIA

Jetzt lässt er mich so stehn, der grobe Ding!
Und das ist mein Zukünftiger.
Und blattersteppig ist er auch, o mein Gott!

What breeding's this to leave me here alone!
And he my husband that's to be,
And pockmarked also is his face, on my soul!

BARON

(*To Faninal.*)

Seh', Liebden, schau' dir dort den Langen an,
den Blonden, hinten dort.
Ich will ihn nicht mit Fingern weisen,
aber er sticht wohl hervor
durch eine adelige Kontenance.
Ist aber ein ganz besondrer Kerl.
Sag's nicht, weil ich der Vater bin,
hat's aber faustdick hinter den Ohren.

Look well now at that long-legged rascal there,
The fair one at the back.
I cannot point my finger at him,
But you will see at a glance
How he's distinguished by his highborn features.
Is he not truly a splendid fellow?
He has a noble pedigree, but he's the greatest fool of all my houshold.

MARIANNE

Na, wenn er Dir von vorn nicht gefällt,
Du Jungfer Hochmut,

Well, if his front displeases you so,
Young Mistress Haughty,

so schau' ihn Dir von rückwärts an:
da wirst was sehn,
was Dir schon gefallen wird.

Then regard him well from the back;
Then you'll see something
That is good to see.

SOPHIA

Möcht' wissen, was ich da schon sehen werd'!

Then tell me, what it is that I shall find.

MARIANNE
(mimicking her)

Möcht' wissen, was ich da schon sehen werd'.
Dass es ein kaiserlicher Kämmerer ist,
den dir dein Schutzpatron als Herrn Gemahl spendiert hat,
Das kannst seh'n mit einem Blick.

Then tell me, what it is that I shall find.
Why, that your patron saints have sent you this day
One of Her Majesty's chamberlains as a bridegroom,
That is very clear to see.

(The Major-domo approaches the servants of Lerchenau most politely and conducts them out of the room. At the same time Faninal's servants withdraw — all but two, who offer wine and sweets.)

FANINAL
(to the Baron)

Belieben jetzt vielleicht? — ist ein alter Tokaier.

Perhaps you would partake? — 'Tis Tokay, an old vintage.

BARON

Brav, Faninal, er weiss, was sich gehört.
Serviert einen alten Tokaier zu einem jungen Mädel.
Ich bin mit Ihm zufrieden.

Good, Faninal, you know what's right and fitting,
To serve a mellow wine of old vintage to drink to a young bride's health.
You have my commendation.

(To Octavian.)

Musst denen Bagatelladeligen immer zeigen,
dass nicht für unsersgleichen sich ansehen dürfen,
muss immer was von Herablassung dabei sein.

'Tis not amiss to show some condescension
In talking to gimcrack nobility,
And show them clearly
They must not deem themselves equal to such as us.

OCTAVIAN
(pointedly)

Ich muss deine Liebden sehr bewundern.
Hast wahrhaft grosse Weltmanieren.
Konnt'st einen Ambassadeur vorstellen heut oder morgen.

I must admit I do admire your lordship's wisdom.
The great world has no secrets for you.
For an ambassador or a judge might you be taken.

BARON
(roughly)

Ich hol' mir jetzt das Mädl her.
Soll uns jetzt Konversation vormachen,

I'll bring the wench now to my side.
That I may see if her talk pleases me,

(Crosses over, takes Sophia by the hand and leads her back with him.)

damit ich seh', wie sie beschlagen ist.
Eh bien: Nun plauder' Sie uns eins, mir und dem Vetter Taverl.
Sag' Sie heraus, auf was Sie sich halt in der Eh' am meisten freut.

That of her points and paces I may judge.
Eh bien! Now, let us hear you talk, me and your cousin Tavy.
Tell me now, what in marriage, do you think, will please you most?

SOPHIA
(*withdrawing from him*)

Wo denkt Er hin?

What mean these ways?

BARON
(*at his ease*)

Pah! Wo ich hindenk'! Komm' Sie da ganz nah zu mir,
dann will ich Ihr erzählen, wo ich hindenk'.

Pooh! Why this fuss? Now come here quite close to me
And I will tell you quickly all my meaning.

(*Same by-play. Sophia tries to withdraw still more angrily.*)

Wär Ihr leicht präferabel, dass man gegen Ihrer
den Zeremonienmeister sollt' hervortun?
Mit "mille pardons" und "dévotion"
und "Geh da weg" und "hab' Respekt"?

Would your la'ship perhaps prefer it if one came
Like a dancing master, bowing and congeeing,
With *"Mille pardons"* and *"Dévotion"*
And "By your leave" and "My respects"?

SOPHIA

Wahrhaftig und ja gefiele mir das besser!

Most surely, yes, 'twould please me more!

BARON

Mir auch nicht! Das sieht Sie! Mir auch ganz und gar nicht!
Bin einer biedern offenherzigen Galanterie recht zugetan.

I think not! All flim-flam, fudge and silly whimsies —
My taste is all for free and easy ways, and open-hearted gallantry.

(*He tries to kiss her. She resists energetically.*)

FANINAL
(*offering a chair to Octavian, who refuses*)

Wie ist mir denn! Da sitzt ein Lerchenau
und karessiert in Ehrbarkeit mein Sopherl, als wär' sie ihm schon angetraut.
Und da steht ein Rofrano, grad' als müsst's so sein,
ein Graf Rofrano, sonsten nix,
der Bruder vom Marchese Obersttruchsess.

What! Can it be? There sits a Lerchenau
Paying his addresses to my Sophy, as if they had been wed and all,
And there stands a Rofrano, just as natural!
A Count Rofrano, nothing less —
The brother of the Empress's Lord High Steward.

OCTAVIAN
(*to himself*)

Das ist ein Kerl, dem möcht' ich wo begegnen
mit meinem Degen da,
wo ihn kein Wächter schreien hört.
Ja, das ist alles, was ich möcht'.

What a boor! How I would like to meet him
Alone with my good sword —
No watchman to hear him shout for help —
Yes, I could wish for nothing more!

SOPHIA

(to the Baron)

Ei, lass Er doch, wir sind nicht so vertraut!

I pray you desist, we are still but strangers!

BARON

(to Sophia)

Geniert Sie sich leicht vor dem Vetter Taverl?
Da hat Sie Unrecht.
Hör' Sie, in Paris,
wo doch die hohe Schul' ist für Manieren,
gibt's frei nichts,
was unter jungen Eheleuten geschieht
wozu man nicht die Einladungen liess ergehn
zum Zuschau'n, ja an den König selber.

Is it my cousin Octavian that makes you bashful?
That's without reason.
Look here, in Paris,
Where surely they know most about good manners
There's nothing
That will not be allowed, and freely pardoned,
If it be done correctly with a courtly grace,
Befitting people of birth and breeding.

(The Baron grows more and more importunate — Sophia is at her wits' end.)

OCTAVIAN

(furiously)

Dass ich das Mannsbild sehen muss,
so frech, so unverschämt mit ihr.
Könnt' ich hinaus und fort von hier!

Oh, that I must look on at this,
So coarse and so unmannerly.
Could I but up and fly from here!

FANINAL

(to himself)

Wär' nur die Mauer da von Glas,
dass alle bürgerlichen Neidhammeln von Wien uns könnten
so en famille beisammen so sitzen sehn!
Dafür wollt' ich mein Lerchenfelder Eckhaus geben, meiner Seel'!

Would that the walls could be of glass . . .
If only all the townsfolk could see them sitting there,
Quite en famille, how green would they turn with envy!
Gladly for that I'd give the best of all my houses, on my soul!

BARON

(to Sophia)

Lass Sie die Flausen nur! Gehört doch jetzo mir!
Geht all's recht! Sei Sie gut! Geht alles so wie am Schnürl!

Put your airs aside, for I have got you now!
All goes well! Never fear! 'Tis all just as I wish it!

(Half to himself, fondling her.)

Ganz meine Massen! Schultern wie ein Henderl!
Hundsmager noch — das macht nichts, aber weiss
mit einem Glanz darauf, wie ich ihn ästimier'!
Ich hab' halt ja ein lerchenauisch Glück!

Just as I like it! Tender as a pullet!
Not very plump — no matter — but so white,
White — and what a bloom — there's nothing I like more!
I have the luck of all the Lerchenaus!

(Sophia tears herself away and stamps her feet.)

Ist Sie ein rechter Kapricenschädel!	Gad, what a mettlesome little filly!

(Rises and runs after her.)

Steigt Ihr das Blut gar in die Wangen, dass man sich die Hand verbrennt?	And see how hot her cheeks are burning — Full hot enough to burn one's hands!

SOPHIA
(pale with anger)

Lass Er die Hand davon!	Hands off, I say! Be gone!

(Octavian, in silent anger, crushes the glass he holds in his hand and throws the pieces to the ground. Marianne runs with affected grace toward Octavian, picks up the pieces and confides her delight to him.)

MARIANNE

Ist recht ein familiärer Mann, der Herr Baron! Man delektiert sich, was er all's für Einfäll' hat!	'Tis most uncommon easy ways his lordship has, The jests he thinks of, oh, they make me laugh till I could cry.

BARON
(near Sophia)

Geht mir nichts darüber. Könnt' mich mit Schmachterei und Zärtlichkeit nicht halb so glücklich machen, meiner Seel!	Oh! what sport for princes! Languishing airs and tender moods Could never give me half such pleasure, on my soul!

SOPHIA
(furious, to his face)

Ich denk' nicht dran, dass ich Ihn glücklich mach'!	I don't care at all Whether I please you or not!

BARON
(pleasantly)

Sie wird es tun, ob Sie daran wird denken oder nicht.	You will please me, Whether you care or not.

MARIANNE
(to Faninal)

Ist recht ein familiärer Mann, der Herr Baron! Man delektiert sich, was er all's für Einfäll' hat!	'Tis most uncommon easy ways his lordship has, The jests he thinks of, oh, they make me laugh till I could cry.

OCTAVIAN
(to himself, pale with anger)

Hinaus, hinaus und kein Adieu! Sonst steh' ich nicht dafür, dass ich nicht was Verwirrtes tu! Hinaus aus diesen Stuben! Nur hinaus!	Could I but go without farewell! Else heaven alone can tell What foolish things I might do! This house, these rooms choke me! Just let me get away!

(In the meantime the attorney has entered with his clerk, introduced by Faninal's Majordomo. He announces them in a whisper to Faninal: Faninal goes to the back to the attorney, speaks with him and looks through a bundle of documents presented to him by the clerk.)

SOPHIA

(with clenched teeth)

Hat nie kein Mann dergleichen Reden nicht zu mir geführt!
Möcht wissen, was ihm dünkt von mir und Ihm?
Was ist Er denn zu mir?

There is no man has ever dared to speak to me like this!
What can you think of me, and of yourself?
What are you, pray, to me?

BARON

(contentedly)

Wird kommen über Nacht,
dass Sie ganz sanft
wird wissen, was ich bin zu Ihr.
Ganz wie's im Liedel heisst — kennt Sie das Liedel?
Lalalalala —

One day you'll wake and find
That you have just
Discovered what I am to you.
Just as the ballad says — Do you know it?
Lalalalala.

(Very sentimentally.)

Wie ich dein alles werde sein!
Mit mir, mit mir keine Kammer dir zu klein,
ohne mich, ohne mich jeder Tag dir so bang,

How to you I'll be all in all!
With me, with me there's no attic seems too small.
Without me, without me slowly will pass all the days,

(Impudently and coarsely.)

mit mir, mit mir keine Nacht dir zu lang?

With me, with me no night will seem too long.

(Sophia, as he tries to draw her still closer to him, frees herself and violently pushes him back.)

OCTAVIAN

(without looking at the Baron, and yet aware of all that is happening)

Ich steh' auf glüh'nden Kohlen!
Ich fahr' aus meiner Haut!
Ich büss' in dieser einen Stund'
all meine Sünden ab!

On coals of fire I'm standing!
'Tis more than I can bear!
In this one hour 'fore Heav'n I do
Penance for all my sins!

MARIANNE

(now hurrying to Sophia)

Ist recht ein familiärer Mann, der Herr Baron!
Man delektiert sich, was er all's für Einfäll' hat!

'Tis most uncommon easy ways his lordship has,
The jests he thinks of make me laugh till I could cry!

(Speaking to Sophia with feverish energy.)

Nein, was er all's für Einfäll' hat, der Herr Baron!

They make me laugh till I could cry, his lordship's jests.

BARON

(to himself, very contented)

Wahrhaftig und ja, ich hab' halt ein lerchenauisch Glück!
Gibt gar nichts auf der Welt, was mich so enflammiert
und also vehement verjüngt als wie ein rechter Trotz!

I always did say, I have all the luck of all the Lerchenaus!
Nothing else in the world so renews my youth
Or whets my appetite so much as a real spitfire does.

(Faninal and the attorney, followed by the clerk, have advanced to the front, on the left.)

BARON

(as soon as he sees the attorney, eagerly to Sophia, without the smallest idea what she is thinking)

Dort gibt's Geschäften jetzt, muss mich dispensieren:
bin dort von Wichtigkeit. Indessen
der Vetter Taverl leistet Ihr Gesellschaft!

But now there's work to do, so for a while excuse me:
They need my presence there. And meanwhile
There's Cousin Tavy, he will entertain you!

FANINAL

Wenn's jetzt belieben tät', Herr Schwiegersohn!

May I beg the honor now, dear son-in-law!

BARON

(eagerly)

Natürlich wird's belieben.

Of course you'll have the honor.

(In passing to Octavian, whom he touches familiarly.)

Hab' nichts dawider,
wenn du ihr möchtest Äugerln machen, Vetter,
jetzt oder künftighin.
Ist noch ein rechter Rühr-nicht-an.
Betracht's als förderlich, je mehr sie degourdiert wird.
Ist wie bei einem jungen ungerittenen Pferd.
Kommt all's dem Angetrauten letzterdings zugut',
wofern er sein eh'lich Privilegium
zunutz zu machen weiss.

'Twould not displease me
If you should cast some sheep's eyes at her, cousin,
Now or at any time:
You're still content with looks alone.
The more she learns from you, the better I shall like it.
For a girl, you see, is just like an unbroken filly:
The husband, in the end, gets all the benefits,
Provided he has but sense enough to use
His opportunities.

(He goes to the left. The servant who had admitted the attorney has in the meantime opened the door on the left. Faninal and the notary make for the door. The Baron fixes his eyes on Faninal and signifies to him he must keep a distance of three paces. Faninal obsequiously retreats. The Baron takes precedence, assures himself that Faninal is three paces behind him, and walks solemnly through the door on the left. Faninal follows, and after him come the attorney and his clerk. The footman closes the door to the left, and goes out, leaving the door which leads to the anteroom open. The footman who was serving refreshments has already left the room. Sophia, on the right, stands confused and humiliated. The duenna curtseys in the direction of the door till it closes. Octavian, quivering with excitement, hurries toward Sophia, after glancing backward so as to be sure that the others have gone.)

OCTAVIAN

Wird Sie das Mannsbild da heiraten, ma cousine?

And will you marry that thing there, *ma cousine?*

SOPHIA

(moving one step toward him, in a whisper)

Nicht um die Welt!

Not for the world!

(With a look to the duenna.)

Mein Gott, wär' ich allein mit Ihm,
dass ich Ihn bitten könnt'! dass ich Ihn bitten könnt'!

Oh my God! Could we but be alone,
That I might beg of you, that I might beg of you . . .

OCTAVIAN

(quickly under his breath)

Was ist's, das Sie mich bitten möcht'? Sag' Sie mir's schnell!

What is it you would beg of me? Tell me now, quick!

SOPHIA

(coming another step nearer to him)

O mein Gott, dass Er mir halt hilft! Und Er wird mir nicht helfen wollen,
weil Er halt sein Vetter ist!

O my God, befriend me in my need! But since he is your friend and cousin,
You will not wish to help me!

OCTAVIAN

(vehemently)

Nenn' ihn Vetter aus Höflichkeit;
Gott sei Lob und Dank,
hab' ihn im Leben vor dem gestrigen Tag nie gesehn!

I am his cousin but by courtesy;
Thank my lucky stars,
I had not even seen his hideous face till yesterday!

(Some of the servant girls rush headlong across the anteroom, hotly pursued by the Baron's attendants. The body-servant and the one with the plaster on his nose are at the heels of a pretty young girl and bring her to bay close to the door of the salon. Faninal's Major-domo runs in much perturbed, to call the duenna to help him.)

MAJOR-DOMO

Die Lerchenauischen sind voller Branntwein gesoffen
und gehn aufs Gesindel los, zwanzigmal ärger
als Türken und Krowaten!

The Baron's menfolk, with our good wine quite besotted,
Have run after all the girls, worse than an army
From Turkey or Croatia!

MARIANNE

Hol' Er von unseren Leuten, wo sind denn die?

Fetch our men quickly to help you. Where have they hid?

(She runs off with the Major-domo. They rescue the girl from her assailants and lead her away. All disappear. The anteroom remains empty.)

SOPHIA

(speaking freely, now that they are unobserved)

Zu Ihm hätt' ich ein Zutrau'n, mon cousin,
so wie zu niemand auf der Welt,

In you I place my trust, *mon cousin,*
Knowing that you, like no one else,

dass Er mir könnte helfen,
wenn Er nur den guten Willen hätt'!

Could be my help, my saviour,
If you would bend your will to it!

OCTAVIAN

Erst muss Sie sich selber helfen,
dann hilf ich Ihr auch.
Tu' Sie das erst für sich,
dann tu' ich was für Sie!

First you must take courage yourself,
Then I too will help.
Till you have helped yourself,
I can do nothing for you!

SOPHIA
(confidingly, almost tenderly)

Was ist denn das, was ich zuerst muss tun?

What is it then, I for myself must do?

OCTAVIAN
(softly)

Das wird Sie wohl wissen!

Surely you know it!

SOPHIA
(looking at him undismayed)

Und was ist das, was Er für mich will tun?
O sag' Er mir's!

And what is it that you will do for me?
Now tell me that!

OCTAVIAN
(decisively)

Nun muss Sie ganz alleinig für uns zwei einstehn!

Now must you strike a blow alone — you for the two of us.

SOPHIA

Wie? Für uns zwei?
O sag' Er's noch einmal.

What, for the two of us?
O say it once again!

OCTAVIAN
(softly)

Für uns zwei!

For the two of us!

SOPHIA
(rapturously)

Ich hab' im Leben so was Schönes nicht gehört!

I have never in my life heard anything sc sweet till now.

OCTAVIAN
(loudly)

Für sich und mich muss Sie sich wehren
und bleiben — was Sie ist.

To save us both you must be steadfast,
And remain — What you are.

(Sophia seizes his hand, bends over it, kisses it quickly before he can withdraw it. He kisses her on the lips.)

OCTAVIAN
(holding her in his arms as she nestles closely to him)

Mit Ihren Augen voll Tränen
kommt Sie zu mir, damit Sie sich beklagt.

With tear-dimmed eyes, in fear,
You seek my aid, telling all your sorrows,

Vor Angst muss Sie an mich sich lehnen,
Ihr armes Herz ist ganz verzagt.
Und ich muss jetzt als Ihren Freund mich zeigen
und weiss noch gar nicht, wie!
Mir ist so selig, so eigen,
dass ich dich halten darf:
Gib antwort, aber gib sie mit Schweigen:
Bist du von selber so zu mir gekommen?
Ja oder nein? Ja oder nein?
Du musst es nicht mit Worten sagen —
Hast du es gern getan?
Sag', oder nur aus no — say yes or no!
Nur aus Not so alles zu mir hergetragen,
dein Herz, dein liebliches Gesicht?
Sag', ist dir nicht, dass irgendwo
in irgendeinem schönen Traum
das einmal schon so war?
Spürst du's wie ich?
Sag', spürst du's so wie ich?
Mein Herz und Seel'
wird bei lhr bleiben,
wo Sie geht und steht,
bis in alle Ewigkeit.

Fear nothing, henceforth to me united,
Fear nothing, whatever may befall!
To save you now must be my one endeavor,
And yet I know not how!
Rapture like this the Gods never did
Grant to a mortal.
Give me an answer, but with eloquent silence —
Did your own free will guide you to me like this?
Say yes or no — say yes or no!
No words could tell me all your meaning.
Was your free will your guide?
Say, or was it your direful need?
Why brought you here these gifts so lavish?
Your loving heart, your face so fair?
Say, seems it not that once in far-off days,
In some dear magic dream
We loved each other like this?
Think you not so?
Dream'd you never like this, as I?
My heart, my soul,
Will remain by your side
Wherever you are
For all eternity.

Sophia

Ich möchte mich bei Ihm verstecken
und nichts mehr wissen von der Welt.
Wenn Er mich so in Seinen Armen hält,
kann mich nichts Hässliches erschrecken.
Da bleiben möcht' ich, da!
Und schweigen, und was mir auch gescheh',
geborgen wie der Vogel in den Zweigen,
stillstehn und spüren: Er ist in der Näh'!
Mir müsste angst und bang im Herzen sein,
statt dessen fühl' ich nur Freud und Seligkeit
und keine Pein,
ich könnt' es nicht mit Worten sagen!
Hab' ich was Unrechtes getan?
Ich war halt in der Not!
Da war Er mir nah!
Da war es Sein Gesicht,
Sein' Augen jung und licht,
auf das ich mich gericht,
Sein liebes Gesicht —
und seitdem weiss ich halt nichts,
nichts mehr von mir.
Bleib' du nur bei mir.
Er muss mir Seinen Schutz vergönnen,
Was Er will, werd' ich können;
Bleib' Er nur bei mir!

What rapture, to hide with you like this
And hear no whisper of the world.
When contented like this in your arms I lie,
I fear nothing, no ill can befall me.
There happily I'd linger, there, forever
Secure from grief and fear,
And know that nothing can sever our union.
Nothing now can harm me: You are always near!
My pulse should cease to beat for fear and shame,
But, lo, I feel only joy and happiness.
All pain is healed,
No words can tell you all my meaning,
Was it sinful what I did?
But my need was dire,
And, lo, you were near!
I saw your face so fair —
Your eyes, your valiant air —
And healed was my despair.
Your face so fair —
And thenceforth nothing I know,
Nothing more of myself —
O stay now with me —
Protect me, save me, stay beside me,

I will follow wherever you guide me.
Forever, forever remain by my side!

(From the fireplaces to the left and right respectively come Valzacchi and Annina noiselessly and watch the lovers. They approach silently on tiptoe. Octavian draws Sophia to him and kisses her on the lips. At this moment the two Italians are close behind them. They duck behind the armchairs. Then they jump forward. Annina seizes Sophia, Valzacchi takes hold of Octavian.)

VALZACCHI AND ANNINA
(screaming together)

Herr Baron von Lerchenau! — Herr Baron von Lerchenau! —

Quick, Baron Lerchenau, quick, Baron Lerchenau!

(Octavian leaps aside to the right.)

VALZACCHI
(holding him with difficulty, breathless to Annina)

Lauf und 'ole Seine Gnade!
Snell, nur snell, ik muss 'alten diese 'err!

Run, bring 'izzer 'is lords'ip —
Quick, make 'aste: I must 'old zis young man!

ANNINA

Lass ich die Fräulein aus, läuft sie mir weg!

If I not 'old zis lady, she escape me!

VALZACCHI AND ANNINA

Herr Baron von Lerchenau,
Herr Baron von Lerchenau!
Komm' zu sehn die Fräulein Braut!
Mit eine junge Kavalier!
Kommen eilig, kommen hier! Ecco!

Quick! Baron Lerchenau!
Quick! Baron Lerchenau!
Come to see your future wife
Discovered viz a gentleman,
Pray come quickly! Pray come 'ere!

(The Baron enters through the door on the left. The Italians let their victims go, spring aside, bow low to the Baron with significant gestures. Sophia nestles timidly close to Octavian.)

BARON
(with folded arms, contemplates the group. Ominous pause)

Eh bien, Mamsell, was hat Sie mir zu sagen?

Eh bien, Ma'mselle! What would you wish to tell me?

(Sophia remains silent. The Baron retains his composure.)

Nun, resolvier' Sie sich!

Well, do not hesitate.

SOPHIA

Mein Gott, was soll ich sagen,
Er wird mich nicht verstehn!

My God! What could I tell you?
You would not understand —

BARON
(genially)

Das werden wir ja sehn!

We'll see about that!

OCTAVIAN

(moving a step nearer the Baron)

Eu'r Liebden muss ich halt vermelden, dass sich in Seiner Angelenheit was Wichtiges verändert hat!	'Tis my duty to inform your lordship That most important changes have been wrought In matters that much concern you.

BARON

(genially)

Verändert? Ei, nicht dass ich wüsst'!	Important? Changes? Not that I know!

OCTAVIAN

Darum soll Er es jetzt erfahren! Die Fräulein —	And therefore I now have to tell you, This lady . . .

BARON

Ei, Er ist nicht faul! Er weiss zu profitieren, mit Seine siebzehn Jahr'! Ich muss Ihm gratulieren!	Well, you lose no time, and take the best advantage For all your seventeen years — I must congratulate you!

OCTAVIAN

Die Fräulein —	This lady —

BARON

Ist mir ordentlich, ich seh' mich selber! Muss lachen über den Filou, den pudeljungen.	Gad I like you well. Was I not just the same? The rascal! I must laugh, egad — to start so early!

OCTAVIAN

Die Fräulein —	This lady —

BARON

Ei! Sie ist wohl stumm und hat Ihn angestellt für Ihren Advokaten!	Ah! She's dumb, I presume, and is employing you To plead as her attorney.

OCTAVIAN

Die Fräulein —	This lady —

(He pauses again, as though to let Sophia speak.)

SOPHIA

(terror-struck)

Nein! Nein! Nein! Ich bring' den Mund nicht auf. Sprech' Er für mich!	No, no, no! I cannot speak the word. Speak for me!

OCTAVIAN

(with determination)

Die Fräulein —	This lady —

BARON

(mimicking him)

Die Fräulein, die Fräulein! Die Fräulein! Die Fräulein!	This lady, this lady, this lady, this lady!
Ist eine Kreuzerkomödi wahrhaftig!	This is jack-pudding foolery, by heaven!
Jetzt echappier' Er sich, sonst reisst mir die Geduld.	And now you'd best depart. I've been patient with you too long.

OCTAVIAN

(very determined)

Die Fräulein, kurz und gut,	This lady, once and for all now,
die Fräulein mag Ihn nicht.	This lady will have none of you.

BARON

Sei Er da ausser Sorg'. Wird schon lernen mich mögen.	As for that, have no fear — she will soon enough have me.

(Moving toward Sophia.)

Komm' Sie da jetzt hinein: wird gleich an Ihrer sein, die Unterschrift zu geben.	Come with me now in there — you will be needed soon to sign the marriage contract.

SOPHIA

(retreating)

Um keinen Preis geh' ich an seiner Hand hinein!	No, not for all the world will I let you lead me in!
Wie kann ein Kavalier so ohne Zartheit sein!	How can a gentleman be so indelicate!

OCTAVIAN

(who has now taken his place between them and the door on the left)

Versteht Er deutsch? Die Fräulein hat sich resolviert.	Don't you understand? The lady has finally decided
Sie will Euer Gnaden ungeheirat' lassen in Zeit und Ewigkeit!	That she will let your lordship stay unmarried For now and evermore!

BARON

(with the air of a man in a great hurry)

Mancari! Jungfernred' ist nicht gehaun und nicht gestochen!	Baby-talk! By hard words ne'er a bone is broken!
Verlaub' Sie jetzt!	And time is short.

OCTAVIAN

(firmly planted in front of the door).

Wenn nur so viel in Ihm ist von einem Kavalier,	If but one spark you have in you of true gentility,
so wird Ihm wohl genügen, was Er g'hört hat von mir.	Then what I just told you would make your duty clear.

BARON

(pretending not to hear; to Sophia)

Gratulier' Sie sich nur, dass ich ein Aug' zudrück'!	Thank your lucky stars that I choose to close one eye,

Daran mag Sie erkennen, was ein Kavalier ist!

As is correct and seemly for a gentleman!

Octavian

(pointing to his sword)

Wird doch wohl ein Mittel geben Seinesgleichen zu bedeuten!

There's a way to make my meaning understood by such as you!

Baron

(he attempts to pass with Sophia)

Ei, schwerlich, wüsste nicht!

That I can scarce believe!

Octavian

(losing all self-control)

Ich acht' Ihn mit nichten für einen Kavalier.

Of the name of gentleman you are unworthy, sir.

Baron

(pompously)

Wahrhaftig, wüsst ich nicht, dass Er mich respektiert,
und war' Er nicht verwandt, es wär mir jetzo schwer,
dass ich mit Ihm nicht übereinander käm'!

Indeed, were I not sure you know my due,
And were you not my kinsman, I could hardly
Restrain myself from measures of violence!

(Takes Sophia by the hand. He attempts, with feigned unconcern, to lead Sophia toward the center door, after the Italians have signaled to him by lively gestures to take that way.)

Komm' Sie! Gehn zum Herrn Vater dort hinüber!
Ist bereits der nähere Weg!

Come, now! Go to your father, who awaits us.
By this door's the speedier way!

Octavian

(following him close to her)

Ich hoff', er kommt vielmehr jetzt mit mir hinters Haus,
ist dort recht ein bequemer Garten.

I beg you rather come with me — at the back of the house
I know a most convenient garden.

(The Baron continues in the same direction still with simulated unconcern, trying to lead away Sophia, whom he still holds by the hand, and speaks over his shoulder.)

Baron

Bewahre. Wär' mir jetzo nicht genehm.
Lass um all's den Notari nicht warten.
Wär' gar ein Affront für die Jungfer Braut!

Enough of this. Your jests are most ill-timed —
We must not keep the notary waiting.
'Twould be an insult to this lady here.

Octavian

(seizing him by the sleeve)

Beim Satan, Er hat eine dicke Haut!
Auch dort die Tür passiert Er mir nicht!
Ich schrei's Ihm jetzt in Sein Gesicht:

By Satan, I never knew so tough a hide!
And through this door I swear you'll not pass —

Ich schrei's Ihn für einen Filou,
einen Mitgiftjäger,
einen durchtriebenen Lügner und schmutzigen Bauer,
einen Kerl ohne Anstand und Ehr'!
Und wenn's sein muss, geb' ich ihm auf dem Fleck die Lehr'!

That you may know it, to your face:
I saw that you are but a cheat,
And a dowry-hunter,
Nothing but a rascally, lying, unmannerly clown, sir,
But a boor, vile in thought and in deed,
And with my sword I'll give you the sharp lesson you need!

(Sophia has freed herself from the Baron and takes refuge behind Octavian. They stand to the left, almost in front of the door.)

BARON

(putting two fingers into his mouth and giving a shrill whistle)

Was so ein Bub' in Wien mit siebzehn Jahr
schon für ein vorlaut Mundwerk hat!

How soon these boys do learn here in Vienna
To set their tongues a-wagging.

(Looking toward the center door.)

Doch Gott sei Lob, mann kennt in hiesiger Stadt
den Mann, der vor ihm steht,
halt bis hinauf zu kaiserlicher Majestät!
Man ist halt was man ist, und braucht's nicht zu beweisen.
Das lass Er sich gesagt sein und geb' mir den Weg da frei.

But, God be praised, the court and all the town
Know him that you affront,
E'en to the throne of Her Imperial Majesty!
We all are what we are, and there's no need to prove it.
Now, young sir, I have said my say, and let me pass.

(Lerchenau's servants, in full numbers, have appeared at the center door. The Baron, by a backward glance, assures himself of their presence. He now approaches Sophia and Octavian, determined to secure Sophia and his retreat.)

Wär mir wahrhaftig leid, wenn meine Leut' da hinten —

Truly I should regret it if my people yonder —

OCTAVIAN

(furious)

Ah, untersteht Er sich, Seine Bedienten
hineinzumischen in unsern Streit!
Jetzt zieh Er oder gnad' ihm Gott!

Now, as you value your life, sir, do not dare
To drag your grooms and lackeys into our quarrel.
Draw, sir, or God save your soul!

(The Baron's servants, who had already approached a few steps, hesitate as they see what is happening and pause in their advance. The Baron takes a step forward in order to secure Sophia.)

SOPHIA

O Gott, was wird denn jetzt geschehn?

Oh! Heaven! Oh, what will happen now?

OCTAVIAN

Zum Satan, zieh' Er oder ich stech' Ihn nieder!

Draw, ruffian, draw! Or on my sword I'll split you.

BARON

(withdraws a step)

Vor einer Dame, pfui! So sei Er doch gescheit!

What! In a lady's presence! Is the boy possessed?

(Octavian rushes at him furiously, the Baron draws and lunging clumsily receives the point of Octavian's sword in his upper arm. Lerchenau's servants rush forward.)

BARON

(dropping his sword)

Mord! Mord! Mein Blut! Zu Hilfe! Mörder! Mörder! Mörder!

Help! Help! I bleed! A surgeon! Murder! Murder! Murder!

(All the servants rush toward Octavian. He springs to the right and keeps them at arm's length whirling his sword about him. The almoner, Valzacchi and Annina hurry to the Baron, and supporting him, lead him to one of the chairs in the middle of the room.)

BARON

(surrounded by his servants and the Italians, who conceal him from the public)

Ich hab' ein hitzig' Blut! Um Ärzt', um Leinwand!
Verband her! Ich verblut' mich auf eins, zwei!
Aufhalten den! Um Polizei! Um Polizei!

I have most fiery blood! A doctor! Linen!
A bandage! I bleed to death before you count three!
Don't let him go! And call the police! And call the police!

LERCHENAU'S SERVANTS

(closing round Octavian with more swagger than courage)

Den haut's z'samm!
Spinnweb' her! Feuerschwamm!
Reisst's ihn den Spadi weg!
Schlagt's ihn tot auf'm Fleck!

Break his crown!
Cobwebs here! Sponge him down!
Quick, take his sword,
Kill him dead. Why delay?

(All Faninal's servants, the female domestics, the kitchen staff and the stable hands, have streamed in by the center door.)

ANNINA

(going to them, haranguing them)

Der junge Kavalier
und die Fräulein Braut, versteht's?
Waren im Geheimen
schon recht vertraut, versteht's?

Yes, zis young gentleman
And ze lady, understand?
Vere already in secret
Familiar, understand?

(Valzacchi and the almoner divest the Baron, who groans uninterruptedly, of his coat.)

FANINAL'S SERVANTS

G'stochen is einer? Wer?
Der dort? Der fremder Herr?
Welcher? Der Bräutigam?
Packt's den Duellanten z'samm!
Wer is der Duellant?
Der dort im weissen G'wand!
Wer? Der Rosenkavalier?

Somebody wounded? Who?
That one? The stranger there?
Which one? The son-in-law?
Seize the brawler, hold him tight!
Who is it, that first drew?
That one, all dressed in white!
Who? The Rose Cavalier?

Wegen was denn? Wegen ihr!	For what cause, then? Just for her!
Angepackt! Niederg'haut!	Hold him tight, tan his hide!
Wegen der Braut?	Just for the bride?
Wegen der Liebschaft!	They were a-courting!
Schaut's nur die Fräulein an,	Look after the lady,
Schaut's, wie sie blass is'! G'stochen der Bräut'gam.	Look how pale she is! Look how the bridegroom bleeds.

SOPHIA

Alles geht durcheinand'!	Oh, what confusion is this!
Furchtbar war's, wie ein Blitz,	Wondrous! Quicker than lightning
wie er's erzwungen hat!	He drove them all away!
Ich spür' nur seine Hand,	I feel nothing but the thrill
die mich umschlungen hat.	Of his embraces still.
Ich verspür' nichts von Angst,	I feel nothing of fear,
ich verspür' nichts von Schmerz,	I feel nothing of shame,
nur das Feuer, seinen Blick	His bright glances have consumed
durch und durch, bis in Herz!	All my heart with their flame!

OCTAVIAN

Wer nur zu nah kommt,	Short shrift for all
der lernt beten!	Who come too near me!
Was da passiert ist,	I will explain all,
kann ich vertreten!	When you can hear me!

LERCHENAU'S SERVANTS

(having left Octavian, now rush at all the maids near them)

Leinwand her! Verband machen!	Bandages! Linen bands we're needing!
Fetzen aus'm G'wand machen!	Sponges to staunch the bleeding!
Vorwärts, keine Spanponaden!	Bring us quickly salve and plaster!
Leinwand her für Seine Gnaden!	Bring them quick for our dear master!

SOPHIA

(calling to Octavian, in despair)

Liebster!	Dearest!

FANINAL'S SERVANTS

Schaut's nur die Fräulein an,	Look after the lady!
Schaut's, wie sie blass is'!	Look how pale she is!

OCTAVIAN

(calling to Sophia, in despair)

Liebste!	Dearest!

(Lerchenau's servants make as if to tear up the clothes of the younger and prettier servant maids. Mêlée till Faninal comes. At this moment the duenna, who had rushed out, returns, breathless, bringing linen for bandages, behind her two maids with sponges and basins. They surround the Baron and busy themselves about him. Faninal rushes in by the door to the left, followed by the attorney and his clerk, who remain standing, in great alarm, in the doorway.)

BARON

(his voice is heard, but he is scarcely visible)

Ich kann ein jedes Blut mit Ruhe fliessen sehen,
nur bloss das meinig' nicht! Oh! Oh!

I can see other people's blood unmoved,
My own makes me flinch! Oh! Oh!

(Shouting to the duenna.)

So tu' Sie doch was G'scheidt's, so rett' Sie doch mein Leben!
Oh! Oh!

Stop whining! Stir yourself! Don't stand and watch me dying!
Oh! Oh!

(Sophia, as soon as she has seen her father, has run across the front of the stage to the right, and stands by Octavian, who sheathes his sword.)

ANNINA

(curtseying and crossing over to Faninal, eagerly)

Der junge Kavalier
und die Fräulein Braut, Gnaden,
waren im Geheimen
schon recht vertraut, Gnaden!
Wir voller Eifer
für'n Herrn Baron, Gnaden,
haben sie betreten
in aller Devotion, Gnaden!

Ze gentleman 'ere
And Mistress Sophia zere, yes sir,
Secretly were intimate,
I declare, yes sir,
Ve, full of zeal
For his lords'ip's cause, yes sir,
Kept a watch and found zem,
And zere was no mistake, yes sir.

MARIANNE

(busied about the Baron)

So ein fescher Herr! So ein gross' Malheur,
so ein schwerer Schlag, so ein Unglückstag!

Such a highborn Lord! Such a great misfortune!
Such a heavy blow! Such a day of woe!

FANINAL

(at first speechless, wrings his hands and breaks out)

Herr Schwiegersohn! Wie ist Ihm denn? Mein Herr und Heiland!
Dass Ihm in mein' Palais das hat passieren müssen!
Gelaufen um den Medikus! Geflogen!
Meine zehn teuren Pferd' zu Tod gehetzt!
Ja hat denn niemand von meiner Livree
dazwischen fahren mögen! Füttr' ich dafür
ein Schock baumlanger Lackeln, dass mir solche Schand'
passieren muss in meinem neuchen Stadtpalais!
Hätt' wohl von Euer Liebden eines and'ren Anstands mich versehn!

Dear son-in-law, how is it with you? The saints preserve us!
That such a brawling boy should so disgrace my palace!
Send someone for a surgeon, quick! Delay not!
Ride all my costly thorough breds to death.
How is it none of my men had the sense,
To interfere between them? Do I feed a whole troop
Of long-legged good-for-nothings, just that such disgrace
Should fall on me in my new palace here in town?
Truly, far other manners I had hoped your lordship would provide!

BARON

Oh! Oh! Oh! Oh!

Oh! Oh! Oh! Oh!

FANINAL

Oh! um das schöne freiherrliche Blut, was auf den Boden rinnt!
O pfui! So eine ordinäre Metzgerei!

Oh, that such blood of priceless pedigree should run to waste like this!
Pah, oh, what a common vulgar butchery!

BARON

Hab' halt so ein jung' und hitzig Blut, ist nicht zum Stillen! Oh!

I have blood so young and so full of fire,
Nothing can staunch it! Oh!

FANINAL

(Going to Octavian, with suppressed fury)

Wär mir von Euer Liebden
hochgräfliche Gegenwart allhier
Wahrhaftig einer anderen Freud' gewärtig!

Truly, from your most noble presence
In my humble dwelling here
I ventured to expect far other pleasures!

OCTAVIAN

(courteously)

Er muss mich pardonieren
Bin ausser Massen sehr betrübt über den Vorfall.
Bin aber ausser Schuld. Zu einer mehr gelegenen Zeit
erfahren Euer Liebden wohl den Hergang
aus Ihrer Fräulein Tochter Mund.

I beg you, sir, forgive me;
I too am grieved beyond all measure by this accident;
But I am free from blame. At some more fitting time and place
Your lordship will discover from your daughter
How these events came to pass.

FANINAL

(controlling himself with difficulty)

Da möcht' ich recht sehr bitten!

'Twould please me — nothing better!

SOPHIA

(determined)

Wie Sie befehlen, Vater. Werd' Ihnen alles sagen.
Der Herr dort hat sich nich so, wie er sollt', betragen.

As you command me, Father, I will tell you the truth of it all:
His lordship did not treat me as would a man of honor.

FANINAL

(angrily)

Ei, von wem red't Sie da? Von Ihrem Herrn Zukünft'gen?
Ich will nicht hoffen, wär' mir keine Manier.

What? Of whom do you speak? Of my future son-in-law?
I hope 'tis not so: I should think it a sin —

SOPHIA

(quietly)

Ist nicht der Fall. Seh' ihn mit nichten an dafür.

It is not so — I do not look on him as such.

FANINAL

(still more angry)

Sieht ihn nicht an?

What? Not as such?

SOPHIA

Nicht mehr. Bitt' Sie dafür um gnädigen Pardon.

No more — I ask your gracious pardon, if what I do is wrong.

(The doctor arrives and at once goes to the Baron.)

FANINAL

(at first muttering to himself)

Sieht ihn nicht an. Nicht mehr. Mich um Pardon.
Liegt dort gestochen. Steht bei ihr. Der Junge.

Looks not on him? No more? Pardon she asks?
And he lies wounded. By her side this schoolboy!

(Breaking out.)

Blamage. Mir auseinander meine Eh',
Alle Neidhammeln von der Wieden und der Leimgrub'n
auf! in her Höh! Der Medikus! Stirbt mir womöglich.

A scandal! What? This great marriage broken off!
All the jealous fools of the quarter and the streets around,
How they will laugh! The surgeon, quick! What if't were fatal?

(To Sophia, in utmost fury.)

Sie heirat' ihn!

You marry him!

(To Octavian, subduing his rudeness, because of Rofrano's rank, to obsequious civility.)

Möchte Euer Liebden recht in aller Devotion
gebeten haben, schleunig sich von hier zu retirieren
und nimmer wieder zu erscheinen!

And may I now, in all humility, request
Your lordship to retire speedily from here
And never again darken this door!

(To Sophia.)

Hör' Sie mich!
Sie heirat' ihn! Und wenn er sich verbluten tät',
so heirat' Sie ihn als Toter!

Mark my words!
You marry him, and if he now should bleed to death,
His lifeless corpse will be your bridegroom!

(The doctor indicates by a reassuring gesture that the wounded man is in no danger. Octavian looks for his hat, which had fallen under the feet of the servants. A maid hands it to him with a curtsey. Faninal makes an obeisance to Octavian of exaggerated civility, but unmistakable meaning. Octavian realizes that he must go, but is longing to speak one more word to Sophia. He replies to Faninal's obeisance by an equally ceremonious bow. Sophia hastens to speak the following words before Octavian is out of earshot. With a curtsey.)

SOPHIA

Heirat' den Herrn dort nicht lebendig und nicht tot!
Sperr' mich zuvor in meine Kammer ein!

That man I will not marry living, and not dead.
First I'll lock me in my chamber and starve!

FANINAL

(furious, after he has again made an angry bow to Octavian, to which Octavian promptly responds)

Ah! Sperrst dich ein. Sind Leut' genug im Haus,
die dich in Wagen tragen werden.

Ah! Lock yourself in — I've men enough to drag you
To the coach if I command it.

DER ROSENKAVALIER
AT THE MET

Premiere of the current production,
January 23, 1969
CONDUCTOR, Karl Böhm
PRODUCTION, Nathaniel Merrill
SET AND COSTUME DESIGNER, Robert O'Hearn
(Photographs of the story of the opera by Frank Dunand.
Courtesy of the Education Department, Metropolitan Opera Guild)

ACT I

THE PRINCESS'S BEDCHAMBER, WERDENBERG PALACE, VIENNA.

1. Morning sun. Young Octavian (Christa Ludwig) leaves the bed where he has spent the night with his lover, Marie Therese, Princess von Werdenberg, wife of the Field Marshal (Leonie Rysanek).

2. The arrival of the Marschallin's cousin, Baron Ochs (Walter Berry). He has come to talk about his imminent marriage. But no sooner does he set his eyes on Octavian, disguised now as the maid Mariandel, than he starts to make advances toward "her" and begs for an assignation.
3. The Marschallin's levée, her daily appointment with her hairdresser and her milliner, with tradesmen and petitioners. Baron Ochs confers with the Princess's attorney (Paul Plishka), sets out his terms for taking Herr von Faninal's daughter, Sophie, as his wife.
4. The Marschallin and Octavian alone. The Marschallin broods about their affair. She knows that it must end — "if not now, then tomorrow" — and sends Octavian away.
5. The Marschallin sends her servant (Celeste Scott) after Octavian with the silver rose. The Count will "know what he must do."

2.

3.

5.

4.

ACT II

THE RECEPTION ROOM OF VON FANINAL'S TOWN HOUSE.

6. The presentation of the silver rose to Sophie (Reri Grist).
7. Octavian and Sophie. They realize that it is "love at first sight."
8. Faninal (Rudolf Knoll) introduces Baron Ochs to Sophie. The Baron tries to fondle his intended.
9. Octavian defends Sophie's honor, draws his sword, scratches the Baron's arm. Ochs makes the most of his "wound."
10. Octavian plots with Valzacchi and Annina (Rosalind Elias). Annina reads a letter to the Baron from Mariandel: the "maid" has agreed to an assignation. It is the "luck of the Lerchenaus!"

6.

7.

8.

10.

9.

A PRIVATE ROOM IN AN INN.

11. Baron Ochs and Mariandel drinking wine. The Baron tries to caress her, but Octavian gives the signal for the plot to begin.
12. Annina emerges out of the darkness, accuses the Baron of being her long-lost husband and the father of her four children.
13. The Marschallin arrives. Baron Ochs pleads for her help in explaining the mistaken identity.
14. The Marschallin comes to the Baron's rescue, but not before his final humiliation when the staff of the inn crowd in on him and present their bill.
15. The Marschallin meets Sophie, reflects on the fate of her love for Octavian, on the fate of her life. Octavian is forced to choose between the "wisdom" of one and the "innocence" of the other.

11.

12.

14.

13.

15.

16. The Marschallin leaves. Octavian and Sophie remain alone, lost in their bliss, in the love for each other that will last for "all time and all eternity."

SOPHIA

Spring' aus dem Wagen noch, der mich zur Kirch'n führt!

Then on the way to church I'll jump out of the coach.

FANINAL

(*with similar by-play between himself and Octavian, who each time takes a step toward the door, but cannot tear himself from Sophia at such a moment*)

Ah! Springst noch aus dem Wagen! Na, ich sitz' neben dir,
werd' dich schon halten!

From the coach you'll jump, miss! Well, I'll be by your side,
And I'll know how to hold you.

SOPHIA

(*curtseys again*)

Geb' halt dem Pfarrer am Altar
Nein anstatt Ja zur Antwort!

Then at the altar I will give the answer
"No," and not "Yes."

(*The Major-domo has in the meantime made the servants leave. The stage is gradually cleared. Only Lerchenau's servants remain with their master.*)

FANINAL

(*with similar by-play*)

Ah! Gibst Nein statt Ja zur Antwort.
Ich steck' dich in ein Kloster stante pede!
Marsch! Mir aus meinen Augen! Lieber heut als morgen!
Auf Lebenszeit!

Ah! Say "No" and not "Yes" at the altar!
I'll send you to a convent in an instant!
March! Out of my sight! Better now than tomorrow.
For all your life!

SOPHIA

(*alarmed*)

Ich bitt' Sie um Pardon! Bin doch kein schlechtes Kind!
Vergeben Sie mir nur dies eine Mal!

Forgive me, I implore you! I am your loving child —
Forgive me, Father, but this once, this once.

FANINAL

(*furious, closing his ears*)

Auf Lebenszeit! Auf Lebenszeit!

For all your life! For all your life!

OCTAVIAN

(*quickly whispers*)

Sei Sie nur ruhig, Liebste, um alles!
Sie hört von mir!

Be nothing but calm, dearest, for my sake!
You'll hear from me.

(*The duenna pushes Octavian toward the door.*)

FANINAL

Auf Lebenszeit!

For all your life!

(*The duenna takes Sophia with her to the left.*)

MARIANNE

So geh' doch nur dem Vater aus den Augen!

Go, get you gone from your father's sight now.

(*Takes her out by the door to the left — closes the door. Octavian goes out by the center door. The Baron, surrounded by his servants, the duenna, two maids, the Italians and the doctor, is now discovered lying on a couch improvised out of several chairs.*)

FANINAL

(*shouts once more through the door after Sophia*)

Auf Lebenszeit!

For all your life!

(*Hurries toward the Baron.*)

Bin überglücklich! Muss Eu'r Liebden embrassieren!

What joy unbounded! I must embrace you, my dear Baron!

BARON

(*whose arm has been hurt by the embrace*)

Oh! Oh! Jesus Maria!

Oh! Oh! Jesus! Mary!

FANINAL

(*turning to the right, his anger rising again*)

Luderei! Ins Kloster!

Hussy you! To the convent!

(*Turning to the center.*)

Ein Gefängnis!
Auf Lebenszeit!

To a prison!
For all your life!

BARON

Is gut! Is gut! Ein Schluck von was zu trinken!

Let be! Let be! Some drink! I am thirsty.

FANINAL

Ein Wein? Ein Bier? Ein Hippokras mit Ingwer?

Some wine? Some beer? Some hippocras with ginger?

(*The doctor makes a nervous deprecating gesture.*)

FANINAL

(*plaintively*)

So einen Herrn zurichten miserabel!
In meinem Stadtpalais! Sie heirat' ihn um desto früher!
Bin Manns genug!

So nobly born, so nobly born, so mauled and so insulted!
And in my palace too! You'll marry him even sooner.
I'm master here!

BARON

(*wearily*)

Is gut, is gut!

All right! All right!

FANINAL

(*toward the door on the left, his anger rising*)

Bin Manns genug!

I'm master here!

(*To the Baron.*)

Küss Ihm die Hand für Seine Güt und Nachsicht.
Gehört alles Ihm im Haus. Ich lauf' — ich bring' Ihm —

I kiss your hand. My thanks for such indulgence.
Command all things in this house! I'll run — I'll bring you —

(*To the left.*)

Ein Kloster ist zu gut!	A convent is too good.

(To the Baron.)

Sei'n ausser Sorg'.	Pray, have no fear.

(Very obsequious.)

Weiss, was ich Satisfaktion Ihm schuldig bin.	I know what satisfaction is your due from me.

(Faninal rushes off. The duenna and the maids follow. The two Italians have already slunk off during the preceding scene.)

BARON

(half sitting up)

Da lieg' ich! Was einem Kavalier nit all's passieren kann in dieser Wienerstadt!	Here am I! What curious adventures may befall a man in this metropolis.
Wär nicht mein Gusto hier — da ist eins gar zu sehr in Gottes Hand,	Not all are to my taste — Here one is far too much the sport of fate!
wär lieber schon daheim!	'Tis better at home.

(A footman enters and serves wine. The Baron tries to drink and makes a movement which causes him pain.)

BARON

Oh! Oh! Der Satan! Oh! Oh! Sakramentsverfluchter Bub',	Oh! Oh! The Devil! Oh! Oh! Oh, a plague upon that boy!
nit trocken hinterm Ohr und fuchtelt mit 'n Spadi!	A baby, scarcely breeched, and plays with swords already.

(With growing passion.)

Wällischer Hundsbub' das! Dich sollt' ich nur erwischen	Cursèd foreign hound! Wait till I catch your lordship!
In Hundezwinger sperr' ich dich, bei meiner Seel',	In my kennel, I'll teach you to fight, upon my soul!
in Hühnerstall! In Schweinekofen!	With cocks and hens I'll house you.
Tät' dich kuranzen! Solltest alle Engel singen hör'n!	Egad, I'll trounce you! Make you hear the angels sing!

(To Faninal's footman.)

Schenk' Er nur ein da, schnell!	Give me some wine there, quick!

LERCHENAU'S SERVANTS

(with hollow voices)

Wenn ich dich erwisch',	We will towzle you!
Du liegst unter'm Tisch.	Beat you black and blue!
Wart', dich richt' ich zu,	Wait, our time will come,
Wällischer Filou!	Vile Italian scum!

(The doctor pours for the Baron and presents the cup.)

BARON

(his good humor gradually returning)

Und doch, muss lachen, wie sich so ein Loder	And yet, 'tis rare sport to think what fancies
mit seine siebzehn Jahr die Welt imaginiert:	A baby like that has — he thinks me quite undone
meint, Gott weiss, wie er mich kontreveniert,	

Haha! Umgekehrt ist auch gefahren! Möcht' um all's nicht,
dass ich dem Mädel sein rebellisch' Aufbegehren nicht verspüret hätt'!

By his talk, thinks he has won the girl —
Ha-ha! Well, we'll see who laughs the longest! Not for much, no,
Would I have lost the chance to see that saucy baggage spitting fire at me!

(*takes the maid's hand*)

's gibt auf der Welt nichts, was mich enflammiert
und also yehement verjüngt als wie ein rechter Trotz.

There's nothing I know of, that so whets my appetite,
Or that renews my youth so well, as real defiance can.

LERCHENAU'S SERVANTS

Wart's dich hau' i z'samm,
Wällischer Filou,
Wart, dich hau' i z'samm,
dass dich Gott verdamm'!

We will do for you,
Vile Italian scum!
We will do for you,
Beat you black and blue!

BARON

(*to the doctor*)

Herr Medicus, verfüg' Er sich voraus!
Mach' Er das Bett aus lauter Federbetten.
Ich komm'. Erst aber trink' ich noch. Marschier' Er nur indessen.

And now, my friend, precede me to my room!
And make my bed, and let it be all feathers.
I come, but first, another draught!
Remember what I told you.

(*The doctor goes out with the body-servant. Annina has entered through the anteroom and comes up to him mysteriously with a letter in her hand.*)

BARON

(*to himself softly, emptying the second cup*)

Ein Federbett. Zwei Stunden noch zu Tisch. Werd' Zeitlang haben.
"Ohne mich, ohne mich, jeder Tag dir so bang,
mit mir, mit mir, keine Nacht dir zu lang."

A feather bed. Two hours yet till I dine, and no distraction.
"Without me, without me, slowly pass all the days.
With me, with me, no night will seem too long."

(*Annina places herself so that the Baron must see her and makes mysterious signs to him with her letter.*)

Für mich?

For me?

ANNINA

(*nearer*)

Von der Bewussten.

From her you know of!

BARON

Wer soll da gemeint sein?

And whom may you mean, pray?

ANNINA

(*coming quite close*)

Nur eigenhändig, insgeheim zu übergeben.

Into your own 'ands I must give it, and in secret.

BARON

Luft da!

Room there!

(His servants retire without more ado, take the wine from Faninal's servant and empty it.)

Zeig' sie den Wisch!

Show me the thing!

(Tears the letter open with his left hand. Tries to read it, holding it as far as possible from him.)

Such' Sie in meiner Tasch' meine Brillen.

Look in my pocket for my glasses.

(Suspiciously, as she is searching.)

Nein! Such' Sie nicht! Kann Sie Geschriebnes lesen? Da.

No! Do not look. Are you a scholar? Read it. There.

ANNINA
(takes the letter and reads)

"Herr Kavalier! Den morgigen Abend hätt' i frei.
Sie ham mir schon g'fall'n, nur g'schamt
hab' i mi von der fürstli'n Gnad'n,
weil i noch gar so jung bin. Das bewusste Mariandel,
Kammerzofel und Verliebte.
Wenn der Herr Kavalier den Namen nit schon vergessen hat.
I wart' auf Antwort."

"Wors'ipful Sir! Tomorrow at nightfall I am free!
I liked you, but I felt it shame,
Ven 'er 'ighness was looking, to say it,
For I am still a young thing,
She you know of, Mariandel,
Chambermaid, and your sweetheart,
And I hope that your lords'ip's 'onor 'as not forgotten me.
I wait an answer."

BARON
(delighted)

Sie wart' auf Antwort.
Geht all's recht am Schnürl so wie z' Haus
und hat noch einen andern Schick dazu.

She waits an answer!
It goes as on wheels — as at home,
And, look you, what an air of fashion it has.

(Very merry.)

Ich hab' halt schon einmal ein lerchenauisch Glück.
Komm' Sie nach Tisch, geb' Ihr die Antwort nachher schriftlich.

I have all the luck of the Lerchenaus.
Come when I've dined, I'll give the answer then in writing.

ANNINA

Ganz zu Befehl, Herr Kavalier. Vergessen nicht die Botin?

Your most obedient servant, my lord. Your lords'ip von't forget me?

BARON
(not noticing her — to himself)

"Ohne mich, ohne mich jeder Tag dir so bang."

"Without me, without me, slowly pass all the days."

ANNINA
(importunately)

Vergessen nicht die Botin, Euer Gnade?

Your lords'ip 'as forgotten ze bearer?

BARON

Schon gut.	Enough —
"Mit mir, mit mir keine Nacht dir zu lang."	"With me, with me, no night will seem too long."

(*Annina makes another begging gesture.*)

Das später. Alls auf einmal. Dann zum Schluss.	Afterwards — all together — at the end.
Sie wart' auf Antwort! Tret' Sie ab indessen.	"I wait an answer." In the meantime leave me,
Schaff' Sie ein Schreibzeug in mein Zimmer, hin dort drüben,	Bring to my room soon all that you need for writing,
dass ich die Antwort dann diktier'.	And I'll dictate to you my reply.

(*Annina goes out, not without indicating by a threatening gesture behind the Baron's back that she will be even with him for his niggardliness. The Baron takes a last sip of wine, and goes toward his room, accompanied by his people.*)

BARON

"Mit mir, mit mir keine Nacht dir zu lang!"	"With me, with me, no night will seem too long!"

ACT THREE

A private room in an inn. At the back to the left a recess (in it a bed). The recess is separated from the room by a curtain, which can be drawn.

At the center, toward the left, a fireplace with a fire, over it a mirror. In front on the left, a door leading to a side room. Opposite the fireplace is a table laid for two, on which stands a large, many-branched candlestick. At the back, in the center, a door leading to the corridor. Next to it, on the right, a sideboard.

At the back, on the right, a blind window; in front, on the right, a window looking on the street. Candelabra with candles on the sideboard and on the chimneypiece, and sconces on the walls.

Only one candle is burning in each candlestick on the chimneypiece. The room is in semi-darkness.

Annina discovered, dressed as a lady in mourning. Valzacchi is arranging her veil, putting her dress right; he takes a step backward, surveys her, takes a crayon from his pocket and paints her eyes.

The door on the left is opened cautiously, a head appears, and vanishes. Then a not unsuspicious-looking but decently dressed old woman slips in, opens the door silently and respectfully introduces Octavian, in female clothes, with a cap such as girls of the middle classes wear. Octavian, followed by the old woman, moves toward the others. Valzacchi is at once aware of them, stops what is occupying him, and bows to Octavian. Annina does not at once recognize him in his disguise. She cannot restrain her astonishment, and curtseys low. Octavian feels in his pocket (not like a woman, but like a man, and one sees that under his skirt he is wearing riding boots without spurs) and throws a purse to Valzacchi; Valzacchi and Annina kiss his hands. Annina puts a finishing touch to his kerchief.

Five suspicious-looking men enter very cautiously from the left. Valzacchi makes them a sign to wait. They stand at the left, near the door.

A clock strikes the half-hour. Valzacchi takes out his watch; shows it to Octavian; it is high time. Octavian hurries out to the left, followed by the old woman, who acts as his duenna. Valzacchi leads the suspicious-looking men to the front, impressing on them with every gesture the necessity of extreme caution. Annina goes to the mirror (all the while cautiously avoiding every noise) and completes her disguise; then draws from a pocket a piece of paper, from which she seems to be learning a part. The suspicious-looking men follow Valzacchi on tiptoe to the center. He signals to one of them to follow him noiselessly, quite noiselessly, leads them to the wall on the right, noiselessly opens a trapdoor not far from the table, makes the men descend, closes the trapdoor; then he summons the others to his side, slinks in front of them to the door of the room, puts his head out, assures himself that they are not observed, makes a sign to the two to come to him, and lets them out. Then he closes the door, directs the two remaining men to precede him to the door which leads to the side room, pushes them out, signals to Annina to come to him, goes out with her silently to the left, and noiselessly closes the door behind him. He returns — claps his hands.

The man who is hidden rises to his waist from the trapdoor. At the same moment heads appear above the bed and in other places. At a sign from Valzacchi they disappear as suddenly — the secret panels close without a sound. Valzacchi again looks at his watch, goes to the back, opens the door. Then he produces a tinderbox and busily lights the candles on the table.

A waiter and a boy run in with tapers for lighting candles, and light the candles on the chimney, on the sideboard, and the numerous sconces. They have left the door open behind them, dance music is heard from the anteroom at the back.

Valzacchi hurries to the center door, opens it respectfully (both wings) and bowing low springs aside.

Baron Ochs appears, his arm in a sling, leading Octavian at his left, followed by his body-servant. The Baron surveys the room. Octavian looks around, runs to the mirror, and arranges his hair. The Baron notices the waiter and the boy, who are about to light more candles, and signals to them to stop. In their preoccupation they do not notice him. The Baron, in his impatience, pulls the boy from the chair on to which he has climbed, and extinguishes some of the candles nearest him with his hand. Valzacchi discreetly points out the recess to him (and, through an opening of the curtains, the bed). Enter the innkeeper.

INNKEEPER

(hurrying forward to greet the noble guest)

Haben Euer Gnaden noch weitre Befehle? — Has your lordship any further wishes?

WAITERS

Befehln mehr Lichter? — More candles?

INNKEEPER

Ein grösseres Zimmer? — A larger room?

WAITERS

Befehlen mehr Silber auf den Tisch? — Do you desire more silver on the table?

BARON

(busily engaged in extinguishing all the candles in his reach with a napkin which he has taken from the table and unfolded)

Verschwindt's! Macht mir das Mädel net verruckt. — Be off! Such talk will turn the girl's brain.

(Extinguishes more candles.)

Was will die Musik? Hab' sie nicht bestellt. — What is that music? I ordered none.

INNKEEPER

Schaffen vielleicht, dass man sie näher hört
Im Vorsaal da als Tafelmusik.

They can come near if 'tis your lordship's wish —
To play to you in yonder anteroom.

BARON

Lass Er die Musik, wo sie ist.

Best let them stay there, as they are.

(Notices the blind window to the right behind the table.)

Was ist da für ein Fenster da?

Tell me, what means that window there?

(Tries it.)

INNKEEPER

Ein blindes Fenster nur.

That window? That is blind.

(Bows.)

Darf aufgetragen werd'n?

Can supper now begin?

(All five waiters make as if to hurry off.)

BARON

Halt, was woll'n die Maikäfer da?

Stop! What mean those grinning apes there?

WAITERS

Servier'n, Euer Gnaden.

To wait upon your lordship.

BARON

(makes a sign to them to go)

Brauch' niemand nicht.
Packt's Euch! Servieren wird mein Kammerdiener da.
Einschenken tu' ich selber. Versteht Er?

I need no help. Be off!
My man there will serve all the meats to us.
I'll fill the glasses myself. Now leave us.

(Valzacchi signals to them to respect his lordship's wishes without demur, pushes them all out of the door. The Baron continues to extinguish the candles, among them some high on the walls which he reaches with difficulty.)

BARON

(to Valzacchi)

Er ist ein braver Kerl. Wenn er mir hilft, die Rechnung 'runterdrucken,
Dann fallt was ab für Ihn. Kost' sicher hier ein Martergeld.

You are an honest fellow. If you can help me now reduce the bill,
There will be something in it for you. 'Tis surely very costly here.

(Exit Valzacchi, bowing. Octavian has now finished arranging his hair. The Baron leads him to the table. The body-servant at the sideboard contemplates the developments of the tête-à-tête with impudent curiosity. He places bottles of wine from the sideboard on the table. The Baron pours out wine. Octavian takes a sip. The Baron kisses Octavian's hand. Octavian withdraws his hand. The Baron signals to the lackey to withdraw, but he has to repeat the signal several times before he goes.)

OCTAVIAN

(pushing back his glass)

Nein, nein, nein, nein! I trink' kein Wein.

No, no, no, no. I don't drink wine.

BARON

Geh', Herzerl, was denn? Mach' doch keine Faxen.	Come, sweetheart, why not? Now let's have no flim-flam.

OCTAVIAN

Nein, nein, i bleib' net da.	No, no, I will not stay.

(*Jumps up as if he would go away.*)

BARON

(*seizing him with his left hand*)

Sie macht mich desperat.	I'm quite beside myself.

OCTAVIAN

Ich weiss schon, was Sie glaub'n! Oh Sie schlimmer Herr!	I know now what you think. Oh, you wicked man!

BARON

Saperdipix! Ich schwör bei meinem Schutzpatron!	Plague on the wench! I swear by all my ancestors.

OCTAVIAN

(*feigns great terror, runs as if by mistake to the recess instead of to the door, opens the curtains and sees the bed. As if astonished, he returns, quite disconcerted, on tiptoe.*)

Jesus Maris, steht a Bett drin, a mordsmässig grosses.	Jesus and Mary, there's a bed there, a tremendous big one.
Ja mei, wer schläft denn da?	Bless me, who sleeps in it?

BARON

(*leads him back to the table*)

Das wird Sie schon sehn.	You'll know in good time,
Jetzt komm' Sie. Setz' Sie sich schön.	Sit down now, take your place, here.
Kommt gleich wer mit'n Essen. Hat Sie denn kein' Hunger nicht?	They'll soon bring supper . . . Aren't you hungry at all?

(*Puts his arm round his waist. Octavian casts languid glances at him.*)

OCTAVIAN

O weh, wo Sie doch ein Bräutigam tun sein.	Oh dear! Oh, to think you're promised and all!

(*Keeping him off.*)

BARON

Ach, lass Sie schon einmal das fade Wort!	Have done with such old wives' tales once and for all!
Sie hat doch einen Kavalier vor sich	You see here nothing but a gentleman,
und keinen Seifensieder:	None of your common fellows —
Ein Kavalier lässt alles,	A gentleman forgets
was ihn nicht konveniert,	And leaves behind him everything
da draussen vor der Tür. Hier sitzt kein Bräutigam	That is not to his taste. Here sits no promised man,
und keine Kammerjungfer nicht:	Here at my side is no waiting-maid —

Hier sitzt mit seiner Allerschönsten ein Verliebter beim Souper.	Here sit we two and sup, a lover and his lass. That merely — nothing more.

(Draws him to his side. Octavian leans back coquettishly in his chair, with half-closed eyes. The Baron rises. The moment for the first kiss seems to have come. As his face is close to that of his companion, the resemblance to Octavian strikes him like a blow. He starts back and half unconsciously feels his wounded arm.)

BARON

Ist ein Gesicht! Verfluchter Bub'!	One face, I swear! Accursèd boy . . .
Verfolgt mich alser wacher und im Traum!	Pursues me when I'm awake and when I dream!

OCTAVIAN

(opening his eyes and looking at him with impudent coquetry)

Was meint Er denn?	What do you mean?

BARON

Sieht einem ähnlich, einem gottverfluchten Kerl!	You're like someone — an accursèd scurvy boy!

OCTAVIAN

Ah geh'! Das hab' i no net g'hört!	Go on! Who can it be I'm like?

(The Baron has once again assured himself that it is the chambermaid and forces a smile. But he is not quite rid of his fright. He must take breath, and the kiss is postponed. The man under the trapdoor opens it too soon and appears. Octavian, who is sitting opposite him, makes violent signs to him to get out of sight. He vanishes at once. The Baron, who to shake off the unpleasant impression has taken a few steps and is on the point of embracing Octavian from behind, just catches a last glimpse of the man. He is violently alarmed and points to the spot.)

OCTAVIAN

(as if he did not understand)

Was ist mit Ihm?	What's wrong with you?

BARON

(points to the spot where the apparition has vanished)

Was war den das? Hat Sie den nicht gesehn?	Gad! What was that? Did you see that man there?

OCTAVIAN

Da is ja nix.	There's nothing there.

BARON

Da is nix?	Nothing there?

(Again anxiously scanning Octavian's face.)

So?	No?
Und da ist auch nix?	Nothing there, neither?

(Passing his hand over his face.)

OCTAVIAN

Da is mei' G'sicht. — That is my face.

BARON

(breathing heavily, pours out a glass of wine)

Da is Ihr G'sicht — und da is nix — mir scheint,
ich hab' die Kongestion.

There is your face, and nothing there. It seems
I have a feverish brain.

(Falls into a chair heavily; he is ill at ease. The door opens. The music from outside is heard again. The body-servant comes and serves.)

OCTAVIAN

(very sentimentally)

Die schöne Musi! — What pretty music!

BARON

(very loud again)

Is mei Leiblied, weiss Sie das? — 'Tis the song that I like best.

OCTAVIAN

(listens to the music)

Da muss ma weinen. — It sets me weeping.

BARON

Was? — What?

OCTAVIAN

Weil's gar so schön is. — 'Cause it is so pretty.

BARON

Was, weinen? Wär nicht schlecht.
Kreuzlustig muss Sie sein, die Musi geht ins Blut.

What? Weeping? Why, what next?
Full of joy you must be. The music fires the blood.

(Sentimentally.)

G'spürt Sie's jetzt — — Is it clear now, my dear?

(Signals to the body-servant to go.)

Auf die letzt, g'spürt Sie's dahier,
Dass Sie aus mir
kann machen alles frei, was Sie nur will.

Do you not see how it is with me?
You now can make of me
Your willing slave.

(The body-servant goes reluctantly — then opens the door again, and looks in with insolent curiosity and does not go till the Baron has made an angry sign.)

OCTAVIAN

(leaning back in his chair as though to himself with exaggerated melancholy)

Es is ja eh als eins, es is ja eh als eins,
was ein Herz noch so jach begehrt.

'Tis all one, 'tis all one,
All our joys, and all our bitter pain.

(The Baron takes his hand.)

Geh', es is ja all's net drumi wert. — In the end are they not all in vain?

BARON

(dropping his hand)

Ei, was denn? Is sehr wohl der Müh wert.	Why, what's this? No, sweetheart, not in vain.

(Octavian casts languishing glances at him.)

OCTAVIAN

(still very melancholy)

Wie die Stund hingeht, wie der Wind verweht, so sind wir bald alle zwei dahin. Menschen sin' ma halt. Richtn's nichts mit G'walt,	As the hours that go, as the winds that blow, So the two of us will pass away; Flesh and blood are we, ruled by Fate's decree.

(With another languishing glance.)

Weint uns niemand nach, net dir net und net mir.	When we die there's none to cry for us, not for you and not for me.

BARON

Macht Sie der Wein leicht immer so? Is ganz gewiss Ihr Mieder, das aufs Herzerl Ihr druckt.	Does wine always make you so sad? 'Tis surely your bodice that is pressing your heart.

(Octavian, with closed eyes, does not answer. The Baron rises and tries to open his dress.)

Jetzt wird's frei mir a bisserl heiss.	It grows warm — I will be more at ease.

(Without ado he takes off his wig, and seeks a place to deposit it. At this moment he spies a face which shows itself in the recess and glares at him. The face vanishes in an instant. He says to himself "Brainsick" and struggles with his fright, but has to mop his forehead. His eyes fall once again on the chambermaid, sitting there helpless with relaxed limbs. That makes him decide, and he approaches tenderly. Then again he sees Octavian's face close to his own. He starts back again. "Mariandel" scarcely stirs. Once more the Baron fights with his terror, and forces himself to take a cheerful mien. Then his eyes alight again on a strange face, staring at him from the wall. Now he is beside himself with fright — he gives a muffled scream, seizes the handbell from the table and swings it distractedly.)

BARON

Da und da und da und da!	There, and there, and there, and there!

(Suddenly the presumed blind window is torn open. Annina in mourning appears and with outstretched arms points to the Baron.)

BARON

(beside himself with fear)

Da und da und da und da!	There, and there, and there, and there!

(Tries to protect his back.)

ANNINA

Er ist es! Es ist mein Mann! Er ist's!	My husband! Yes, it is he! 'tis he! 'tis he!

(Vanishes.)

BARON

(alarmed)

Was ist denn das?	What was that?

OCTAVIAN

Das Zimmer ist verhext.	The room is bewitched!

("Mariandel" makes the Sign of the Cross. Annina, followed by Valzacchi who makes pretence of holding her back, the innkeeper, and three waiters, rushes in at the center door.)

ANNINA

(speaking with a Bohemian accent, but like a woman of education)

Es ist mein Mann, ich leg' Beschlag auf ihn! Gott ist mein Zerge, Sie sind meine Zeugen! Gerichte! Hohe Obrigkeit! Die Kaiserin muss ihn mir wiedergeben!	I am his wife! I make a claim to him! Heav'n is my witness — you shall be my witness! The Law, the Ministers, Her Majesty must restore him to my arms!

BARON

(to the innkeeper)

Was will das Weibsbild da von mir, Herr Wirt! Was will der dort und der und der und der?	Landlord, what does this female want of me? What does he want? and he? and that one there?

(Pointing all round the room.)

Der Teufel frequentier' sein gottverfluchtes Extrazimmer!	The Devil makes his home in this foul den of thieves!

(The Baron has put a cold compress on his head, holds it in its place with his left hand, then goes close up to the innkeeper, the waiters, and Annina in turn, and scans them closely, as if to convince himself that they are real.)

ANNINA

Er wagt mich zu verleugnen, ah! Tut als ob er mich nicht täte kennen! Ist auch lebendig!	And would you dare deny me. Villain, and make pretence you do not know me?

BARON

(throws the compress away; very precisely)

Ich hab wahrhaft'gen Gott, das Möbel nie gesehn!	Alive! by heaven! This baggage, I protest, I never saw before!

(to innkeeper)

Debarassier' Er mich und lass er fort servier'n! Ich hab', sein Beisl heut zum letzten Mal betreten!	Begone, now, all of you! And let us sup in peace! I vow, I'll never more set foot in your low pothouse!

ANNINA

(as though noticing Octavian for the first time)

Ah! es ist wahr, was mir berichtet wurde, Er will ein zweites Mal heiraten, der Infame, ein zweites unschuldiges Mädchen, so wie ich es war!	Ah! It is true, what all my friends did tell me, That he intends a second marriage, oh the monster, A second innocent maiden, such as once I was!

(The innkeeper is startled.)

INNKEEPER AND THE THREE WAITERS

Oh! oh! Euer Gnaden!	Oh! Oh! Your lordship!

BARON

Bin ich in einem Narrnturm? Kreuzelement!	What, am I in a madhouse? Plague on you all!

(shakes Valzacchi, standing next to him)

Bin ich der Baron von Lerchenau oder bin ich es nicht? Bin ich bei mir?	Am I Baron Ochs of Lerchenau, or am I not? Am I possessed?

(putting his finger in the flame)

Is das ein Kerz'l,	Is that a candle?

(waving the napkin in the air)

Is das ein Serviettl?	Is that a napkin?

ANNINA

Ja, ja, du bist es und so wahr als du es bist, bin ich es auch und du erkennst mich wohl, Leupold bedenk': Anton von Lerchenau, dort oben richtet dich ein Höherer!	Yes, yes, you are he, and as true as you are he, I am your wife, and you know me full well; Leopold, reflect! Anton of Lerchenau, above us dwells a Judge that knoweth all!

(At first the Baron starts violently, so that her speech is interrupted, but soon regains his composure.)

BARON

(stares in amazement at Annina)

Kommt mir bekannt vor.	Surely I know you!

(Looks toward Octavian again.)

Hab'n doppelte Gesichter alle miteinander.	They all have double faces, all of them together!

INNKEEPER AND WAITERS

Die arme Frau, die arme Frau Baronin!	Oh wretched, ill-used lady!

THE FOUR CHILDREN

(between the ages of ten and four, entering too soon, rush toward the Baron)

Papa! Papa! Papa!	Papa! Papa! Papa!

ANNINA

Hörst du die Stimme deines Blutes! Kinder, hebt eure Hände auf zu ihm!	Hear the voices of your offspring? My children, raise your hands to him in pray'r!

BARON

(hitting out at the children with a napkin which he takes from the table; to the innkeeper)

Debarassier' Er mich von denen da, Von der, von dem, von dem!	Take all this crew away from here at once — Take her, take him, and him, and him!

OCTAVIAN
(aside to Valzacchi)

Ist gleich wer fort, den Faninal zu holen?

Have messengers been sent for Faninal yet?

VALZACCHI
(whispers)

Sogleich in Anfang. Wird sogleich zur Stelle sein.

Ere you 'ad come 'ere: in a moment you vill see 'im.

INNKEEPER
(behind the Baron)

Halten zu Gnaden, gehen nit zu weit,
könnten recht böse Folgen g'spüren! Bitterböse!

Asking your pardon, venture not too far,
Else might it end in harm for you — harm most serious.

BARON

Was? ich was g'spür'n? Von dem Möbel da?
Hab's nie nicht angerührt, nicht mit der Feuerzang'!

What? Harm to me from that beldam there?
Never have I touched her — no, not with a pitchfork's end.

ANNINA
(screams shrilly)

Aah!

Ah!

INNKEEPER

Die Bigamie ist halt kein G'spass,
Is ein Kapitalverbrechen!

For bigamy is not a trifle,
It is a hanging matter!

VALZACCHI
(to the Baron softly)

Ik rat' Euer Gnaden, sei'n vorsiktig,
Die Sittenpolizei sein gar nicht tolerant!

I counsel zat your lords'ip 'ave a care,
Ze police in zis town, it 'ave no mercy, sir!

BARON

Die Bigamie? Die Sittenpolizei?

Bigamy! Pooh! A fig for your police!

(Mimicking the voices of the children.)

Papa, Papa, Papa!

Papa! Papa! Papa!

(Striking his head as if in despair, then furiously.)

Schmeiss' Er hinaus das Trauerpferd! Wer? Was? Er will nicht?
Was? Polizei! Die Lackln woll'n nicht? Spielt das Gelichter
Leicht alles unter einem Leder?
Sein wir in Frankreich? Sein wir unter Kurutzen?
Oder in kaiserlicher Hauptstadt?

Throw out that whining Jezebel! Who? What? You will not?
What? The police! The rascals will not stir?
Is all this scurvy crew plotting to do me mischief?
Are we 'mong heathens? Or in France, or Turkey?
Or in this Empire's foremost city?

(Tears open the window that looks on to the street.)

Polizei!
Herauf da, Polizei: Gilt Ordnung herzustellen
Und einer Stand'sperson zu Hilf' zu eilen!

Police!
The police here, hurry! Here! Quick, here, to quell a riot!
Here is a nobleman in danger!

(Loud cries of "Police" are heard from the street.)

INNKEEPER

Mein renommiertes Haus! Das muss mein Haus erleben.	Oh! my old inn disgraced! Oh, my fair reputation!

THE CHILDREN

(*whining*)

Papa! Papa! Papa!	Papa! Papa! Papa!

(*A Commissary of Police enters with two Constables. All stand back to make way for them.*)

VALZACCHI

(*to Octavian*)

Oh weh, was maken wir?	Alas! Vat can ve do?

OCTAVIAN

Verlass' Er sich auf mich und lass' Er's gehen, wie's geht.	You must rely on me, and leave the rest to chance.

VALZACCHI

Zu Euer Exzellenz Befehl!	Your 'umble servant to command!

COMMISSARY

(*roughly*)

Halt! Keiner rührt sich! Was ist los?	Stop! No one stirs now! What's amiss?
Wer hat um Hilf' geschrien? Wer hat Skandal gemacht?	Who was it called for help? Who was it broke the peace?

BARON

(*going toward him with the self-confidence of a great gentleman*)

Is all's in Ordnung jetzt. Bin mit Ihm wohl zufrieden.	The trouble now is passed. Right well done! I commend you.
Hab' gleich verhofft, das in Wien all's wie am Schnürl geht.	I knew at once that in Vienna there's no danger.

(*Relieved.*)

Schaff' Er das Pack mir vom Hals. Ich will in Ruh' soupieren.	Drive this crowd from out the room. I wish to dine in peace.

COMMISSARY

Wer ist der Herr? Was gibt dem Herrn Befugnis?	Who are you, pray? What right have you to intervene?
Ist Er der Wirt?	Is this your house?

(*The Baron stands open-mouthed.*)

Dann halt' Er sich gefällig still	Then hold your peace, withdraw,
und wart' Er, bis man ihn vernehmen wird.	And wait in patience till it is time to question you.

(*The Baron, perplexed, retires and begins to look for his wig, which has disappeared in the confusion and is not to be found. The Commissary seats himself. The two Constables take up their position behind him.*)

Wo ist der Wirt?	The landlord first.

INNKEEPER
(submissively)

Mich dem Herrn Oberkommissarius schön stens zu rekommandieren.

By'r leave. Report myself. I'm landlord here, very much at your service.

COMMISSARY

Die Wirtschaft da rekommandiert Ihn schlecht.
Bericht' Er jetzt! Von Anfang!

These goings-on do not speak well for you.
Now, your report! The whole truth!

INNKEEPER

Herr Kommissar! Der Herr Baron —

Herr Commissar! His lordship here —

COMMISSARY

Der grosse Dicke da? Wo hat er sein Paruckl?

That very fat man there? Where have you put your wig, sir?

BARON
(who has been searching all the time)

Um das frag' ich Ihn!

I'd ask that from you!

INNKEEPER

Das ist der Herr Baron von Lerchenau!

That is his lordship, Baron Lerchenau —

COMMISSARY

Genügt nicht.

Prove it.

BARON

Was?

What?

COMMISSARY

Hat Er Personen nahebei,
Die für Ihn Zeugnis geben?

Is any person near at hand
Whom you can call as a witness?

BARON

Gleich bei der Hand! Da hier mein Sekretär, ein Italiener.

Yes, close at hand. There! My secretary, an Italian.

VALZACCHI
(exchanges glances of intelligence with Octavian)

Ik exkusier mik. Ik weiss nix. Die Herr
kann sein Baron, kann sein auch nit. Ik weiss von nix.

I can say nozzing! I not know. 'E may
Be Lerchenau — 'e may be not. I do not know.

BARON
(beside himself)

Das ist doch stark, wällisches Luder, falsches!

That is too much. Lying Italian scum, you!

(Goes toward him with raised fist.)

COMMISSARY
(to the Baron, sharply)

Für's erste moderier' Er sich.

'Twere best you keep a civil tongue.

OCTAVIAN

(who up to now has stood quietly, now acts as if he were running about in despair and could not find the way out, and mistook the window for the door)

Oh mein Gott, in die Erd'n möcht' ich sinken!	Oh, I pray that the earth may start to open!
Heilige Mutter von Maria Taferl!	Holy Mother of God!

(The body-servant, who is much alarmed at the situation, suddenly has a hopeful inspiration and hastily rushes out by the center door.)

COMMISSARY

Wer ist dort die junge Person?	That young woman there, who is she?

BARON

Die? Niemand. Sie steht unter meiner Protektion!	That? No one. She stands under my protection here!

COMMISSARY

Er selber wird bald eine Protektion sehr nötig haben.	You yourself will find protection very necessary soon.
Wer ist das junge Ding, was macht Sie hier?	Who is that girl, I say? Why is she here?

(Looks round.)

Ich will nicht hoffen, dass Er ein gottverdammter Debauchierer	I am suspicious that you are one of those abandoned men
und Verführer ist! Da könnt's Ihm schlecht ergehn.	Who lead young girls astray! It would go hard with you.
Wie kommt er zu den Mädel? Antwort will ich!	Once more, how come you by her? Answer quickly!

OCTAVIAN

I geh' ins Wasser!	Farewell! The river!

(He runs toward the alcove, as if fleeing, tears open the curtain so that the bed, softly lit, is revealed.)

COMMISSARY

Herr Wirt, was seh' ich da?	What's this, landlord, what's this?
Was für ein Handwerk treibt denn Er?	What business do you carry on?

INNKEEPER

(embarrassed)

Wenn ich Personen vom Stand zum Speisen oder Nachtmal hab' . . .	When there are persons of rank and fashion come to dine or sup . . .

COMMISSARY

Halt' Er den Mund. Ihn nehm' ich später vor.	Hold your tongue: wait till I question you.

(to the Baron)

Jetzt zähl ich noch bis drei, dann will ich wissen,	Now I will count to three, then you must tell me,
wie Er da zu dem jungen Bürgermädchen kommt!	How it comes that this honest girl is here with you.

Ich will nicht hoffen, dass Er sich einer falschen Aussag' wird unterfangen.	And I would have you know, you had best not try to cheat me with lying answers.

(The innkeeper and Valzacchi indicate to the Baron with gestures the danger of the situation and the importance of this statement.)

Baron

(makes signs to them to show that they may rely on him; he was not born yesterday)

Wird wohl kein Anstand sein bei Ihm, Herr Kommissar,	The Police Officer, for sure, will think no harm,
wenn eine Standsperson mit seiner ihm verlobten Braut	If men of quality with their affianced brides should choose
um neune Abends ein Souper einnehmen tut.	To sit at supper at nine o'clock here in this inn.

(Looks around to see the effect of his explanation.)

Commissary

Das wäre Seine Braut? Geb' Er den Namen an	She your affianced bride? Then state her father's name,
vom Vater und's Logis. Wenn seine Angab' stimmt,	And tell me where he lives. And if you've spoken the truth,
mag Er sich mit der Jungfer retirieren!	You'll be free at once to leave us with the girl.

Baron

Ich bin wahrhaftig nicht gewohnt, in dieser Weise —	Pray, do you know to whom you speak? I'm not accustomed —

Commissary

Mach' Er sein Aussag' oder ich zieh' andre Saiten auf.	Answer without ado. Else I will sing quite another tune.

Baron

Werd' nicht mankieren.	Well then, now listen:
Ist die Jungfer Faninal,	'Tis young Mistress Faninal,
Sophia Anna Barbara, eheliche Tochter	Sophia Anna Barbara, heiress and daughter
des wohlgeborenen Herrn von Faninal.	In lawful wedlock born to the most noble Lord Faninal,
Wohnhaft am "Hof" im eignen Palais.	Domiciled here in the Hof.

(The servants of the inn, other guests, also some of the musicians from the next room have crowded around the door, and look in curiously. Herr von Faninal forces his way through the crowd, much perturbed, in hat and cloak.)

Faninal

Zur Stell'! Was wird von mir gewünscht?	The same, sir. What might you want of me?

(Goes to the Baron.)

Wie sieht Er aus?	Why, how you look,
War mir vermutend nicht zu dieser Stunde,	I scarce expected you would need my presence
in ein gemeines Beisl depeschiert zu werden!	At this untimely hour, here in a common pothouse.

Baron

(very much surprised and annoyed)

Wer hat Ihn hierher depeschiert? In drei Teufels Namen?	And who asked you to meddle, in the name of mischief?

Faninal

Was soll mir die saudumme Frag', Herr Schwiegersohn?	Why ask such a question, like a fool, Sir Son-in-Law?
Wo Er mir schier die Tür einrennen lässt mit Botschaft.	When messengers from you come batt'ring at my house door
Ich soll sehr schnell	And shouting I must come in hottest haste
herbei und ihm in einer üblen Lage soutenieren,	To rescue you from gravest danger,
In die Er unverschuldter Weise geraten ist!	Which by no fault of yours was threatening your liberty.

(The Baron seizes his head in his hand.)

Commissary

Wer ist der Herr? Was schafft der Herr mit Ihm?	Whom have we here? What is your talk with him?

Baron

Nichts von Bedeutung. Ist bloss ein Bekannter,	'Tis nothing — nothing. We are scarcely acquainted.
hält sich per Zufall hier im Gasthaus auf.	'Tis but by chance that he is staying here.

Commissary

(to Faninal)

Der Herr geb' seinen Namen an!	Your name — and tell me why you're here.

Faninal

Ich bin der Edle von Fanninal.	I am the Baron von Faninal.

Commissary

Somit ist dies der Vater . . .	And this young lady's father?

Baron

(standing between them, concealing Octavian from Faninal's eyes; eagerly)

Beileib' gar nicht die Spur. Ist ein Verwandter,	What? He her father? No. A distant kinsman.
ein Bruder, ein Neveu! Der Wirkliche ist noch einmal so dick!	A cousin, it may be! The father is full twice as fat as he!

Faninal

(in amazement)

Was geht hier vor? Wie sieht er aus? Ich bin der Vater, freilich!	What means this, pray? How strange you look. I am her father, surely.

Baron

(tries to draw him aside)

Das Weitre findet sich, verzieh' Er sich!	Now leave it all to me, and get you gone!

FANINAL

Ich muss schon bitten —

What, you presume, sir —

BARON

Fahr' Er heim, in Teufels Namen!

Get you gone, the devil take you!

FANINAL

(*with growing anger*)

Mein Nam und Ehr in einen solchen Händel zu melieren,
Herr Schwiegersohn!

To drag my name into a vulgar brawl in this low tavern,
I'll not submit!

BARON

(*tries to stop his mouth; to the Commissary*)

Ist eine idée fixe.
Benennt mich also nur im G'spass.

It is his fancy.
He calls himself so as a jest.

COMMISSARY

Ja, ja, genügt schon.
Er erkennt demnach
in diesem Herrn hier Seinen Schwiegersohn?

Yes, yes, I follow.
Then you recognize
This gentleman for your son-in-law?

FANINAL

Sehr wohl! Wieso sollt' ich Ihn nicht erkennen?
Leicht, weil Er keine Haar nicht hat?

For sure; how should I fail to recognize him?
Maybe because his pate is bald?

COMMISSARY

(*to the Baron*)

Und Er erkennt nunmehr wohl auch in diesem Herrn
wohl oder übel Seinen Schwiegervater?

And you now recognize this gentleman to be,
For good or evil, the young lady's father?

BARON

(*taking the candlestick from the table and holding it up to Faninal's face*)

So so, la la! Ja, ja, wird schon derselbe sein.
War heut den ganzen Abend gar nicht recht beinand,
kann meinen Augen heut nicht traun. Muss Ihm sagen,
liegt hier was in der Luft, man kriegt die Kongestion davon.

So, so! La, la! Yes, yes! May be that it is he.
My head today has been quite giddy and confused,
I can no longer trust my eyes. I feel
There's something in the air that gives a man a fever'd brain.

COMMISSARY

(*to Faninal*)

Dagegen wird von Ihm die Vaterschaft
zu dieser Ihm verbatim zugeschobenen
Tochter geleugnet.

You, on the other hand, deny you are
The father of this girl here who is said
To be your daughter?

FANINAL

(*now for the first time noticing Octavian*)

Meine Tochter?

That my daughter?

Da, der Fetzen, gibt sich für meine Tochter aus?

That, that hussy? She dares to say she's a child of mine?

BARON

(forcing a smile)

Ein G'spass! Ein purer Missverstand! Der Wirt
hat dem Herrn Kommissarius da was vorerzählt
von meiner Brautschaft mit der Faninalschen!

A jest! A mere mistake! I vow! The landlord
Has told the police officer a tale
Of me and how I shall soon wed your daughter.

INNKEEPER

Kein Wort, kein Wort, Herr Kommissarius!
Laut eigner Aussag'.

No word, no word from me, 'twas he there
That told the story.

FANINAL

(beside himself)

Das Weibsbild arretieren! Kommt am Pranger!
Wird ausgepeitscht! Wird eingekastelt in ein Kloster!
Ich — ich — ich —

Arrest that shameless baggage! To the prison!
I'll have her whipped! I'll have her shut up in a convent!
I — I — I —

BARON

Fahr' Er nach Haus. Auf morgen in der Früh'
ich klär' Ihm alles auf. Er weiss, was er mir schuldig ist.

You'd best go home. Tomorrow I will come,
And tell you the truth. You know how much you owe to me.

FANINAL

Laut eigner Aussag'!
Meine Tochter soll herauf!
Sitzt unten in der Tragchaise. Im Galopp herauf!

'Twas you that said it!
Call my daughter here!
She waits in her sedan-chair. Bid her come up at once.

(Again going to the Baron.)

Das zahlt Er teuer! Bring' Ihn vors Gericht!

You'll pay for this dearly! I will go to court!

BARON

Jetzt macht Er einen rechten Palawatsch
für nichts und wieder nichts. Ein Kavalier
braucht ein Rossgeduld, Sein Schwiegersohn zu sein!
Parole d'honneur! Ich will mei Perükke!

What a mighty pother you are making
About a little thing — to be your son-in-law
A man must have the patience of an ass!
Parole d'honneur! Now bring my wig here!

(Shakes the innkeeper.)

Mei Perükke will ich sehn!

Find my wig! Find me my wig!

(In his wild hunt for his wig, he seizes some of the children and pushes them aside.)

THE FOUR CHILDREN

(automatically)

Papa! Papa! Papa!

Papa! Papa! Papa!

FANINAL

(*starts back*)

Was ist denn das? | Whose brats are these?

BARON

(*in his search he has come across his hat and hits out at the children with it*)

Gar nix, ein Schwindel! Kenn' nit das Bagagi!	Nothing! A lie! Till now I never saw her!
Sie sagt, dass sie verheirat' war mit mir.	She says that she's my lawful wedded wife!
Käm' zu der Schand', so wie der Pontius ins credo!	Heav'n only knows why things like this are sent to try us!

(*At the door appear servants of Faninal, each one holding the pole of a sedan-chair. Sophia comes in, in hat and cloak. All make room for her. The Baron tries to conceal his bald pate from Sophia with his hat, while Sophia goes toward her father.*)

CHORUS

Die Braut. Oh, was für ein Skandal!	The bride! Oh, what a sad disgrace!

FANINAL

(*to Sophia*)

Da schau' dich um! Da hast du den Herrn Bräutigam!	Now look around. See, there your noble suitor stands.
Da die Famili von dem saubern Herrn!	And there his gracious lordship's family!
Die Frau mitsamt die Kinder! Da das Weibsbild	The wife and all her children! She's his too,
g'hört linker Hand dazu. Nein, das bist du, laut eigner Aussag'! Du!	but a morganatic wife! No, that is you, as he himself has said!
Möcht in die Erd'n sinken, was? Ich auch!	Does not the shame overwhelm you? What? Me too!

SOPHIA

(*with joyful relief*)

Bin herzensfroh, seh' ihn mit nichten an dafür.	I'm overjoyed! I never looked on him as mine!

FANINAL

Sieht ihn nicht an dafür! Sieht ihn nicht an dafür!	Not look on him as yours? Not look on him as yours!
Mein schöner Nam'! Ich trau' mi' nimmer über'n Graben!	My name and fame! I'll be the mock of all the city!
Kein Hund nimmt mehr ein Stück'l Brot von mir.	I dare not show my face on 'Change again!

(*He is near to tears.*)

CHORUS

Der Skandal! Der Skandal! Der Skandal!	The scandal! The scandal! The scandal!
für Herrn von Faninal!	For Baron von Faninal!

FANINAL

Die ganze Wienerstadt! Die schwarze Zeitung!	I dare not show my face! The black-edged journal!

MUFFLED VOICES FROM ALL SIDES

Der Skandal! Der Skandal!!	The scandal! The scandal!
Fürn Herrn von Faninal!	For Baron von Faninal!

FANINAL

Da! Aus dem Keller! Aus der Luft! Die ganze Wienerstadt!	From the cellar! From the air! I dare not show my face —

(Going toward the Baron with clenched fist.)

Oh, Er Filou! Mir wird nicht gut! Ein' Sessel!	Scoundrel! I am not well! An armchair!

(His servants run forward and save him from falling. Two of them had already given their poles to the onlookers. Sophia hurries to his aid. They lift him up and carry him to the next room. Several waiters precede them, showing the way and opening the door. At this moment the Baron is aware of his wig, which has reappeared as if by magic, darts toward it, claps it on his pate and, going to a mirror, sets it straight. With this change he regains some of his lost self-confidence, but satisfies himself with turning his back on Annina and the children, whose presence, after all, he regards with uneasiness. The door to the left is closed behind Herr von Faninal and his following. The waiters and the innkeeper after a time emerge quietly and go to fetch drugs, bottles with water and other things, which they carry as far as the door and hand to Sophia through the opening.)

BARON

(going toward the Commissary with self-confidence now fully restored)

Sind desto ehr im Klaren. Ich zahl', ich geh'!	This clears our path all the sooner. I'll pay, and go.

(To Octavian.)

Ich führ' Sie jetzt nach Haus.	And you I'll now take home.

COMMISSARY

Da irrt Er sich. Mit Ihm jetzt weiter im Verhör.	No, not so fast. A few more questions before you go.

(At a sign from the Commissary, the Constables remove from the room everybody except Annina and the children, who remain standing by the wall to the left.)

BARON

Lass' Er's jetzt gut sein. War ein G'spass.	Let it drop for now. 'Twas a jest.
Ich sag' Ihm später wer das Mädel ist.	I'll tell you later, who she truly is.
Geb' Ihm mein Wort, ich heirat' sie wahrscheinlich auch einmal.	I pledge my word: I'll marry her, I tell you, in good time.
Da hintern dort, das Klumpert ist schon stad.	The other one, in yonder, may go hang.
Da sieht Er wer ich bin und wer ich nicht bin.	You'll know now, what I am and what I am not.

(Prepares to lead Octavian off.)

OCTAVIAN

(freeing himself)

I geh' nit mit dem Herrn!	I will not go with him!

BARON

(in an undertone)

I heirat' Sie, verhält Sie sich mit mir.	I'll marry you, if you behave well with me.

Sie wird noch Frau Baronin, so gut gefällt Sie mir!

So vastly do you please me, you'll be my baroness.

OCTAVIAN

Herr Kommissar, i geb' was zu Protokoll,
Aber der Herr Baron darf nicht zuhörn dabei.

I have something that I would say to you, officer,
but the Baron must not hear it.

(At a sign from the Commissary, the two Constables shepherd the Baron to the front of the stage to the right. Octavian says something to the Commissary which seems to surprise him very much. The Commissary accompanies him to the recess and Octavian disappears behind the curtain.)

BARON

(familiarly to the Constables, pointing to Annina)

Kenn' nicht das Weibsbild dort, auf Ehr'. War grad' beim Essen!
Hab' keine Ahnung, was sie will.

She is unknown to me, I swear. We were at supper —
I have no inkling what she wants.

(The Commissary seems to be vastly entertained and unconcernedly approaches the open curtain.)

Hätt' sonst nicht selber um die Polizei —

Or I would not have called the police —

(Suddenly much perturbed at the inexplicable proceeding)

Was g'schieht denn dort? Is wohl nich möglich das? Der Lackl!
Das heisst Ihr Sittenpolizei? Ist eine Jungfer!

What is happening there? Can I believe my eyes? The rascal!
He, too, who dared to threaten me! It is a maiden, yes, a girl!

(They have difficulty in holding him back.)

Steht unter meiner Protektion! Beschwer' mich!
Hab' ein Wörtel drein zu reden!

She's under my protection. I warn you,
You'll pay for this behavior.

(He frees himself and goes toward the recess; they pursue him and seize him again. From the recess are thrown Mariandel's clothes, piece by piece. The Commissary makes a bundle of them. The Baron struggles with his captors. They hold him with difficulty, while Octavian puts his head out of the opening of the curtains.)

INNKEEPER

(rushes in)

Ihre hochfürstliche Gnaden, die Frau Fürstin Feldmarschall!

It is the Princess, her highness the Princess of Werdenberg!

(First some men in the Princess's livery appear, then the Baron's body-servant. They form a line. Then the Princess enters, the little blackamoor carrying her train.)

BARON

(who has shaken off his captors, mops his forehead and hurries toward the Princess)

Bin glücklich über Massen, hab' die Gnad' kaum meritiert,
Schätz' Dero Gegenwart hier als ein Freundstück ohnegleichen.

Your highness overwhelms me. This is more than I deserve.
Your presence, here, your highness, does betoken truest friendship.

OCTAVIAN

(his head appearing behind the curtain)

Marie Theres', wie kommt Sie her?	Marie Theres'! How come you are here?

(The Princess stands motionless and does not answer. She looks around with a questioning glance.)

COMMISSARY

(going toward the Princess, at attention)

Fürstliche Gnaden, melde mich gehorsamst Als vorstädtischer Unterkommissarius.	May't please your highness, my most humble duty. The Commissary of this district.

BARON

Er sieht, Herr Kommissar, die Durchlaucht haben selber sich bemüht. Ich denk', Er weiss, woran Er ist.	Her highness, as you see, has deigned to come in person to my aid. And now perhaps you'll know the man I am.

(The body-servant, proud and pleased with himself, goes toward the Baron. The Baron gives him signs of his satisfaction.)

PRINCESS

(to the Commissary, paying no attention to the Baron)

Er kennt mich? Kenn' ich Ihn nicht auch? Mir scheint beinah'.	You know me? Do I know you, too? I almost think —

COMMISSARY

Sehr wohl.	Yes, well!

PRINCESS

Dem Herrn Feldmarschall seine brave Ordonnanz gewest?	Were you not long ago the Prince Field Marshal's orderly?

COMMISSARY

Fürstliche Gnaden, zu Befehl!	'Tis so, your highness, at your command!

(Octavian puts his head through the curtains. The Baron makes a sign to Octavian to vanish, and is at the same time in great anxiety lest the Princess should observe him.)

BARON

Bleib' Sie, zum Sakra, hinten dort!	Plague on you, stay there! Hide yourself!

(The Baron hears steps approaching the door on the left to the front, rushes there and places himself with his back to the door, trying by means of gestures in the direction of the Princess to appear quite at his ease. The Princess steps toward the left and looks at the Baron expectantly. Octavian comes from behind the curtain, in male clothes, as soon as the Baron has turned his back.)

OCTAVIAN

War anders abgemacht! Marie Theres', ich wunder' mich!	It was not this we hoped, Marie Theres'. It makes me wonder!

(The Princess, as though not hearing Octavian, fixes a courteous expectant look on the Baron, who with the utmost perplexity is dividing his attention between the Princess and the door. The door on the left is opened violently, so that the Baron, who has been leaning against it in a vain attempt to keep it closed, is pushed forward. Two of Faninal's servants now stand aside to let Sophia pass.)

SOPHIA

(without seeing the Princess, who is hidden from her by the Baron)

Hab' ihm von mei'm Herrn Vater zu vermelden!	I have to bring you a message from my father!

BARON

(interrupting her, in an undertone)

Is jetzo nicht die Zeit, Kreuzelement!	'Tis most untimely now, can you not wait!
Kann Sie nicht warten, bis dass man Ihr rufen wird?	Can you not wait until the proper time has come?
Meint Sie, dass ich Sie hier im Beisl präsentieren werd'?	Think you this pothouse here is fitting for an introduction?

OCTAVIAN

(who now comes quietly from the recess, aside to the Princess)

Das ist die Fräulein — die — um derentwillen —	That is the lady — who — to whom you sent me —

PRINCESS

(aside to Octavian, over her shoulder)

Find' Ihn ein bissl empressiert, Rofrano.	Surely there's a little hastiness here, Rofrano.
Kann mir wohl denken, wer sie ist. Find' sie charmant.	It is not hard to guess who she is. Your taste is good.

(Octavian slips back behind the curtain.)

SOPHIA

(her back to the door, so angrily that the Baron instinctively starts back a step)

Er wird mich keinem Menschen auf der Welt nicht präsentieren,	You will not here, nor anywhere, to anyone present me,
dieweilen ich mit Ihm auch nicht so viel zu schaffen hab.	For I would have you know that I have done with you, once and for all.

(The Princess converses in a low voice with the Commissary.)

Und mein Herr Vater lässt Ihm sagen: wenn Er alsoweit	And this my father bids me tell you: should you ever
die Frechheit sollte treiben, dass man seine Nasen nur	Carry your presumption so far as to dare to let your face
erblicken tät' auf hundert Schritt von unserm Stadtpalais,	Be seen within a hundred yards of where our mansion is,
so hätt' Er sich die bösen Folgen selber zuzuschreiben,	You'll have yourself alone to thank for all that will befall you.
das ist, was mein Herr Vater Ihm vermelden lässt.	That is the message that my father sends to you.

BARON

(very angrily)

Corpo di Bacco!	Corpo di Bacco!

Was ist das für eine ungezogene Sprach'!	What impertinence is this, what ill-bred language?

SOPHIA

Die Ihm gebührt.	It is what suits you.

BARON

(beside himself, tries to pass her and reach the door)

He, Faninal, ich muss —	Ha, Faninal, I must —

SOPHIA

Er untersteh' sich nicht!	Stand back, sir! Do not dare!

(The two footmen of Faninal come forward, bar his passage and push him back. Sophia passes out. The door is closed behind her.)

BARON

(shouting against the door)

Bin willens, alles Vorgefall'ne	I am content that all that's happened
Vergeben und vergessen sein zu lassen!	Shall henceforth be forgiven and forgotten!

(The Princess approaches the Baron from behind and taps him on the shoulder.)

PRINCESS

Lass' Er nur gut sein und verschwind' Er auf eins, zwei!	Leave well alone, now, and before I count to two, withdraw!

(The Baron turns around and stares at her.)

BARON

Wieso denn?	What do you mean?

PRINCESS

(gaily, sure of victory)

Wahr' Er sein Dignité und fahr' Er ab!	Think of your dignity and take your leave!

BARON

(speechless)

Ich? Was?	I? What?

PRINCESS

Mach Er bonne mine à mauvais jeu:	Make your "bonne mine à mauvais jeu."
So bleibt Er quasi doch noch eine Standsperson.	As a gentleman, make virtue of necessity.

(The Baron stares at her in speechless amazement. Sophia again comes quietly out of the other room. Her eyes seek Octavian.)

PRINCESS

(to the Commissary, who is standing at the back on the right with the two Constables)

Er sieht, Herr Kommissar:	And now, 'tis quite clear;
das Ganze war halt eine Farce und weiter nichts.	It all has been just a diversion and nothing more.

COMMISSARY

Genügt mir! Retirier' mich ganz gehorsamst.

Enough! I humbly beg to leave you.

(Exits, followed by the two Constables.)

SOPHIA

(aside, afraid)

Das Ganze war halt eine Farce und weiter nichts.

The whole has been just a diversion and nothing more.

(The eyes of the two women meet; Sophia makes an embarrassed curtsey.)

BARON

(standing between Sophia and the Princess)

Bin gar nicht willens!

Not so, your highness!

PRINCESS

(impatiently, stamping her foot)

Mon Cousin, bedeut' Er Ihm!

Mon cousin, explain it to him!

(Turns her back on the Baron.)

OCTAVIAN

(approaches the Baron from behind. Very mannish)

Möcht Ihn sehr bitten!

Will you permit me?

BARON

(turns on him sharply)

Wer? Was?

Who? What?

PRINCESS

(on the right, where she now takes up her position)

Sein' Gnaden, der Herr Graf Rofrano, wer denn sonst?

The Count Rofrano, my dear kinsman, who else?

BARON

(resignedly, after careful scrutiny of Octavian's face)

Is schon a so!

I thought as much!

(To himself.)

Hab' g'nug von dem Gesicht,
sind doch nicht meine Augen schuld. Is schon ein Mandl.

That face, I'm sick of it,
My eyes did not mislead me then. It was that boy, then.

(Octavian stands there, arrogant and defiant.)

PRINCESS

(approaching a step nearer)

Ist eine wienerische Maskerad' und weiter nichts.

A Viennese masquerade and nothing more.

SOPHIA

(half sadly, half ironically to herself)

Ist eine wienerische Maskerad' und weiter nichts.

A Viennese masquerade and nothing more.

BARON

(*greatly amazed*)

Aha!	Aha!

(*To himself.*)

Spiel'n alle unter einem Leder gegen meiner!	I see now they are all conspiring to fool me!

PRINCESS

(*laughing*)

Ich hätt' Ihm nicht gewunschen,	'Tis well for you it was not
Dass Er mein Mariandl in der Wirklichkeit mir hätte debauchiert!	Really my Mariandel whom you had debauched.

(*Baron as before deep in thought.*)

PRINCESS

(*as before and without looking at Octavian*)

Hab' jetzt einen montierten Kopf gegen die Männer —	I feel just now a bitter grudge, a deep resentment
so ganz im allgemeinen!	Against all men in general!

BARON

(*gradually realizing the situation*)

Kreuzelement! Komm' aus dem Staunen nicht heraus!	God bless my soul! I'm in a maze without a clue!
Der Feldmarschall — Octavian — Mariandl — die Marschallin — Octavian.	The Field Marshal — Octavian — Mariandel — the Marschallin — Octavian.

(*With a comprehensive glance which wanders from the Princess to Octavian and from Octavian back to the Princess.*)

Weiss bereits nicht, was ich von diesem ganzen qui-pro-quo mir denken soll!	In all this crazy comedy I'm at a loss to know What I should think.

PRINCESS

(*looking at him fixedly, then emphatically*)

Er ist, mein' ich, ein Kavalier? Da wird Er sich halt gar nichts denken.	It best befits a gentleman in such case to refrain from thinking.
Das ist's, was ich von Ihm erwart'.	That is what I expect of you.

(*Pause.*)

BARON

(*with a bow and the manner of a man of the world*)

Bin von so viel Finesse charmiert, kann gar nicht sagen, wie.	Such refinement of feeling excites my admiration,
Ein Lerchenauer war noch nie kein Spielverderber nicht.	And none could ever say of any Lerchenau that he would ever spoil good sport.

(*Approaching the Princess.*)

Find' deliziös das ganze qui-pro-quo,	I find it charming, all this comedy,
bedarf aber dafür nunmehro Ihrer Protektion.	But as quid pro quo I need your highness's help and interest.

Bin willens, alles Vorgefallene
vergeben und vergessen sein zu lassen.

I will consent to let these incidents
And all that's passed from henceforth be forgotten.

(Pause.)

Eh bien, darf ich den Faninal —

Eh bien, may I tell Faninal —

(Approaching the door to the left.)

PRINCESS

Er darf — Er darf in aller Still' sich retirieren.

You may — you may without a word withdraw and leave us.

(The Baron is thunderstruck with surprise.)

Versteht Er nicht, wenn eine Sach' ein End' hat?
Die ganze Brautschaft und Affär' und alles sonst.
Was drum und dran hängt,

Do you not know when you can go no further?
Your great alliance and whate'er it meant, both now
And in the future,

(Emphatically.)

Ist mit dieser Stund' vorbei.

From this hour is finished.

SOPHIA

(in great astonishment, aside)

Was drum und dran hängt, ist mit dieser Stund' vorbei!

Whatever it meant, from this hour it is finished.

BARON

(aside, indignantly, softly)

Mit dieser Stund' vorbei! Mit dieser Stund' vorbei!

From this hour it is finished. From this hour it is finished!

PRINCESS

(seems to look for a chair. Octavian hurries forward and gives her one. The Princess takes a seat to the right and says significantly, aside)

Ist halt vorbei.

It is quite finished!

SOPHIA

(on the left, pale)

Ist halt vorbei!

It is quite finished.

(The Baron finds it difficult to accept the new developments and rolls his eyes in anger and perplexity. In this moment the man emerges from the trapdoor. Valzacchi enters from the left, his suspicious accomplices following him. Annina takes off her widow's cap and veil, wipes off the paint and shows her natural face. The Baron watches this in growing astonishment. The innkeeper carrying a long bill in his hand enters by the center door, followed by the waiters, musicians, servant boys and coachmen.)

BARON

(when he sees this, knows that his game is lost, calls out quickly and decisively)

Leupold, wir gehn!

Leopold, we go!

(Makes a deep but angry bow to the Princess. His body-servant takes a candle from the table and precedes his master.

ANNINA
(insolently bars the Baron's passage)

"Ich hab' halt schon einmal ein Lerchenauisch Glück."	"For sure I have the luck of all the Lerchenaus."

(Pointing to the landlord's bill.)

"Komm' Sie nach Tisch, geb' Ihr die Antwort nachher schriftlich!"	"Come when I've dined, I'll give the answer then in writing."

(The children run between the Baron's legs. He hits out at them with his hat.)

CHILDREN

Papa! Papa! Papa!	Papa! Papa! Papa!

WAITERS
(pressing around the Baron)

Entschuld'gen Euer Gnaden! Uns gehen die Kerzen an!	May it please you, your lordship, Item, the candlelight!

INNKEEPER
(pressing forward with his bill)

Entschuld'gen Euer Gnaden!	May it please you, your lordship.

ANNINA
(dancing backwards in front of the Baron)

"Ich hab' halt schon einmal ein Lerchenauisch Glück!"	"I surely have the luck of all the Lerchenaus!"

VALZACCHI
(ironically)

"Ich hab' halt schon einmal ein Lerchenauisch Glück!"	"I surely have the luck of all the Lerchenaus!"

MUSICIANS
(coming in front of the Baron)

Tafelmusik über zwei Stunden!	Item, music two hours and more.

(The body-servant forces a passage to the door. The Baron tries to follow him.)

COACHMEN
(pressing round the Baron)

Für die Fuhr', für die Fuhr', Rösser g'schund'n ham ma gnua!	Coach hire, coach hire! Our poor horses whipped to death!

SERVANT BOY
(insolently shouting at the Baron)

Sö fürs Aufsperrn, Sö, Herr Baron!	For opening the doors, your lordship!

INNKEEPER
(still presenting his bill)

Entschuld'gen Euer Gnaden.	May it please you, your lordship.

WAITERS

Zwei Schock Kerzen, uns gehen die Kerzen an.	Two score candles, item, the candlelight!

BARON

(in the middle of the crowd)

Platz da, Kreuzmillion.	Make room, make room, make room, I say!

CHILDREN

Papa! Papa! Papa!	Papa! Papa! Papa!

(The Baron struggles violently toward the door, all follow him in confusion.)

SERVANT BOY

Führa g'fahr'n, aussa g'ruckt. Sö. Herr Baron!	I am the boy that opened the doors, may it please your lordship!

(The whole crowd is in the doorway, someone wrests the candlestick from the body-servant. The Baron rushes off. All tear after him. The noise grows fainter. Faninal's two footmen have in the meanwhile gone through the door on the left. Sophia, the Princess, and Octavian are left alone.)

SOPHIA

(standing on left, pale)

Mein Gott, es war nicht mehr als eine Farce. Mein Gott, mein Gott! Wie Er bei ihr steht und ich bin die leere Luft für Ihn.	My God, the whole affair has been a mere diversion And nothing more. How he leans over her, and I am like empty air for him!

OCTAVIAN

(behind the Princess's chair, embarrassed)

War anders abgemacht, Marie Theres', ich wunder' mich.	It was not this we hoped, Marie Theres' — I stand amazed.

(In extreme perplexity.)

Befiehlt Sie, dass ich — soll ich nicht — die Jungfer — der Vater —	Perhaps you wish — shall I not — the lady — her father —

PRINCESS

Geh' Er doch schnell und tu' Er, was Sein Herz Ihm sagt.	Go quickly, go, and do all that your heart commands.

SOPHIA

(in despair)

Die leere Luft. O mein Gott, o mein Gott!	Like empty air! Oh God! Oh God!

OCTAVIAN

Theres', ich weiss gar nicht —	Theres', I have no words!

PRINCESS

Geh' Er und mach' Er seinen Hof.	Woo her and win her love.

OCTAVIAN

Ich schwör Ihr —	I wonder —

PRINCESS

Lass Er's gut sein.	'Tis no matter.

OCTAVIAN

Ich begreif' nicht, was Sie hat.	On my honor, what you mean —

PRINCESS

(laughs angrily)

Er ist ein rechtes Mannsbild, geh' Er hin.	How like the rest! How like a man! Go to her!

OCTAVIAN

Was Sie befiehlt.	As you command!

(Crosses to Sophia, who stands silent.)

Eh bien, hat Sie kein freundlich Wort für mich?	Eh bien, have you no kindly word for me?
Nicht einen Blick, nicht einen lieben Gruss?	No smile, no look, no greeting, not one sign?

SOPHIA

(hesitating)

War mir von Euer Gnaden Freundschaft und Behilflichkeit	I had hoped, truly, that your lordship would quite otherwise
wahrhaftig einer andern Freud' gewärtig.	Befriend me, and would bring me help and comfort —

OCTAVIAN

(eagerly)

Wie — freut Sie sich denn nicht?	What? Are you then not glad?

SOPHIA

(angrily)

Hab' wirklich keinen Anlass nicht.	Pray, tell me, what cause I have?

OCTAVIAN

Hat man Ihr nicht den Bräutigam vom Hals geschafft?	Is it not cause enough that you are rid of him?

SOPHIA

Wär' all's recht schön, wenn's anders abgegangen wär'.	Had it been done quite otherwise, it would have been well,
Schäm mich in Grund und Boden. Versteh' sehr wohl,	Anger and shame oppress me. I feel the scorn and pity
mit was für einen Blick Ihre fürstliche Gnaden mich betracht'.	Of every glance her highness casts at me.

OCTAVIAN

Ich schwör Ihr, meiner Seel' und Seligkeit.	You wrong her, on my soul, by such a thought!

SOPHIA

Lass Er mich gehn.	Leave me in peace!

OCTAVIAN

Ich lass Sie nicht.	That cannot be!

(Seizes her hand.)

SOPHIA	
Der Vater braucht mich drin.	My father needs my help.
OCTAVIAN	
Ich brauch' Sie nötiger.	My need is far greater.
SOPHIA	
Das sagt sich leicht.	'Tis lightly said.
OCTAVIAN	
Ich hab' Sie übermässig lieb.	My love for you has no bounds.
SOPHIA	
Das ist nicht wahr, Er hat mich nicht so lieb, als wie Er spricht. Vergess' Er mich!	No, 'tis not so. Your love is not as great as you declare. Forget me quite!
OCTAVIAN	
Ist mir um Sie und nur um Sie.	You are my all — you are my all.
SOPHIA	
Vergess' Er mich!	Forget me quite!
OCTAVIAN *(vehemently)*	
Mag alles drunter oder drüber gehn!	Beside you, the whole world is worth nothing!
SOPHIA *(passionately)*	
Vergess' Er mich!	Forget me quite!
OCTAVIAN	
Hab' keinen andern Gedanken nicht. Seh' allweil Ihr lieb Gesicht.	My thoughts are ever of you alone! Nothing but you I see.
(Seizes both her hands in his.)	
SOPHIA *(defending herself weakly)*	
Vergess' Er mich!	Forget me quite!
PRINCESS *(rises abruptly, but controls herself and sits again; aside, solemnly, at the same time with Sophia and Octavian)*	
Heut oder morgen oder den übernächsten Tag. Hab' ich mir's denn micht vorgesagt? Das alles kommt halt über jede Frau. Hab' ich's den nicht gewusst? Hab' ich nicht ein Gelübde tan, Dass ich's mit einem ganz gefassten Herzen	"Now or tomorrow: if not tomorrow, very soon" — Did I not say the words myself? There is no woman can escape her fate! Did I not know the truth? Did I not swear by all the saints That I with chastened heart and tranquil spirit

Ertragen werd' . . .	Would bear the blow . . .
Heut oder morgen oder den übernächsten Tag.	"Now or tomorrow: if not tomorrow, very soon."

(Wipes her eyes and rises.)

SOPHIA
(softly)

Die Fürstin da! Sie ruft Ihn hin! So geh' Er doch.	Her highness! Look! She calls to you! Then go to her!

(Octavian, after advancing a few steps toward the Princess, now stands undecided between the two. Sophia, in the doorway, is hesitating whether to go or to remain. Octavian, between them, turns his head from one to the other. The Princess notices his perplexity and a melancholy smile flits over her countenance.)

SOPHIA
(by the door)

Ich muss hinein und fragen, wie's dem Vater geht.	I must go in and ask how my dear father is.

OCTAVIAN

Ich muss jetzt was reden, und mir verschlagt's die Red'.	There's much would I tell her, but thought and language fail.

PRINCESS

Der Bub', wie er verlegen da in der Mitten steht.	Look how the boy stands there perplexed between the two of us.

OCTAVIAN
(to Sophia)

Bleib' Sie um alles hier.	Stay here for all you love.

(To the Princess.)

Wie, hat Sie was gesagt?	What? did you speak to me?

(The Princess, paying no heed to Octavian, crosses to Sophia and looks at her, critically but kindly. Sophia, much embarrassed, curtseys. Octavian retreats a step.)

PRINCESS

So schnell hat Sie ihn gar so lieb?	So quickly did you learn to love him?

SOPHIA
(very quickly)

Ich weiss nicht, was Euer Gnaden meinen mit der Frag'.	Indeed, madam, I can hardly understand your question.

PRINCESS

Ihr blass Gesicht gibt schon die rechte Antwort drauf.	Your cheek so pale gives me the answer plain enough.

SOPHIA

(very timid and embarrassed. Still very quickly)

War gar kein Wunder, wenn ich blass bin, Euer Gnaden.
Hab' einen grossen Schreck erlebt mit dem Herrn Vater.
Gar nicht zu reden von gerechtem Emportement
gegen den skandalösen Herrn Baron.
Bin Euer Gnaden recht in Ewigkeit verpflichtet,
dass mit Dero Hilf' und Aufsicht —

Small wonder, too, it is, your highness, if I am pale.
With my dear father's illness I was very frightened.
Did not all the vile things that hateful Baron
Said and did also give me cause for great anger?
And to your highness I shall be grateful always
That your timely intervention —

PRINCESS

(deprecatorily)

Red' Sie nur nicht zu viel, Sie ist ja hübsch genug!
Und gegen den Herrn Papa sein Übel weiss ich etwa eine Medizin.
Ich geh' jetzt da hinein zu ihm und lad' ihn ein,
Mit mir und Ihr und dem Herrn Grafen da
in meinem Wagen heimzufahren — meint Sie nicht —
dass ihn das rekreieren wird und allbereits
ein wenig munter machen?

Waste not your words on me, you're pretty, that's enough!
And for your worthy father's humors, a most sovereign cure I think I know.
I'll go, say a word to him, and bid him ride
With me and you and Count Octavian,
In my own coach, and bring him home — Don't you think
That will soon restore his health
And cheer his drooping spirits?

SOPHIA

Euer Gnaden sind sie Güte selbst.

Your highness is goodness itself.

PRINCESS

Und für die Blässe weiss vielleicht mein Vetter da die Medizin.

And for your poor pale cheeks I think my cousin there will know the cure.

OCTAVIAN

(with deep feeling)

Marie Theres', wie gut Sie ist.
Marie Theres', ich weiss gar nicht —

Marie Theres', how good you are.
Marie Theres', I do not know —

PRINCESS

(with an enigmatical expression, softly)

Ich weiss auch nix.

I know nothing.

(Quite toneless.)

Gar nix.

Nothing.

(She makes a sign to him to remain.)

OCTAVIAN

(uncertain, as if he wished to follow her)

Marie Theres'!

Marie Theres'!

(The Princess remains standing in the door. Octavian stands next to her, Sophia farther to the right.)

PRINCESS

(to herself)

Hab' mir's gelobt, ihn lieb zu haben in der richtigen Weis'.
Dass ich selbst sein Lieb' zu einer andern
noch lieb hab! Hab' mir freilich nicht gedacht,
dass es so bald mir auferlegt sollt' werden!

I made a vow to love him in the right way as a good woman should,
Even to love the love he bore another
I promised! But in truth I did not think
That all so soon the task would await me.

(Sighing.)

Es sind die mehreren Dinge auf der Welt,
so dass sie ein's nicht glauben tät'
wenn man sie möcht' erzählen hör'n.
Alleinig wer's erlebt, der glaubt daran und weiss nicht wie —
Da steht der Bub' und da steh' ich, und mit dem fremden Mädel dort
wird er so glücklich sein, als wie halt Männer
das Glücklichsein verstehen. In Gottes Namen.

Full many a thing is ordained in this world,
Which we should scarce believe could be
If we heard others tell of them . . .
But soon those they wound believe in them, and know not how —
There stands the boy, and here stand I, and with his love, new found this day,
He will have happiness,
Such as a man thinks the best of the world can give. 'Tis done — so be it.

OCTAVIAN

(together with the Princess and Sophia, first aside, then gazing into Sophia's eyes)

Es ist was kommen und ist was g'schehn.
Ich möcht' Sie fragen: darf's denn sein? und grad' die Frag',
die spür ich, dass sie mir verboten ist.
Ich möcht' Sie fragen: warum zittert was in mir? —
Ist denn ein grosses Unrecht geschehn? Und grad' an Sie
darf ich die Frag' nicht tun — und dann seh' ich dich an,
Sophie, und seh' nur dich und spür' nur dich,
Sophie, und weiss von nichts als nur: dich hab' ich lieb.

What has come over me, what has come to pass?
I want to ask her. Can it be? And just that question,
I know I cannot ask of her.
I want to ask her: oh, why trembles all my soul? —
Has a great wrong, a sinful deed been done? And just of her
I may not ask the question — and then on your dear face, Sophia,
I gaze, and see but you, and know but you,
Sophia, and I know but this: you, you I love!

SOPHIA

(together with the Princess and Octavian, first aside, then gazing into Octavian's eyes)

Mir ist wie in der Kirch'n, heilig ist mir und so bang.
Und doch ist mir unheilig auch! Ich weiss nicht, wie mir ist.

I feel as one at worship — holiest thoughts fill my soul.
And yet unholy and sinful thoughts possess me. I know not how I feel.

(With much expression.)

Ich möcht mich niederknien dort vor der Frau und möcht ihr
was antun, denn ich spür', sie gibt mir ihn
und nimmt mir was von ihm zugleich. Weiss gar nicht, wie mir ist!
Möcht' all's verstehen und möcht' auch nichts verstehen.

At yonder lady's feet I would kneel, yet would I
Harm her, for I feel that she gives him to me
And yet robs me of part of him. I don't know what I feel.
I would know all things, yet I fear to know the truth.

Möcht fragen und nicht fragen, wird mir heiss und kalt.
Und spür nur dich und weiss nur eins: dich hab' ich lieb!

Now longing to ask, all now fearing, hot am I and cold.
And know but you and know but this one thing, that I love you!

(The Princess goes quickly into the room on the left; the two others do not notice her. Octavian has come quite near to Sophia. A moment later she is clasped in his arms.)

OCTAVIAN
(together with Sophia)

Spür nur dich, spür nur dich allein
und dass wir beieinander sein!
Geht all's sonst wie ein Traum dahin
vor meinem Sinn!

You alone I know, only you
That you love me and I love you!
All besides like a vision seems
Of passing dreams.

SOPHIA
(together with Octavian)

Ist ein Traum, kann nicht wirklich sein,
dass wir zwei beieinander sein,
beieinand' für alle Zeit
und Ewigkeit!

'Tis a dream of heaven: is it true,
That you love me and I love you?
Never in this world to part,
For all time and all Eternity.

OCTAVIAN
(louder)

War ein Haus wo, da warst du drein,
und die Leute schicken mich hinein,
mich gradaus in die Seligkeit!
Die waren g'scheit!

It was a great house, in it you were;
On a foolish quest folk sent me there,
But sent me to my bliss.
Wise things they knew.

SOPHIA

Kannst du lachen? Mir ist zur Stell'
bang wie an der himmlischen Schwell'!
Halt' mich, ein schwach Ding, wie ich bin,
sink' dir dahin!

Dare you still laugh? I fear my fate,
Trembling as a soul at Heaven's Gate!
Hold me closer, friendless and weak,
Your arms I seek.

(She leans on him for support. At this moment Faninal's footmen open the door and enter, each carrying a candlestick. Faninal, leading the Princess by the hand, enters through the door. The two young people stand for a moment confused, then they make a deep bow, which Faninal and the Princess return. Faninal pats Sophia with paternal benevolence on the cheek.)

FANINAL

Sind halt aso, die jungen Leut'!

'Tis just their way — youth will be youth!

PRINCESS

Ja, ja.

Yes, yes.

(Faninal gives his hand to the Princess, conducts her to the center door which the suite of the Princess, among them the little blackamoor, at that moment throw open. Bright light outside, inside a half-light, as the two footmen with the candlesticks precede the Princess.)

OCTAVIAN
(*dreamily*)

Spür nur dich, spür nur dich allein
und dass wir beieinander sein!
Geht all's sonst wie ein Traum dahin
vor meinem Sinn!

You alone I know, only you,
That you love me and I love you!
All besides like a vision seems
Of passing dreams.

SOPHIA
(*dreamily*)

Ist ein Traum, kann nicht wirklich sein,
dass wir zwei beieinander sein.
beieinand' für alle Zeit
und Ewigkeit!

'Tis a dream of heaven: is it true,
That you love me and I love you?
Never in this world to part,
For all time and all Eternity.

OCTAVIAN AND SOPHIA

Spür nur dich allein!

I know you alone!

(*She sinks into his arms. He kisses her quickly. Without her noticing it, her handkerchief drops from her hand. Then they run off quickly, hand in hand. The stage remains empty. Then the center door is opened again. Through it comes the little blackamoor with a taper in his hand. Looks for the handkerchief — finds it — picks it up — trips out. The curtain falls quickly.*)

Appendix

Productions of *Der Rosenkavalier* in Europe and the USA

The roles interpreted by the singers listed below are in the following order: Marschallin (soprano), Octavian (soprano or mezzo soprano), Sophie (soprano), Ochs (bass), Faninal (baritone), Leitmetzerin (soprano), Annina (mezzo soprano), Valzacchi (tenor) and Italian singer (tenor).

Dresden

World premiere, 26 January 1911: Margarethe Siems, Eva von der Osten, Minnie Nast, Karl Perron, Karl Scheidemantel, Riza Eibenschutz, Erna Freund, Hans Rüdiger, Fritz Soot
c. Ernst von Schuch
This production, with various cast changes, remained in the repertory until 1934 by which time it had been given nearly 200 times.

NEW PRODUCTIONS:
1934: Martha Fuchs, Tiana Lemnitz, Maria Cebotari, Ludwig Ermold, Rudolf Schmalnauer, Walburga Vogel, Helene Jung, Hanns Lange, Mario Parlo
c. Karl Böhm
1948: Dora Zschille, Christel Goltz, Elfriede Weidlich, Kurt Böhme, Hans Löbel, Angela Kolniak, Helena Roth, Erich Zimmermann, Helmut Schindler
c. Joseph Keilberth
1961: Brünnhild Friedland, Gisela Schröter, Renate Reinecke, Theo Adam, Arno Schetlenberg, Angela Kolniak, Brigitte Pfretzschner, Johannes Kemter, Gerd Hösel
c. Otmar Suitner

Great Britain

First performance, Covent Garden, 26 January 1913: Margarethe Siems, Eva von der Osten, Claire Dux, Paul Knüpfer, Friedrich Brodersen, Elsa Julich, Anna Gura-Hummel, Hans Bechstein, Frederick Blamey
c. Thomas Beecham
(During this first season there were several cast changes: the Marschallin was sung by Louise Petzl-Perard, Hedy Iracema-Brügelmann and Sophie Wolff; Octavian by Marie Gutheil-Schoder, Hermine Bosetti and Arlene Sanden; Ochs by Rudolf Gmur and Arthur Pacyna; and Faninal by Hermann Gura and Hermann Wiedemann. Herr Schilling-Ziemssen conducted two of the eight performances.)

REVIVALS:

London

1914 (Theatre Royal, Drury Lane): Margarethe Siems/Frieda Hempel, Charlotte Uhr/Johanna Lippe, Claire Dux/Lotte Lehmann, Paul Knüpfer/Michael Bohnen, Friedrich Brodersen, Seiter, Muriel Terry, Hans Bechstein, Marescotti
c. Thomas Beecham

1924 (Covent Garden): Lotte Lehmann/Frida Leider, Delia Reinhardt, Elisabeth Schumann, Richard Mayr/Paul Bender/Alfred Jerger, Eduard Habich/Karl Renner, Rosel Landwehr/Seiter, Helene Jung, Hermann Gallos, Karl Fischer-Niemann
c. Bruno Walter
1931 (Covent Garden): Lotte Lehmann, Margit Angerer, Elisabeth Schumann, Richard Mayr, Eduard Habich, Odette de Foras, Anna Tibell, Heinrich Tessmer, Heddle Nash
c. Bruno Walter/Robert Heger
1933 (Covent Garden): Lotte Lehmann, Eva Hadrabova, Adele Kern, Alexander Kipnis, Eduard Habich, Odette de Foras, Gladys Parr, Hans Fleischer, Heddle Nash
c. Thomas Beecham
1936 (Covent Garden): Elisabeth Rethberg, Tiana Lemnitz, Stella Andreva, Emanuel List, Karl August Neumann, Constance Willis, Margery Booth/ Gladys Parr, Hans Fleischer, Heddle Nash
c. Fritz Reiner
1936 (Dresden State Opera at Covent Garden): Martha Fuchs, Marta Rohs/Elsa Wieber, Maria Cebotari, Ludwig Ernold, Arno Schellenberg, Walburga Vogel, Helene Jung, Hanns Lange, Martin Kremer
c. Karl Böhm
1938 (Covent Garden): Lotte Lehmann/Hilde Konetzni, Tiana Lemnitz, Erna Berger/Irma Beilke, Fritz Krenn, Eduard Habich/Hermann Wiedemann, Constance Willis/Eclas-Schurr, Marie-Louise Schilp, Heinrich Tessmer/Karl Laufkötter, Webster Booth
c. Erich Kleiber/Fritz Zweig
1939 (Sadler's Wells Theatre): Joan Cross, Joy McArden, Ruth Naylor, Ronald Stear, Redvers Llewellyn/Denis Dowling, Muriel Burnett, Valetta Iacopi, D. M. Jones, Booth/Herbert Tree
c. Lawrance Collingwood
1947 (Covent Garden): Doris Doree, Victoria Sladen, Virginia MacWalters/Leni Lynn, David Franklin, Graham Clifford, Muriel Burnett, Constance Shacklock, Hubert Norville, Kenneth Neate
c. Karl Rankl
1950 (Covent Garden): Sylvia Fisher, Constance Shacklock, Elisabeth Schwarzkopf/Uta Graf, Howell Glynne, Graham Clifford, Muriel Burnett, Jean Watson, Parry Jones, Murray Dickie/James Johnston
c. Karl Rankl/Erich Kleiber
1954 (Covent Garden): Sylvia Fisher, Constance Shacklock, Ruth Guldbaek, Frederick Dalberg, Lewis, Estelle Valery, Barbara Howitt, Raymond Nilsson, William McAlpine
c. Rudolf Kempe
1958 (Covent Garden): Claire Watson/Una Hale, Hertha Töpper/Constance Shacklock, Joan Carlyle, James Pease, Lewis, Judith Pierce, Barbara Howitt, Raymond Nilsson, William McAlpine
c. Rudolph Kempe/Downes
1959 (Covent Garden): Elisabeth Schwarzkopf, Sena Jurinac, Hertha Töpper, Hanny Steffek, Kurt Boehme, Lewis, Judith Pierce, Monica Sinclair, Raymond Nilsson, Kenneth Macdonald
c. Georg Solti
1963 (Covent Garden): Régine Crespin, Merstin Meyer, Barbara Holt, Joan Carlyle, Michael Langdon, Lewis, Judith Pierce, Monica Sinclair, Robert Bowman, Kenneth Macdonald
c. Heinz Walberg
1966 (Covent Garden): Sena Jurinac, Josephine Veasey, Joan Carlyle, Michael

Langdon, Lewis, Margaret Kingsley, Yvonne Minton, John Dobson, Kenneth Macdonald
c. Georg Solti
1968 (Covent Garden): Lisa Della Casa, Yvonne Minton, Elizabeth Robson, Michael Langdon, Gwyn Griffiths, Margaret Kingsley, Anne Howells, John Dobson, Kenneth Macdonald
c. Georg Solti
1971 (Covent Garden): Sena Jurinac, Brigitte Fassbänder, Lucia Popp, Michael Langdon, Derek Hammond-Stroud, Gwyneth Price, Gillian Knight, John Dobson, Ermanno Mauro
c. Josef Krips
1974 (Covent Garden): Helga Dernesch, Yvonne Minton, Teresa Cahill, Jules Bastin, Derek Hammond-Stroud, Gwyneth Price, Gillian Knight, John Dobson, Ermanno Mauro
c. Carlos Kleiber
1975 (English National Opera at the Coliseum): Anne Evans, Josephine Barstow, Valerie Masterson, Neil Warren-Smith, Eric Shilling, Judith Turner, Sarah Walker, Paul Crook, Tom Swift
c. Charles Mackerras

The Denhof Grand Opera Company toured Great Britain in the autumn of 1913 giving the first performances in English with: Agnes Nicholls, Elizabeth Schiller, Caroline Hatchard, Arthur Pacyna, Frederick Austin, Muriel Jerry, Hans Bechstein, Frederick Blamey
c. Schilling-Siemssen

Glyndebourne

1959: Régine Crespin, Elisabeth Söderström, Anneliese Rothenberger, Oscar Czerwenka, Willy Ferenz, Elizabeth Crook, Nancy Evans, John Kentish, William McAlpine
c. Leopold Ludwig
1965: Montserrat Caballe/Erika Schmidt, Teresa Zylis-Gara/Josephine Veasey, Edith Mathis/Liselotte Hammes, Manfred Jungwirth/Otto Edelmann, John Modenos, Angela Jenkins, Anna Reynolds, David Hughes, Jon Andrews
c. John Pritchard
1980: Rachel Yakar/Elizabeth Harwood, Felicity Lott, Krisztina Laki, Donald Gramm/Artur Korn, Derek Hammond-Stroud, Rae Woodland, Nucci Condo, John Fryatt, Dennis O'Neill
c. Bernard Haitink

Scottish Opera

1971: Helga Dernesch, Janet Baker, Elizabeth Harwood, Noel Mangin, Michael Langdon, Thomas Hemsley, Judith Pierce, Joan Davies, Nigel Douglas, Derek Blackwell
c. Alexander Gibson

Berlin (east)

Hofoper (later State Opera)
First performance, 14 November 1911: Frieda Hempel, Lola Artôt de Padilla, Claire Dux, Paul Knüpfer, Baptist Hoffmann, Ida von Schoele-Müller, Therese Rothauser, Valdemar Henke, Karl Jörn
c. Karl Muck

(This production with various cast changes remained in repertory until June 1933 and received 367 performances.)
1935: Viorica Ursuleac, Tiana Lemnitz, Adele Kern, Jaro Prohaska, Hilde Scheppan, (rest unknown)
c. Clemens Krauss

Staatsoper at the Admiralspalast
1948: Paula Buckner, Anneliese Müller, Erna Berger, Jaro Prohaska, Kurt Rehm, Gerda Wismar, Karola Goerlich, Paul Schmidtmann, Hans Hopf
c. Leopold Ludwig
At the rebuilt *Staatsoper unter den Linden*
1960: Clara Ebers, Ludmila Dvorakova, Ingeberg Wenglar, Reiner Süss, Gerhard Wiese, Irmgard Klein, Gertrud Stilo, Gerhard Stolze, Gerhard Unger
c. Franz Konwitschny
1973: Wilma Schmidt, Ludmila Dvorakova, Ingeborg Springer, Isabella Nave, Reiner Süss, Erich Siebenschuh, Ilona Papenthil, Annelies Burmeister, Horst Hiestermann, Ruggiero Orofino
c. Otmar Suitner

BERLIN (WEST)

Stadtische (later Deutsche Opera)
1950: Aga Joesten, Elisabeth Grümmer, Lisa Otto, Josef Greindl, Robert Koffmane, Karina Kutz, Emmi Hagemann, Georg Gerhardt, Sebastian Hauser
c. Arthur Rother
1959: Elizabeth Grümmer, Kerstin Meyer, Lisa Otto, Josef Greindl, Robert Koffmane, Karina Kutz, Emmi Hagemann, Georg Gerhardt, Sebastian Hauser
c. Arthur Rother
1959: Elisabeth Grümmer, Kerstin Meyer, Lisa Otto, Josef Greindl, Ernst Krukowski, Marlies Siemling, Sieglinde Wagner, Martin Vantin, Helmut Krebs
c. Silvio Varviso
1970: Leonie Rysanek, Tatyana Troyanos, Edith Mathis, Franz Mazura, Tomislav Neralic, (*unknown*), Sieglinde Wagner, Loren Driscoll, Carlo Cossuta
c. Josef Krips

MILAN

La Scala
First performance in Italy, 1 March 1911: Adelina Agostinelli, Lucrezia Bori, Ines Maria Ferraris, Pavel Ludikar, Hevina Lollini, Guiseppe Pacini, Marcello Garoni, (*unknown*), Armondo Marescotti
c. Tullio Serafin
1927: Mercedes Llopart, Conchita Supervia, Ines Maria Ferraris, Umberto Di Lelio, Gino Vanelli, Ida Conti, Gina Pedroni, Guiseppe Nessi, Piero Menescaldi
c. Ettore Panizza
1928: Iva Pacetti, Conchita Supervia, Ines Maria Ferraris, Umberto Di Lelio, Gino Vanelli, Ida Conti, Gina Pedroni, Guiseppe Nessi, Piero Menescaldi
c. Strauss
1947: Adriana Guerrini, Elsa Cavelti, Liana Cortini, Italo Tajo, Ornella Rovero, Anna Maria Canali, Guiseppe Nessi, Amerigo Gentilini
c. Ettore Panizza

1952: Elisabeth Schwarzkopf, Sena Jurinac, Lisa Della Casa, Otto Edelmann, Erich Kunz, Jarmila Barton, Else Schimhoff, Erich Majkut, Antonio Pirino
c. Herbert von Karajan
1961: Elisabeth Schwarzkopf, Christa Ludwig, Anneliese Rothenberger, Otto Edelmann, Erich Kunz, Judith Hellwig, Hihle Rössel-Hajdan, Renato Evcolari, Guiseppe Zampieri
c. Karl Böhm
1976: Evelyn Lear, Brigitte Fassbänder, Lucia Popp, Hans Sotin, Raynard Wolansky, Silvana Zanolli, Stefania Malagù, Franco Castellana, Veriano Luchetti
c. Carlos Kleiber

Paris, Opera

First performance, 8 February 1927: Jeanne Campredon, Germaine Lubin, Jane Laval, Albert Hubarty, Henri Fabert, Germaine Humy, Ketty Lapeyrette, Edmond Warnéry, Robert Delbos
c. Philippe Gaubert
1941: Germaine Lubin, Jacqueline Courtin, Janine Micheau, Albert Hubarty, Louis Noguera, Germaine Humy, Ketty Lapeyrette, Raoul Gilles, Carmille Rouquetty
c. Philippe Gaubert
1949: Hilde Konetzni, Risë Stevens, Julia Moor, Emanuel List, Marko Rothmüller, Jarmila Barton, Dagmar Hermann, Hans-Georg Hartig, Raphael Romagnoni
c. Louis Fourestier
1957: Régine Crespin, Suzanne Sarroca, Janine Micheau, Lorenzo Alvary, Louis Noguera, Claude Alland, Suzanne Darbons, Louis Railland, Alain Vanzo
1962: Elisabeth Schwarzkopf, Suzanne Sarroca, Liliane Berton, Michael Langdon, Emanuel Laffage, Georgette Sponellys, Isabelle Andreani, Jacques Mars, Alain Vanzo
c. Louis Fourestier
1976: Christa Ludwig, Yvonne Minton, Lucia Popp, Hans Sotin, Raymond Wolansky, Janine Berbié, Jane Berbié, Michel Sénéchal, Alain Vanzo
c. Horst Stein

Salzburg

First performance, 13 August 1929: Lotte Lehmann, Vera Schwarz, Adele Kern, Richard Mayr, Hermann Wiedemann, Karola Jovanovic, Marta Fuchs, Hermann Gallos, Koloman von Pataky
c. Clemens Krauss
1935: Lotte Lehmann, Eva Hadrabova/Jarmila Novotna/Margit Angerer, Witz Krenn, Victor Madin, Hermann Wiedemann, Aenne Michalsky, Polly Batic, Hermann Gallos, Charles Kullman
c. Josef Krips
1937: Lotte Lehmann/Hilde Konetzni, Jarmila Novotna/Margit Bokor, Esther Réthy, Witz Krenn, Hermann Wiedemann, Aenne Michalsky, Rosette Anday, Hermann Gallos, Emmerich von Goden
c. Hans Knappertsbusch
1938: Hilde Konetzni, Marta Rohs, Esther Réthy/Maria Cebotari, Witz Krenn, Walter Grossmann/Victor Madin, Aenne Michalsky, Dora With/Olga Levko-Antoch, Hermann Gallos, Helge Roswänge/Emmerich von Goden
c. Karl Böhm
1941: Anny Konetzni, Marta Rohs, Esther Réthy/Elisabeth Rutgers, Witz Krenn, Hermann

Wiedemann/Victor Madin, Aenne Michalsky, Olga Levko-Antoch, Hermann Gallos, Anton Dermota/Karl Friedrich
c. Hans Knappertsbusch
1946: Hilde Konetzni, Maud Cunitz, Rosl Schwaiger, Witz Krenn, Georg Hann/Karl Schmidt, Jarmila Barton, Rosette Anday, Peter Klein, Hermann Gallos, Anton Dermota
c. Hans Swarowsky
1949: Maria Reining, Jarmila Novotna, Hilde Gueden, Jaro Prohaska, Georg Hann, Stefanie Holeschovsky, Dagmar Hermann, Peter Klein, Helge Roswänge
c. Georg Szell
1953: Marta Reining, Lisa Della Casa, Hilde Gueden, Kurt Böhme, Alfred Poell, Judith Hellwig, Sieglinde Wagner, László Szemore, Karl Terkal
c. Clemens Krauss/Karl Böhm
1960 (for opening of New Festpielhaus — 26 July): Lisa Della Casa/Elisabeth Schwarzkopf, Sena Jurinac, Hilde Gueden/Anneliese Rothenberger, Otto Edelmann, Erich Kunz/Alfred Poell, Judith Hellwig, Hilde Rössel-Majdon, Renato Ercolani, Guiseppe Zampieri
c. Herbert von Karajan
1978: Gundula Janowitz, Yvonne Minton, Lucia Popp, Kurt Moll, Ernst Gutstein, Doris Soffel, Liselotte Rebmann, David Thaw, Luciano Pavarotti
c. Christoph von Dohnanyi

Vienna

First performance, 8 April 1911: Lucie Weidt, Marie Gutheil-Schoder, Gertrude Förstel, Richard Mayr, Alexander Haydter, (*unknown*), Bella Paalen, Artur Preuss, Georg Maikl
c. Franz Schalk
(This production with innumerable changes of cast and conductors remained in the repertory every season until 1944, receiving 342 performances.)

REVIVALS:
1946 (Theater an der Wien): Anny Kotenzni, Elisabeth Hoengen, Emmy Loose, Ludwig Weber, Karl Karmann, Jarmila Barton, Rosette Anday, Hermann Gallos, Karl Friedrich
c. Rudolph Moralt
1955 (In rebuilt Staatsoper): Maria Reining, Sena Jurinac, Hilde Gueden, Kurt Böhme, Alfred Poell, Judith Hellwig, Hilde Rössel-Majdan, Làszlò Szemore, Karl Terkal
c. Hans Knappertsbusch
1968: Christa Ludwig, Gwyneth Jones, Reri Grist, Walter Berry, Ernst Gutstein, Emmy Loose, Margarita Lilova, Murray Dickie, Waldemar Kmnett
c. Leonard Bernstein

New York

Metropolitan Opera
First performance, 9 December 1913: Frieda Hempel, Margarete Ober, Anna Case, Otto Goritz, Hermann Weil, Rita Fornia, Marie Mattfeld, Albert Reiss, Carl Jörn
c. Alfred Hertz
1914: Frieda Hempel, Margarete Ober, Elisabeth Schumann, Otto Goritz, Hermann Weil, Vera Curtis, Maria Mattfeld, Albert Reiss, Paul Althouse
c. Alfred Hertz

1922: Florence Easton, Maria Jeritza, Marie Sundelius, Paul Bender, Gustav Schützendorf, Grace Anthony, Kathleen Howard, Angelo Bada, Orville Harrold
c. Artur Bodanzky
1927: Florence Easton, Grete Stückgold, Editha Fleischer, Richard Mayr, Gustav Schützendorf, Dorothee Manski, Kathleen Howard, Angelo Bada, Alfio Tedesco
c. Artur Bodanzky
1928: Florence Easton, Grete Stückgold, Queena Mario, Michael Bohnen, Gustav Schützendorf, Dorothee Manski, Kathleen Howard, Angelo Bada, Alfio Tedesco
c. Artur Bodanzky
1935: Lotte Lehmann, Maria Olszewska, Editha Fleischer, Emanuel List, Gustav Schützendorf, Dorothee Manski, Doris Doe, Angelo Bada, Alfio Tedesco
c. Artur Bodanzky
1941: Irene Jessner, Risë Stevens, Eleanor Steber, Emanuel List, Walter Olitzki, Thelma Votipka, Irra Petina, Karl Laufkötter, Kurt Baum
c. Erich Leinsdorf
1949: Eleanor Steber, Risë Stevens, Erne Berger, Emanuel List, Hugh Thompson, Thelma Votipka, Martha Lipton, Peter Klein, Guiseppe Di Stefano
c. Fritz Reiner
1951: Helen Traubel, Risë Stevens, Erne Berger, Fritz Krenn, John Brownlee, Thelma Votipka, Herta Glaz, Alessio De Paolis, Kurt Baum
c. Fritz Reiner
1959: Lisa Della Casa, Christa Ludwig, Elisabeth Söderström, Oskar Czerwenka, Ralph Herbert, Thelma Votipka, Belen Amparan, Alessio De Paolis, Eugenio Fernandi
c. Erich Leinsdorf
1960: Leonie Rysanek, Risë Stevens, Hilde Güeden, Oskar Czerwenka, Marko Rothmuller, Thelma Votipka, Martha Lipton, Charles Kullman, Albert Da Costa
c. Erich Leinsdorf
1962: Régine Crespin, Hertha Töpper, Anneliese Rothenberger, Otto Edelmann, Karl Dönch, Thelma Votipke, Rosalind Elias, Paul Franke, Daniele Barioni
c. Lorin Maazel
1964: Elisabeth Schwarzkopf, Lisa Della Casa, Anneliese Rothenberger, Otto Edelmann, Norman Mittelmann, Lynn Owen, Mignon Dunn, Andrea Velis, Sandor Konyst
c. Thomas Schippers
1969: Christa Ludwig, Evelyn Lear, Judith Raskin, Walter Berry, Rudolf Knoll, Judith DePaul, Rosalind Elias, Andrea Velis, John Alexander
c. Karl Böhm
1974: Christa Ludwig, Brigitte Fassbänder, Judith Blegen, Manfred Jungwirth, William Dooley, Carlotta Ordassy, Mildred Miller, Andrea Velis, Leo Goeke
c. Karl Böhm
1976: Teresa Zylis-Gara, Tatiana Troyanos, Judith Blegen, Walter Berry, William Dooley, Marcia Baldwin, Shirley Love, Andrea Velis, Luciano Pavarotti
c. James Levine
1977: Gwyneth Jones, Yvonne Minton, Reri Grist, Marius Rintzler, Derek Hammond-Stroud, Elizabeth Coss, Shirley Love, James Atherton, Neil Shicoff
c. Leopold Hager
1979: Anna Tomowa-Sintow, Agnes Baltsa, Judith Blegen, Aage Haugland, Ernst Gutstein, Elizabeth Coss, Shirley Love, James Atherton, Seth McCoy
c. Erich Leinsdorf

Buenos Aires

First performance, 26 May 1915: Rosa Raisa, Gilda Dalla Rizza, Amelita Galli-Curci, Guilio Cirino, Ernesta Caronna, Anita Giacomucci, Flora Perini, Giordano Paltrinier, Luigi Nardi
c. Gino Marinucci
1922: Helene Wildbrunn, Gilda Dalla Rizza, Thea Vitulli, Guilio Cirino, Salvatore Persichetti, Agnese Ricci, Elena Ruabdi, Luigi Nardi, Franco Tedeschi
c. Vinago Bellezza
1928: Berta Salter-Kottlar, Marion Olczewska, Adele Kern, Alexander Kipnis, Emil Schipper, Elly Krasser, Paula Weber, Harry Steiner, Carlos Rochriguez
c. Egon Pollak
(First time in Buenos Aires in German)
1939: Rose Pauly, Risë Stevens, Janine Micheau, Emanuel List, Andreas Boehm, Maria Alberti, Lydia Kindermann, Rogelio Baldrich, Koloman von Pataky
c. Erich Kleiber
1956: Brigit Nilsson, Constance Shacklock, Emmy Loose, Lorenzo Alvary, Angelo Maiello, M. Cherry, Ruzena Horokova, Eugenio Valori, Renato Sassola
c. Ferdinand Leitner
1961: Régine Crespin, Kerstin Meyer, Anneliese Rothenberger, Kurt Böhme, Heinz Friedrich, Martha Benegas, Noemi Sousza, Eugenio Valori, Fritz Wünderlich
c. Heinz Walberg
1969: Sena Jurinac, Christa Ludwig, Sylvia Geszty, Walter Berry, Renato Cesari
c. Erich Leinsdorf

Selected Discography

[EDITOR'S NOTE: * indicates recordings not currently available; (I) indicates recordings available as imports from Europe.]

Complete Recordings

[EDITOR'S NOTE: Only the recordings conducted by Kleiber and Solti are absolutely complete; the others make various more-or-less standard cuts.]

CONDUCTOR:	Artur Bodanzky
COMPANY/ORCHESTRA:	Metropolitan Opera Orchestra and Chorus
RECORDED:	Performance of January 7, 1939 (matinee)
MARSCHALLIN:	Lotte Lehmann
OCTAVIAN:	Risë Stevens
SOPHIE:	Marita Farell
OCHS:	Emanuel List
FANINAL:	Friedrich Schorr
ANNINA:	Doris Doe
VALZACCHI:	Karl Laufkoetter
MARIANNE:	Dorothee Manski
POLICE COMMISSARY:	Norman Cordon
ITALIAN TENOR:	Nicholas Massue
COMPLETE SET:	Metropolitan Opera MET-5

CONDUCTOR:	Clemens Krauss
COMPANY/ORCHESTRA:	Bavarian State Opera Chorus and Orchestra
RECORDED:	Performance in April, 1944
MARSCHALLIN:	Viorica Ursuleac
OCTAVIAN:	Georgine von Milinkovic
SOPHIE:	Adele Kern
OCHS:	Ludwig Weber
FANINAL:	Georg Hann
ANNINA:	Luise Willer
VALZACCHI:	Trojan Reger
MARIANNE:	—
POLICE COMMISSARY:	Georg Wieter
ITALIAN TENOR:	Franz Klarwein
COMPLETE SET:	Vox PL 7774*; OPBX 140*
EXCERPTS:	Acanta BB 22322(I)

CONDUCTOR:	Rudolf Kempe
COMPANY/ORCHESTRA:	Saxon State Opera Chorus and Orchestra
RECORDED:	December 21–23, 1950
MARSCHALLIN:	Margarete Bäumer
OCTAVIAN:	Tiana Lemnitz
SOPHIE:	Ursula Richter
OCHS:	Kurt Böhme
FANINAL:	Hans Lobel
ANNINA:	Emilia Walther-Sacks
VALZACCHI:	Franz Sautter
MARIANNE:	Angela Kolniak
POLICE COMMISSARY:	—
ITALIAN TENOR:	Walter Liebing
COMPLETE SET:	Urania URLP 201*; Acanta JA 23039(I)
EXCERPTS:	Urania URLP 7062*

CONDUCTOR:	Erich Kleiber
COMPANY/ORCHESTRA:	Vienna State Opera Chorus and Vienna Philharmonic Orchestra
RECORDED:	June, 1954
MARSCHALLIN:	Maria Reining
OCTAVIAN:	Sena Jurinac
SOPHIE:	Hilde Gueden
OCHS:	Ludwig Weber
FANINAL:	Alfred Poell
ANNINA:	Hilde Rössl-Majdan
VALZACCHI:	Peter Klein
MARIANNE:	Judith Hellwig
POLICE COMMISSARY:	Walter Berry
ITALIAN TENOR:	Anton Dermota
COMPLETE SET:	London XLLA 22*; A 4404* Richmond RS 64001*
EXCERPTS:	London 5615*

CONDUCTOR:	Herbert von Karajan
COMPANY/ORCHESTRA:	Philharmonia Chorus and Orchestra
RECORDED:	December 12–22, 1956
MARSCHALLIN:	Elisabeth Schwarzkopf
OCTAVIAN:	Christa Ludwig
SOPHIE:	Teresa Stich-Randall
OCHS:	Otto Edelmann
FANINAL:	Eberhard Wächter

ANNINA:	Kerstin Meyer
VALZACCHI:	Paul Kuen
MARIANNE:	Ljuba Welitsch
POLICE COMMISSARY:	Franz Bierbach
ITALIAN TENOR:	Nicolai Gedda
COMPLETE SET:	Angel 3563 DL/S; 3563 DL
EXCERPTS:	Angel 35645/S; 35645

CONDUCTOR:	Karl Böhm
COMPANY/ORCHESTRA:	Dresden State Opera Chorus and Saxon State Orchestra
RECORDED:	December 8–16, 1958
MARSCHALLIN:	Marianne Schech
OCTAVIAN:	Irmgard Seefried
SOPHIE:	Rita Streich
OCHS:	Kurt Böhme
FANINAL:	Dietrich Fischer-Dieskau
ANNINA:	Sieglinde Wagner
VALZACCHI:	Gerhard Unger
MARIANNE:	Ilona Steingruber
POLICE COMMISSARY:	Albrecht Peter
ITALIAN TENOR:	Rudolf Francl
COMPLETE SET:	Decca D.G.G. DGM 301/DGS 7301* D.G.G. LPM 18570-3/SLPM 138040-3* D.G.G. 2721 162
EXCERPTS:	D.G.G. LPM 18656/SLPM 138656*

CONDUCTOR:	Georg Solti
COMPANY/ORCHESTRA:	Vienna State Opera Chorus and Vienna Philharmonic Orchestra
RECORDED:	November, 1968 and June, 1969
MARSCHALLIN:	Régine Crespin
OCTAVIAN:	Yvonne Minton
SOPHIE:	Helen Donath
OCHS:	Manfred Jungwirth
FANINAL:	Otto Wiener
ANNINA:	Anne Howells
VALZACCHI:	Murray Dickie
MARIANNE:	Emmy Loose
POLICE COMMISSARY:	Herbert Lackner
ITALIAN TENOR:	Luciano Pavarotti
COMPLETE SET:	London OSA 1435
EXCERPTS:	London OS 26200

CONDUCTOR:	Leonard Bernstein
COMPANY/ORCHESTRA:	Vienna State Opera Chorus and Vienna Philharmonic Orchestra
RECORDED:	March 29–April 10, 1971
MARSCHALLIN:	Christa Ludwig
OCTAVIAN:	Gwyneth Jones
SOPHIE:	Lucia Popp
OCHS:	Walter Berry
FANINAL:	Ernst Gutstein
ANNINA:	Margarita Lilowa
VALZACCHI:	Murray Dickie
MARIANNE:	Emmy Loose
POLICE COMMISSARY:	Herbert Lackner
ITALIAN TENOR:	Placido Domingo
COMPLETE SET:	Columbia M4X 30652
EXCERPTS:	Columbia M 31959

CONDUCTOR:	Edo de Waart
COMPANY/ORCHESTRA:	Helmond Concert Choir, Netherlands Opera Chorus and Rotterdam Philharmonic Orchestra
RECORDED:	June–July, 1976
MARSCHALLIN:	Evelyn Lear
OCTAVIAN:	Frederica von Stade
SOPHIE:	Ruth Welting
OCHS:	Jules Bastin
FANINAL:	Derek Hammond-Stroud
ANNINA:	Sophia van Sante
VALZACCHI:	James Atherton
MARIANNE:	Nelly Morpurgo
POLICE COMMISSARY:	Henk Smit
ITALIAN TENOR:	José Carreras
COMPLETE SET:	Philips 6707 030

Abridged Recording

CONDUCTOR:	Robert Heger
COMPANY/ORCHESTRA:	Vienna State Opera Chorus and Vienna Philharmonic Orchestra
RECORDED:	September 20–24, 1933
MARSCHALLIN:	Lotte Lehmann
OCTAVIAN:	Maria Olszewska
SOPHIE:	Elisabeth Schumann
OCHS:	Richard Mayr

FANINAL:	Viktor Madin
ANNINA:	Bella Paalen
VALZACCHI:	Hermann Gallos
MARIANNE:	Anne Michalsky
POLICE COMMISSARY:	Karl Ettl
COMPLETE SET:	Seraphim IC 6041

HIGHLIGHTS

CONDUCTOR:	Ferdinand Leitner
COMPANY/ORCHESTRA:	Württemburg State Orchestra, Stuttgart
RECORDED:	October 9–10, 1951
MARSCHALLIN:	Tiana Lemnitz
OCTAVIAN:	Georgine von Milinkovic
SOPHIE:	Elfriede Trötschel
	Decca DL 9606*; Heliodor 89698*

CONDUCTOR:	Wilhelm Schüchter
COMPANY/ORCHESTRA:	Berlin Philharmonic Orchestra
RECORDED:	October 1955
MARSCHALLIN:	Leonie Rysanek
OCTAVIAN:	Elisabeth Grümmer
SOPHIE:	Erika Köth
OCHS:	Gustav Neidlinger
ANNINA:	Sieglinde Wagner
ITALIAN TENOR:	Josef Traxel
	EMI/Electrola
	C-047-28566

CONDUCTOR:	Silvio Varviso
COMPANY/ORCHESTRA:	Vienna Philharmonic Orchestra
RECORDED:	September 1964
MARSCHALLIN:	Régine Crespin
OCTAVIAN:	Elisabeth Söderström
SOPHIE:	Hilde Gueden
	London OS 25905

CONDUCTOR:	Rudolf Neuhaus
COMPANY/ORCHESTRA	Dresden State Opera Orchestra
RECORDED:	August 2, 1966
MARSCHALLIN:	Lisa della Casa

OCTAVIAN:	Anneliese Rothenberger (Act I); Lisa della Casa (Acts II, III)
SOPHIE:	Anneliese Rothenberger
	Angel S 36436*

Vocal Excerpts

Act I: Entrance of Ochs

Emanuel List et al. (1928)	Preiser LV 114(I)

Act I: Italian Tenor's Aria ("Di rigori armato")

Richard Tauber (1920)	Seraphim 60086
Helge Roswaenge (1939)	Arabesque 8003
Luciano Pavarotti (1968–69)	London OS 26373

Act I: Marschallin's Monologue ("Da geht er hin . . . Kann mich auch")

Margarethe Siems (1911)	Rococo 20*; 40*; 5217*
Frieda Hempel (1913)	Top Classic 708/9 (I)
Lotte Lehmann (1925)	Seraphim IB-6015
Astrid Varnay (1951)	Acanta DE 22645(I)

Act II: Presentation of the Rose ("Mir ist die Ehre": Sophie and Octavian)

Minnie Nast, Eva von der Osten (1911)	Belcantodisc BC 248*
Elisabeth Schwarzkopf, Irmgard Seefried (cond. Karajan; 1947)	Angel ZX 3915
Erna Berger, Risë Stevens (cond. Reiner; 1951)	Metropolitan Opera Guild MET 114

Act II: Duet of Sophie and Octavian ("Mit Ihren Augen")

Minnie Nast, Eva von der Osten (1911)-	Belcantodisc BC 248*

Act II: Letter Scene and Finale ("Da lieg ich . . . Herr Kavalier": Ochs and Annina)

Richard Mayr, Anny Andrassy (cond. Bruno Walter; 1929	Preiser LV 10; LV 42 (I)
Alexander Kipnis, Else Ruziczka (1931)	Seraphim 60124
Ludwig Weber, Dagmar Herrmann (1949)	World Records SH 286 (I)
Walter Berry, Christa Ludwig (1964)	Eurodisc XB 25971 R (I)
Michael Langdon, Yvonne Minton (cond. Solti; 1968)	London OSA 1276*

Act III: Exit of Ochs

Emanuel List et al. (1928)	Preiser LV 114 (I)

Act III: Trio ("Hab mir's gelobt": Marschallin, Sophie, Octavian)

Margarethe Siems, Minnie Nast, Eva von der Osten (1911)	Rococo 41*; 20*; 5217*

Act III: Final Duet ("Ist's kein Traum": Sophie, Octavian)

Minnie Nast, Eva von der Osten (1911)	Rococo 5217*
Erna Berger, Risë Stevens (cond. Reiner; 1951)	Metropolitan Opera Guild MET 114

Orchestral Excerpts

Suite

Eugene Ormandy, Philadelphia Orchestra	Columbia MS 6678
Eugene Ormandy, Philadelphia Orchestra	RCA Gold Seal AGL1 4291

WALTZ MOVEMENTS (various arrangements)

R. Strauss, Berlin State Opera Orchestra (1927)	DG 2740 160 (I)
R. Strauss, Bavarian State Orchestra (1941)	DG 2740 160 (I)
Bruno Walter, Berlin Philharmonic Orchestra (1929)	EMI/Electrola C-137-54095/9(I)
Fritz Reiner, Chicago Symphony Orchestra (1957)	RCA Gold Seal AGL1 3367
Lorin Maazel, Vienna Philharmonic Orchestra	London CS 6537
Thomas Schippers, Cincinnati Symphony Orchestra	Turnabout TV 34666

SELECTED BIBLIOGRAPHY

Del Mar, Norman. *Richard Strauss.* 3 Volumes. London: Barrie and Rockliff, 1962–1972.

Hartmann, Rudolf. *Richard Strauss: The Staging of His Operas and Ballets.* New York: Oxford University Press, 1981.

Jefferson, Alan. *The Life of Richard Strauss.* Newton Abbot: David and Charles, 1973.

Jefferson, Alan. *Richard Strauss Opera* (Discography Series, XVII) Utica, N.Y.: J. F. Weber, 1977.

Lehmann, Lotte. *Five Operas and Richard Strauss.* New York: Macmillan, 1964.

Mann, William. *Richard Strauss: A Critical Study of the Operas.* London: Cassell, 1964.

Marek, George R. *Richard Strauss: The Life of a Non-Hero.* New York: Simon and Schuster, 1967.

Nicoll, Allardyce. *World Drama: From Aeschylus to Anouilh.* New York: Barnes and Noble, 1976.

Priestley, J. B. *Literature and Western Man.* New York: Harper and Row, 1960.

Strauss, Richard. *Recollections and Reflections.* Ed. Willi Schuh, Tr. L. J. Lawrence. London: Boosey & Hawkes, 1953.

Strauss, Richard, and Hofmannsthal, Hugo von. *Correspondence.* Trs. Hanns Hammelmann and Ewald Osers. London: Collins, 1961.

Strauss, Richard, and Zweig, Stefan. *A Confidential Matter: The Letters of Richard Strauss & Stefan Zweig, 1931–1935.* Tr. Max Knight. Berkeley: University of California Press, 1977.

Tuchman, Barbara. *The Proud Tower.* New York: Macmillan, 1966.

Hamburger, Michael. *Hofmannsthal: Three Essays.* Bollingen Series. Princeton, New Jersey: Princeton University Press, 1971.

Hofmannsthal, Hugo von. *Selected Plays and Libretti.* Ed. Michael Hamburger. Bollingen Series. New York: Pantheon Books, 1963.

Notes on the Contributors

Anthony Burgess was born in Manchester, England, in 1917. He attended Manchester University, where he studied languages. He started his career as a composer and then, later, turned to literature and criticism. In recent years, he has returned to writing music. His novels include *Enderby, A Clockwork Orange, MF, Napoleon Symphony,* and *Earthly Powers.* He has written nonfiction books on Shakespeare and on James Joyce. His musical compositions include "Symphony in C," "Waste Land," the song-cycle "The Bridges of Enderby," and in 1980, a ballet suite entitled "Mr. WS."

George R. Marek emigrated to the United States from his native Austria. For many years he was vice-president and general manager at RCA Records. He has also written numerous articles for *Opera News* and other magazines. His books include *The World Treasury of Grand Opera; Puccini: A Biography; Richard Strauss: The Life of a Non-Hero; Beethoven: Biography of a Genius; Toscanini;* and, in 1981, *Cosima Wagner.*

John Cox was born in Bristol, England, and attended Oxford University. He has directed for the theater and for numerous opera houses throughout the world. From 1971 until 1981 he was Director of Production at the Glyndebourne Festival Opera. In 1980, he directed a new production of *Der Rosenkavalier* at Glyndebourne with sets and costume designs by Erté. In 1982, he directed a new production of *Il Barbiere di Siviglia* at the Metropolitan Opera. Currently, he is the General Administrator of the Scottish Opera in Glasgow.